D0850730

The Spirit of Language
in Civilization

AMS PRESS
NEW YORK

The Spirit of Language in Civilization

BY

KARL VOSSLER

TRANSLATED BY

OSCAR OESER

LONDON

KEGAN PAUL, TRENCH, TRUBNER & CO. LTD.

BROADWAY HOUSE, 68–74 CARTER LANE, E.C.

1932

Library of Congress Cataloging in Publication Data

Vossler, Karl, 1872-1949.
  The Spirit of Language in Civilization.

    Reprint of the 1932 ed. published by K. Paul, Trench,
Trubner, London, in series: International library of
psychology, philosophy, and scientific method.
    Translation of Geist und Kultur in der Sprache.
    Includes bibiographical references and index.
    1. Language and languages. I. Title. II. Series:
International library of psychology, philosophy, and
scientific method.
P105.V5713 1977   400   75-41285
ISBN 0-404-14625-2

Reprinted from the edition of 1932, London
First AMS edition published in 1977
Manufactured in the United States of America

AMS PRESS INC.
NEW YORK, N.Y.

To J. E. Spingarn.

Dear friend,

Twenty-five years ago we both began our researches, and were attracted to the same subjects ; and since the problems of Renaissance poetics drew us together, our friendship has remained alive in spite of the dividing ocean and a world war. Indeed, hard times served only to prove further your nobility of character ; and our ties are even closer now that you are a benefactor and an honorary graduate of the University of Munich, at which I have the honour of teaching.

In the past years you have risen more and more to creative work, while I have had to go down to the fundamentals of philology and literature. The subject, language and poetry, has remained the same ; but where you have the gift of creation, I can only analyse. Still, there may be some poetry even in that ; and so I venture to hope that in the following essays I may, as a sign of my deep and lasting gratitude, be offering you something not wholly unacceptable.

My earlier efforts in the philosophy of language were mainly concerned with the methods of investigation. In the present volume I consider the interweaving of language with the other activities of mind. Some of the chapters have appeared before in a fragmentary form : Ch. II in the *Deutsche Vierteljahrsschrift für Literaturwissenschaft und Geistesgeschichte, I* ; Chs. III and VII/c in *Die Neueren Sprachen*, vols. 28 and 26 ; Ch. IV in the *Festschrift für Ph. A. Becker* ; Ch. V in the *Festschrift für H. Wölfflin* ; Ch. VII/a in the *Neue Rundschau*, vol. 35 ; Ch. VII/d in Italian in *Cultura*, vol. 3 ; Ch. VII/e in *Sitzungsberichte der Bayrischen Akademie der Wissenschaften*, Jan. 1924 ; Ch. VII/f in *Logos*, vol. 13. Recast, corrected, amplified and rounded off into a systematic unity, they were given as a course of lectures on the philosophy of language in our university.   Now that the fruits of seven years' labour seem to some extent mature, I venture to publish them as a whole.

Sincerely yours,

KARL VOSSLER.

MUNICH, *May* 1925.

CONTENTS

THE SPIRIT OF LANGUAGE
IN CIVILIZATION

CHAPTER I

ASSUMPTIONS AND EXPERIENCES

THERE comes a time when the thoughts of every thinker who is immersed in his subject take a personal turn. Some experience this at the deep levels of their thinking, others more on the surface. In any case, it is considered fitting to disguise one's own perplexities, so that they may appear to be all the more profound. We shall conform to this custom, and keep our own conception of language in the background. To begin with, we shall use the definition which everyone uses. For everyone thinks he knows what language is : a meaningful sound, a sociable noise, a passing to and fro of signs, which men make chiefly with the mouth and take in through the ears and by means of which they communicate with each other—though gestures, hands, eyes, etc., also help. No one denies that behind this shifting pattern something is at work that may be called Force, or Meaning, or Will, or Mind, or Body and Soul of Man, or anything else. But as soon as we inquire what this ' something ' is, opinions begin to diverge widely. The pious see in it the divine breath, the enlightened a natural disposition that is to some extent shared by the animals. The origin of language is attributed by psychologists to the psychic part of this disposition, by phoneticians to the bodily part, by sociologists to the communal life of man. The clash of opinions becomes most violent when it comes to the problem of the *value* of language. Overestimation stands against underestimation. On the one hand language is thought to be error and illusion, a veil hiding truth,

A   1

self-deception ; on the other it is looked upon as the first and most important educator of our thought, even as itself thought.   If we wish to pick our way among these clashing views, we have to realize that we need the help of philosophy and even metaphysics, which will lead us to the ultimate foundations of the human spirit.

In his *Prinzipien der Sprachgeschichte* (1st. edn., Halle, 1880), Hermann Paul has given us the most important work on the philosophy of language which has appeared for many years.   But he will not admit that his book is mainly philosophical.   Apparently he understood by philosophy something rather vague, as indeed it was in those days, and did not wish to endanger his views by wedding them to this or that *Weltanschauung*.   It was the modesty of a great scholar no less than his caution that made him take up this attitude.   Since his observations referred only to the Indo-Germanic languages, he did not wish his ' Principles ' to be applied to all languages or to ' language ' in general.   Everyone, however, who thinks about the ' principles ' of a science is a philosopher whether he likes it or not, and is secretly attached to one or other *Weltanschauung*.   It is a good thing, and a form of honesty and modesty to be conscious of this.   If every philologist were to realize how limited, how bound by his inner self are the problems, the possibilities, and the specific knowledge which distinguish him, he would, I am sure, become more certain within *himself* and more tolerant towards others.

It can do no harm, therefore, if we preface our work with a consideration of the ultimate and decisive attitudes of the human mind.

In prehistoric times man already had a dual conception of language ; to-day our science is still trying to harmonize the two aspects.

" And out of the ground the Lord God formed every beast of the field, and every fowl of the air ; and brought them unto Adam to see what he would call them : and whatsoever Adam called every living creature, that was the name thereof." When Adam saw Eve for the first time he said, " This is now bone of my bones, and flesh of my flesh : she shall be called Woman, because she was taken out of Man." In short, having insight into the origin and purpose of things, he gave each of them a name. These names were not arbitrary, they had a meaning. Whatsoever he called each of them in his language, that was the name thereof. The names should have validity because they were based on a knowledge of circumstances, and also because Adam was lord of the earth and had the power to define the purpose of things. In the legend his language is thought to be that of a wise and powerful superman. Adam was a magician whom all living things in Paradise obeyed, since he called them by their right name. He was the master of all things, not by force, but by the power of his speech alone, which was a spiritual eye and a spiritual hand at the same time. But the charm is shattered by the curse of reality ; and in reply to the names by which we invoke her, the world remains petrified and dumb. And now doubt begins to assail the power and with it the concept-forming value of language. The Mystic arises against the Magician :

> Name ist Schall und Rauch,
> Umnebelnd Himmelsgut. . . .
> Gefühl ist alles. . . .
> Und wenn du ganz in dem Gefühle selig bist,
> Nenn' es dann wie du willst.

He who names things as he wills, because " names are sound and smoke " to him, will soon be unable to understand them or his neighbours, or finally himself. He becomes the sport of things, loses himself to them, and completely sinks his identity in them—but this is the heart's desire of the mystic. Instead of speaking to them, he is silent ; listening to them he perceives the unspeakable harmony of their being. He learns from them a new language, with a deeper significance. Now it is no longer the dead formulæ of magic that come to him in outworn words ; he is immersed in living sounds and visions. From the primordial foundations of the world he receives her secrets. But if he wishes to speak the unspeakable and to communicate it to his fellows, he will once more have to make use of those hated names and words and old formulæ. Anything else would not be understood. As soon as he returns from his trance and opens his mouth, he falls under the spell of his language and has to wrestle with the difficulty of making himself understood. What was a tool for the magician becomes a fetter for him. If he does not wish to falsify and stunt the best and most intimate part of his inner life, he has to remain silent. Language is no longer an eye or a hand of the spirit ; it is a veil and a hindrance.

Magi and Mystics are types of spiritual being that cannot be removed from the world.[1] There is constant strife between magic, which uses language as a tool and thereby tries to bring as much as possible, even God, under its control, and mysticism, which breaks, makes valueless, and rejects all forms. This is always making itself felt in the antitheses between classical and romantic, apollinic and dionysic, mythical and symbolic forms of art ; between the æsthetic and the grammatic history of language ; between the theory of meanings and the theory of forms.[2]

Fortunately the average man is neither wholly a mystic nor wholly a magician, but has a foot in each world. He pays tribute to the magical conception by assuming that language has power over human beings, if not over the world, and that he can at any rate transmit some truths to men. He also agrees with the mystic and

[1] Cf. Georg Mehlis, " Formen der Mystik ", *Logos*, II (1912), p. 242 ff., and Anna Tumarkin, " Dichtung und Weltanschauung ", *ibid.*, VIII 1919), p. 195 ff.

[2] Cf. Fritz Strich, *Deutsche Klassik und Romantik, oder Vollendung und Unendlichkeit, ein Vergleich*, Munich, 1922, and my review, " Un nuovo metodo di stilistica ", *La Cultura*, Rome, 15. August, 1922 ; " Form und Bedeutung, die Grundfrage der Sprachwissenschaft ", in the second supplement to the *Berliner Tageblatt*, 10. December, 1916. For the relation between language and religion cf. Ch. III.

admits that the sense of what is meant is liable to confusion and misunderstanding through the spoken words and the names imposed by language. He believes, though not without reservations, in the magic potency of language, and within reason doubts its power and its value as an instrument of knowledge. And so we shall not take the battle between the magicians of the word and the knights of the mind too seriously, as Nietzsche and his followers do. For the opponents are not ideals, but types of humanity. No one can be a pure psychological type, and he who attempts to be so is like a fool who always tries to get out of bed with his left leg only.

Arbitrary concessions to left or right are of no value in science. If one trusts oneself to a mystically or magically inclined thinker, one should foresee whither the journey will lead. One cannot, as Paul believed, lean on the psychology of Herbart, without taking the metaphysics of that philosopher into the bargain. True metaphysics cannot be left behind at the threshold of the empirical sciences. Indeed, Herbart's agnostic mysticism, with its unknowable *Dingen an sich*, has thrown a dark shadow over Paul's whole science of language, so that the fundamental problem as to the nature of language can never come into the light.

On one point, however, Paul is right. He does not wish to take over a complete philosophy and apply it to philology. He wants to arrive at his ' principles ' independently through a study of known languages. For the philosophy of language is not the application of this or that *Weltanschauung* to science ; it means independent thought and research into the nature of language. By deepening and clearly following up these thoughts, a definite *Weltanschauung* will grow up as the natural reward of work. Empiricism can be separated from metaphysics as little as research from thought. Every empirical science makes no ' assumptions ' only in so far as its exponents are intellectually independent, and not in so far as they ignore the hypotheses with which they are working or hand them over to a metaphysical expert for vicarious treatment. Above all we wish to combat that much favoured division of labour, whereby the philosopher undertakes to think and the empiricist to collect and to 'know'. On the one hand so many shadowy, empty concepts have accumulated, on the other so many 'assumptionless', *i.e.* dry facts, that it is time to break down the barrier.

CHAPTER II

THE first and most obvious assumption of the science of language is that there is a language. But this is precisely what is uncertain. For just as it does not follow from the existence of theology that there is a God, nor from geometrical theorems about the circle or triangle that such things exist in reality, so the whole of philology is no proof of the existence of a language. To begin with, there actually is no language, but only speech: my speech, your speech, our speech now and here, to-day and yesterday. But *our* speech is not yet a language, it is at most conversation. And even this would have to be doubted if *my* speech were not heard and understood and answered in some way by someone else. If I were the only one in the whole world who spoke, there would not only be no language, there would not even be speech, not even *my* speech. How can I be sure, how can I know that I am speaking when no one hears me, no one understands, no one answers—no one ; therefore not even myself ? In order to be sure of my speaking, I must at least be able to hear, understand and answer my own speech. Speaking, hearing, understanding, answering or speaking again : all these belong together and form a circle, within which real speech or conversation are circumscribed and guaranteed.

We have already used the expression *speaking* in two senses : first in the abstract one of an individual act of speaking, and then in the fuller one of conversation. It is only the second kind, speaking that is listened to with understanding, is answered, and is assured of reality, in other words, conversation, which is living and concrete speech.

7

It is generally assumed that for conversation several persons are necessary, or at least two : a Jones who speaks to a Smith. That is not so ; everyone can speak to himself. At least three or four factors such as feeling, thinking, speaking, understanding, hearing, answering, are necessary to speech, but not two persons. This does not mean that soliloquy is the original form of conversation ; but it is the simplest. It is the simplest conceivable, which does not mean the most natural, but only the most simplified.

There is little sense in asking which came first, conversation with oneself or with others, monologue or dialogue. Quite primitive people, children and drunkards, often talk to themselves. One can, of course, assume that they believe someone else to be present who is talking to them. On the other hand there are many highly educated people who never say an audible word to themselves, and yet spend their whole life in inner soliloquy : great recluses, silent dreamers and thinkers, who from without can hardly be induced to break their silence, so deeply are they immersed in dialogue with their Self. It is as useless for the history of language to inquire whether monologue or dialogue came first, as it is for the history of literature to inquire whether the lyric, the epic, or the drama is the first-born. Both questions resemble the jejune problem, which of the numbers one, two, three came first. The lyric is the outpouring of the lonely heart ; for the epic a hearer is needed ; and the drama presupposes at least three persons or situations : protagonist, antagonist, and spectator, all of which, it is true, the poet can represent himself, just as in a song a hundred minds and voices can flow together into a choir. So here, too, it is a question of situations, not of persons ; and if we begin to number such aspects one, two, three, we shall have grasped the first one fully only after the third and last has been apprehended. No one can speak who cannot understand and answer. The parrot can perform the external act of speaking ; but he cannot make conversation. He does not understand himself. He is at most an individual, and not a personality.

In attempting to lay the foundation of philology, the concept of the individual should be avoided, and should be replaced by that of the person. For in a conversation only the one who plays a part counts, not one who accidentally happens to be present. Indeed, as we have seen, the *person* has to take the part both of hearer and of speaker ; but then he is sufficient unto himself for carrying on a conversation and needs no second, since he is his own partner. ' Person ' and ' part ' are so closely interwoven with the concept and the meaning of *persona*, that although several parts or persons can be thought of as united in *one* person, no person can be thought of without a part.[1]

If, on the other hand, the concept of ' the individual ' is used, all sorts of misunderstandings are liable to arise, like the controversy between Hermann Paul and Wilhelm Wundt, whether in language the individual or the community is of primary importance ; whether in a science of language individual psychology or social psychology should take the lead.[2] To begin with, since it is real living people who speak and not disembodied souls, the ' science of the soul ' has no business here at all. Since, furthermore, one person as well as a community *can* converse, it is difficult to see why one science should take precedence over the other in this respect. What we need is a concept that will do justice to the individual as well as to the community, and this demand is fulfilled in the concept of ' the person '.

In this concept metaphysical and empirical thinking meet and fructify one another. It is one that contains both an idea and a fact. For on the one hand it points

[1] Cf. Rudolf Hirzel, " Die Person, Begriff und Name derselben im Altertum ", *Sitzungsber. der Bayr. Akad. d. Wissenschaften*, 5. Dec. 1914.

[2] W. Wundt, *Probleme der Völkerpsychologie*, 1st. edn. Leipzig, 1911, 2nd. edn. Stuttgart, 1921 ; and H. Paul, " über die Völkerpsychologie ", *Münchener Rektoratsrede*, 25. June, 1910.

to the part that is played, and this is not a fact without further qualifications ; on the other it expresses the demand that we ourselves should become and be this part. Starting from the mask, the body or the face, in short the external personality, it aims at our innermost, unexpressed Self. We are persons to the extent to which we arrive at ourselves through the part, and through realizing this particular part. We are *not* persons, only individuals, to the extent to which we cling to the mere histrionic aspect of the external part and lose ourselves in it.

The downfall of an autocrat can teach us how the dissolution of the apparent personality proceeds. The monarch used to consider himself a being of state, an *universale fantastico*, as Vico would have said, an objective collective being which, when it thundered, really thundered, was Will when it willed, and Speaker when it uttered words. It was gradually discovered that his thundering, his willing, his speaking, that all his impersonations were only real as a play. The *universale fantastico* was unmasked and found to be an *universale particolare*, the objective-common being a common objective being, and the whole majesty of this ' person ' the hollow affectation of a comedian. Just as the personal God in all his parts *is* the *whole* of reality, so the individual man can only become a person, or, to put it more emphatically, a personality, in so far as he becomes some whole. A whole artist is an artistic, a whole man a human, a whole king a royal personality. On the other hand, just as the pious imagine the infinite variety of the forces of the universe to be fused into unity in the person of their God, so several people, families, tribes, communities of interest of every kind, can coalesce and become persons. Homer, for instance, is such a person or mask, under which the poetic achievement of several individuals appears as a unity. The great founders of religions, philosophies, systems of law, states, the builders, and the conductors of orchestras, may be likened to the apex of a pyramid, in which the aspirations of numberless men find their goal and their consummation. It is often difficult to decide whether such approximations to unity are only apparent, or whether they rest on some actual interconnection. For here, too, there are true and false persons, Christians in spirit, and Christians in name ; men of straw, and protagonists of a common cause. It is the task of critical thought to decide whether and in how far Bismarck was politically a leader ; whilst religious and mystical thought is never weary of paying honour to great personalities, canonizing them, and raising them to the stars, where they shine as images of God. For the concept of personality is not anthropomorphic, it is theomorphic. It elevates human individuality into divinity. In the human sphere, too, the individual is susceptible to degrees of comparison, like those conveyed by the Italian superlatives constructed from individual or national names, *Rossinissimo, Tedeschissimo, Inglesissimo,* which may be translated as ' super-Rossini ', *Ur-Deutscher,* ' John-Bull-Englishman '. But this kind of exaggeration is comic, caricaturing, grotesque and fantastic. If it is meant to be taken seriously it seems merely bombastic, since individuality is essentially egocentric and comparable only to itself. It is of the essence of personality, however, that it lifts above itself the core of its unity, the germ of its greatness, so that it may reach up towards the more comprehensive being that overshadows it. At first, personality lives and grows egoistically on the recognition afforded it by other, lesser persons and the sacrifices they bring ; and then, breaking through the barrier of its selfishness, it grows upwards through denial and sacrifice to a higher and wider greatness.

We have painted an emphatic picture of what constitutes a Person, for the humble circumstances of conversation do not bring out the essentially lofty aspirations of his being. But even in conversation they are active ; for how could a Person answer himself without them, how recognize a personality in his neighbour, honour him as an equal, speak to him and concede validity to his talk ? How could he split his Self into several persons, who practise on each other in the play of words, help each other and unfold their strength in the mutual mastery of words ? It is by the practice of this inner, personal dialectic that the child grows to the height of conversation with adults. For it can only take from them what it can understand in the rôle of listener and utilize again in its own way as a speaker. The concept of the individual does not foresee this possibility at all, for in essence it remains indivisible. If people were merely individuals and not at the same time persons, we should not be able to understand how they could achieve conversation, which consists of imparting, that is, of spiritual division and reunion. Those exponents of the psychology of language who employ the concept of the individual are therefore silent about the origin of the ability to speak possessed by their experimental rabbits ; or, what is even worse, they deduce it from natural reflexes and expressive movements and talk as though the gap between the activities of the body and the activities of the mind were a mere trifle. But this gap is a mere trifle only in so far as it cannot be detected by the purely empirical scientist, even with the most delicate instruments.

In the last resort, therefore, when we look at things from the standpoint of philosophy, the real vehicle and creator of conversation is in every case a single person, who can divide into several and finally into any number of characters or sub-persons. Whenever people converse with one another, a language drama is created which every one of the participators enacts within himself. The general belief that a drama does not take place *in*, but *between* the persons concerned, is due to the observation of sound waves, vibrations in the air which run from the mouth of one to the ear of the other. But it is not the waves in the air that do the speaking, any more than the wires in a telephone call do it. The material world is only the mediator ; it damps, colours, hinders or helps the conversation in a way that is quickly taken into account by us. We do not suffer it passively, but as far as possible actively overcome it. The air, the wire, megaphone and microphone, the whole of natural and manufactured nature are pressed into the service of conversation and utilized in it, just as the musician makes a song out of gut or brass and the author a story out of paper and ink.

The metaphysical view is that all conversations which take place here below, take place in the human personality as such, in a whole made up of an indefinitely large number of parts. Everything that is spoken on this globe in the course of the ages, therefore, must be thought of as a vast soliloquy spoken by the human mind, which unfolds itself in untold millions of persons and characters, and comes to itself again in their reunion.

It follows from this that the human mind as such should be or become a *single* person ; and we must ask whether the concept of personality can stand this extension into the absolute. We can no longer doubt that it can claim some qualities of absolute mind and a certain unity ; but this does not include the possibility of an infinite number of parts played by *one* person. For no mortal has ever been able to be so universal that he could hear, understand, and answer everything that is spoken. But it is true to say that the disposition and desire for this is present to an indefinite extent. Our desire for power or knowledge is essentially the same. It, too, yearns for the infinite, but is baulked and opposed by reality, in a different way for everyone ; for here also the concept of the person with its claim to godlike unity in multiplicity is at work.

The fact that it is the person who converses, not the individual, determines the concept of *language*. Language, too, is characterized by a pendulate swinging between reality and the spheres beyond. It is never wholly real, for it is always in the process of becoming. That is why, to begin with, we had to deny that there is such a thing as language. On the other hand, it is not a pure idea either, and like the concept of person does not admit of being extended to the absolute, although the tendency towards the absolute is inherent in it. The absolute person cannot be thought philosophically ; at most we can think of him as ' God ' in a religious sense. Similarly, an absolute, unified, ' all-language ' would be a religious creation. In so far as all languages are *urverwandt*, as Hugo Schuchardt would say, they are ultimately related, can merge into one another and fuse into unity. They form a spiritual unit since all have the same tendencies and aspirations. Is not the same true of persons in respect of their innermost dispositions and their highest instincts ? For how could language communities and communal languages arise without the personal communities of customs, laws, the family, the nation, and the state ?

The difference between language and conversation is that the former is unthinkable without a plurality as well as a community of persons. A single person, in however many parts and situations he may express himself, can never produce a language, only conversations. I can imagine that a single and personal God has conversations with himself, not that he has a language entirely his own. Several gods would be needed to create one. There can be a language of the gods, but not a god-language. When we talk of a ' national language ', we mean the nation as a *natural* unit, not as a person. A ' language of nations ', however, could only be one that is used by nations as judicial or constitutional persons in their intercourse, over and above their national languages : Esperanto, for instance, or one of the national languages that has been artificially raised to this higher status by special agreement, like diplomatic French, or military German in Austria-Hungary. Concepts like state, church, or school languages are of a somewhat different order. The state, the church, and the school are here not thought of as persons, nor as natural units or individuals that possess their own language. They are not communities of people, but of practical affairs or interests, in whose service a special language is used. This is, therefore, not the language *of* the state or church, but *for* the state or church. There are, it is true, intermediate and transitional forms. The *argot* of criminals, for example, is something that is possessed and used by the community of criminals, as well as being employed in the service of crime. Criminal exploits are both the subject and the object of this language.

Whatever the concern or the aims of language may be, it always needs several persons to be its vehicle. Of language we can assert, what we denied in the case of conversation, that it takes place between persons and not exclusively in them. We must conceive it as a sort of air or wire, metaphorically speaking, of course, for in reality it cannot be captured in the medium. Why do we nevertheless imagine language as something in our environment, which, like a mist or gas, develops as a kind of mental atmosphere between those who speak, listen, and answer ? The fault, I think, lies in the transitory nature of conversational speech, or, looked at from another side, in our desire to capture the passing show of talk in our thought. In conversation, speech is as manifest to our senses as lightning, thunder, and wind ; indeed more manifest, since we can create it ourselves, while we cannot create the storm. In conversation we are not thundered at alone, we thunder in our turn. But like every storm, conversation passes by and dies away. What remains as the permanent effect of all meteorological phenomena is called climate. Language is to conversations as climate is to weather. Language and climate are both something abstract, a mean, an average, something permanent in space-time, though an imaginary thing with no fixed abode. We may doubt its reality, but we need it for understanding the world of reality. It can be doubted whether Munich has a climate ; but it certainly has weather, and bad weather, every day. To anyone who cannot stand this endless change from bad to even worse weather, climate becomes a painful reality, and he cries, " I can't live in it ! " He may be able to stand all sorts of weather, but not the climate, which therefore has potency even if it is not real. The concept is static but at the same time contains something dynamic. The concept of language, under which we subsume that which is permanently active in the conversations of certain times and places, is similarly constituted. Those permanent qualities form themselves through the practice, memory, and habits of the speakers ; they are the usage of speech, and the customs of speech are language.

To satisfy ourselves as to the strength of such a custom, we have only to try and escape its sovereignty by going to a country where no one understands us, or by intentionally opposing its dictates at home. The barrier will be felt as soon as we run up against it. If the law is transgressed, the punishment follows ; and even if one has no sense of justice oneself, one soon recognizes it in others. The laws regulating the customs of speech are peculiarly constituted. The schoolmaster who punishes a boy if he puts the indicative after *ut* is the most glaring example of the force of a language custom. As a rule the sinner against language is not punished with the rod. As a rule the purity of language is left to the tender mercies of the public like certain gardens which betray the fact, or at most to an academy or a language society, and, in the case of beginners, to schoolmasters. But these guardians cannot be present wherever the language is spoken ; and even if they could, what peculiar power has been given them to adjust our tongues ? If no better authority than that of bureaucratic pedants and the general public stands behind the usage of language, we fear that it is in a bad way.

A French colleague in Paris once pointed out to me that the punishment which overtakes the sinner against language is that of being made ridiculous. There may be some truth in this, particularly among the French, who are so ironic, so vain, and so touchy. But the fear of being made ridiculous is not the only guardian. Reverence and regard for traditions have just as much right to the claim. We call our language the mother tongue, *lingua madre*, for the child learns it from the mother, in the bosom of the family, where love rather than irony introduces it. The child will accordingly try to learn it correctly not only from vanity, but from the warmer feelings of trustfulness, devotion and gratitude. And even the adult, if he is sensitive, has a feeling of reverence for the language and even for the dialect he learnt from his father and mother. It may be that in France, where dialect is more vigorously renounced in favour of a barren literary correctness than it is in Germany or Italy, irony is a more successful guardian of language or other traditions than *pietas*. If we remember how in times of revolution the French raged against their own past, against the graves of their kings in St. Denis, against their church and their own beliefs ; how the violation of holy places and memorials becomes at times a burning passion, we shall understand why irony and laughter are necessities to them, to keep them from violating their own customs and discipline. Where reverence does not succeed, vanity will.

On the whole, however, there are no special institutions for the protection of language. That is why doubts as to the validity of language customs are always arising. Some investigators, the so-called neo-grammarians, believed that language customs were a kind of natural law. If that were the case, they would evidently need no guardians, since neither with the best nor the worst intentions could they be violated. For such a law, schools, education, language academies, and nurseries would be superfluous. The neo-grammarians therefore tried to protect the dialects that were growing up wild against every form of linguistic and literary purism, which they abhorred as something forced and unnatural. The science of language

B

no longer wished to have anything to do with the correctness of language.[1] But since the influence of the school, of writing, literature and grammar could not be denied, the grammarians, in a huff, retreated to the investigation of dialects and primitive languages, in the hope that at least among peasants and savages such things did not occur. But they were again deceived ; for even here they came across unpleasant traces of arbitrary interference with the growth of apparently virginal language customs by authorities on language, by priests, and so on.

We are thus faced with the fact that language cannot be adequately protected by human rules or regulations, and is not even protected within itself by the force of natural law. It is the same situation as we find in the case of morals : they can be, to a certain extent may and sometimes even must be transgressed, though we do not do so as a matter of course. Language is a human custom, and the concept of custom implies that it should both be actively and purposively cared for and should passively allow itself to be used. Usage is *solere* and *curare* together. Everyone who speaks, that is, takes part in a conversation between several persons, is, in fact, in a state that is neither pure activity nor pure passivity, but that emphasizes now the one, now the other, according as the person takes the part of speaker or of listener. It is the alternation of these states which is the linguistic and common aspect of conversation. If in a *single* instance someone were able to speak for everyone, he would not need to accept anything in return ; but then there would be no language and no custom. He would not be speaking, he would be *saying* something. The words of God, " Let there be light ! " were said, not spoken. If we nevertheless find in Luther's translation of the Bible : " And God spake ; let there be light ! " the translator means

---

[1] Cf. A. Debrunner, " Sprachwissenschaft und Sprachrichtigkeit ", *Neue Jahrbücher für das klassische Altertum*, vol. L, 1922, p. 201 ff. ; K. Vossler, "Grammatik und Sprachgeschichte," *Logos*, I, 1910, p. 83 ff. ; and *Gesammelte Aufsätze zur Sprachphilosophie*, Munich, 1923, p. 1 ff.

that these words were heard, understood, and answered by chaos, for: "it became light." Saying is an unsociable speaking, for it evokes no receptive passivity and no answer. Law has to be 'spoken', truth has to be 'said'; for the former is social, the latter lonely.

To preserve the usage of a language, a community must alternately make efforts and relax; it must be motoric and sensitive, productive and receptive, active and passive at the same time,[1] like every person in his various rôles during a conversation. The uniting of the active in the passive and the passive in the active is what language has in common with conversation. Both are something mediate, and it is in this mediate behaviour that the individual merges with the language community of which he is a part. He is wrapped up in a language custom, and plays his part in building it up. Every time he says anything, and however he speaks, a language process is taking place in him. It is no accident that Latin and Greek make use of so many middle forms to denote 'speaking' in a language. The ancients had a more immediate intuition than we have of the fact that speaking is something which is happening to us while we are engaged in it, and that the active and the passive aspects can be distinguished, but never separated from one another. Even in conversation, as we saw, listener and speaker are so closely knit into *one* person, that they could only be distinguished as characters, not as independent persons. Even the parts condition each other. Hearing and understanding, questioning and answering, speaking and thinking in a language are all held together by knowledge. No one knows a language who does not practise it in speech and in writing, thinking and articulating in it besides merely hearing and reading it. There are occasions on which the one is of more importance than the other, but they alternate in such a way—as, in walking, the right leg alternates with the left—that only

[1] Cf. K. Vossler, "Der Einzelne und die Sprache", *Logos*, VIII, 1919, p. 266 ff.; and *Gesammelte Aufsätze*, p. 152 ff.

by mutually relieving each other can they fulfil the law of their mutual dependence. As long as the one aspect is active, the others cannot come to rest either. The speaker is his own listener, the writer his own reader. Even in silent thinking our lips often move ; and how can one decipher a manuscript without tracing it in one's imagination ?

It is not easy to associate these twofold aspects of activity and passivity, immediateness and mediateness, freedom and dependence. They always fall apart in the mind. But no one who does not succeed in thinking in this way can ever hope to grasp the concept of language ; for here, as in everything living, opposite attributes are simultaneously present. All living things contradict the law of Identity ; they are active and passive, A and non-A, " the one and the other " at once, since life always carries death in its bosom, or, more accurately, since the one is dependent upon the other. The more we think about one of these aspects, the stronger our attention is directed to the other as something that ought to be distinguished from the first but cannot be separated from it. Life is something different from death ; and because of that, the two can be one. In the same way speaking and hearing, activity and passivity, instinct and custom, speaker and language-community are unities in difference. Thesis and heterothesis belong together ; and only in their union do they form a full concept.[1]

Language is such a unitary manifold. We have defined it as a usage in whose medium conversations take place. These in their turn are something medial, in which speaker and hearer find contact as persons. And the person, again, in so far as he points beyond himself and is in the service of some cause, must be thought of as the medium of this cause. Language thus seems to be the medium of a medium, in which an indefinite number of media meet. The true essence of language is lost to us as it

[1] Cf. Heinrich Rickert, " Das Eine, die Einheit und die Eins ", *Logos*, II, 1911, esp. pp. 30–38.

wanders from custom into conversation, into the various characters and persons, and from there is chased back again through the different media. We see nothing but a network of conductors or roads before us, which fade away into the blue or return upon themselves. What, we ask, is the cause itself, the lightning, the traveller, or the spark that strikes through the persons and characters of conversation and from these into language and back again into the persons, giving coherence, meaning and life to the network ?

Empirical philology gives no answer. Its strength and exactness lie in its view that this cause is something arbitrary, so that it can be either nothing or all possible things, also in its exclusive attention to language alone as the abstract medium for this indefinite ' nothing or all '.

If we nevertheless wish to capture the spark, we must search all the departments of life in which human communities are formed. They are formed only where personalities are growing. A herd without a leader, a mass of individuals, is no language community. If, therefore, we want to understand the life and essence of language, we have to be personalities ourselves and accordingly dissatisfied with merely registering language customs without making any assumptions.

CHAPTER III

LANGUAGE AND RELIGION

WHEN men build up a superindividual life in the family, the nation, or the state, they are not obeying only their natural needs, desires, and instincts, nor are they merely fulfilling moral obligations; but in the first and last instance they are carrying out a religious duty. Family and state cannot be deduced from nature and the moral law alone. Rather do they imply something religious, which the Greeks called εὐσέβεια and the Romans *pietas*.

Pietas is that which is specifically religious in the mundane relationships of human communities, among which we must include language communities. *Pietas magna in parentibus et propinquis, in patria maxima est,* Cicero says in *Somnium Scipionis*.

As a result of the progressive division and separation of the state and other worldly communities from the religious communities, we moderns have lost this pious attitude and with it our insight into the religious basis of our communal life. We do not wish to preach penance to our contemporaries, nor do we predict the downfall of the ' irreligious ' Occident ; for it is in the nature of things that religion as a general concept is less prominent in our thought, the more richly it can unfold itself in its special manifestations as the creative activity of the artist, the scientist, the politician. It is easier to point out the effectiveness of the transcendental impulse in a negro tribe, or in a colony of bees or ants, than in a highly civilized state. From the burnt offerings of cannibals, religion rises as a disgusting smell ; in the lonely work of a conscientiously critical scientist of our ' godless ' age, even the acutest ' smeller-out of souls ' hardly recognizes it. But only a shallow mind will see religion in the former, and deem it to be absent, or only feebly present in the latter. Religion is not measured by the steam or incense it sends up, but by the inward illumination and silence of him who has it. As it becomes more delicate and more refined it vanishes from public manifestations, becomes reserved and shy, withdraws from all communities, even from literary and artistic expression and, in a realm beyond action and talk, where its essence is at home, grows up as a purely personal state of certainty in the individual. Its sphere of validity is then the individual alone.

What is true is valid, whether I as an individual know it or not, and is correct whether I test it or not; even beauty is " blessed in itself ", whether I notice it or not. Only religious certainty lives and dies with me. This does not mean that it depends on my mood or caprice. The way my happiness is fashioned is for me alone; but it does not lie in my power to make it valid or not. If I have it, it has me and bends me to its will. The true believer is possessed by his God. " *Hier stehe ich, ich kann nicht anders,*" Luther said. In such people, attempts to escape from this domination end in a feeling of fear or uncertainty, which can lead to the complete disruption of their psychic balance. Religious mania is the reverse side of religious certainty. The average person, of course, knows neither the one nor the other state, just as he is drowsily insensitive towards impressions of beauty, of truth, and of goodness. He looks upon every man who is in any respect excitable or creative as a dreamer, if not as a fool. But, however small the dose of spiritual values that he can stand, those values exist even for him.

But the peculiar character of religious certainty, which is only to be found in those who have experienced it, and who possess it because it has grown within them, is that to the outsider it appears merely as a belief or an opinion, if not as error and prejudice. Every attempt to communicate it meets with suspicion, for the same reason that every attempt to take over the certainty of someone else results merely in opinion, which remains ' subjective ' and therefore superficial until personal experience leads to ' objectively-subjective ' certainty.   Certainty can no more be communicated than a sense of balance to one trying to learn tight-rope walking or cycling.   The acrobat is born with it, and may have it on a bicycle but not on a tight-rope.   In a similar way the religious sense may be inherent in a plant or an animal, but at the higher level of self-consciousness it has to be acquired again, like the sense of balance on a swaying cord.   Opinion is something external, vacillating, general; it makes us giddy, and within it we can continually lose and recreate our certainty. It is the specific medium of religious certainty, just as language is the specific medium of poetic imagination— a statement that we shall have to prove later.   By itself, that is without certainty, opinion is as unsubstantial, abstract, and valueless as language without imagination ; both must seek a momentary validity outside their own substance, in an eternally elusive and accidental *consensus gentium*.

When one ' means ' something, one is appealing to the *entendement* of others.   Opinion without certainty only has value through others.   Religious certainty is something that cannot be externalized ;   and when I bow to some definite opinion I become a different person with respect to my certainty.   But if I force myself to express my certainty, it, too, becomes opinion, and gazes at me with the eyes of a stranger.

Hence the well-known diffidence of the devout in expressing their certainty.   They are intuitively aware that it will lose itself in the tumult of opinions and come into friendly or inimical contact with all sorts of current opinions of a political, philosophic, or æsthetic nature. This *agoraphobia*, to which every sensitive person is occasionally subject, is a shield for religious modesty. Only those are free from such inhibitions who can build up their certainty and put it to practical use within dogmatically and authoritatively circumscribed spheres of opinion such as the church. Instead of natural modesty, they may even develop a certain unctuousness, since in the circles of the faithful religious sentiment is honoured and is allowed to exhibit its most solemn forms of expression. The church protects the devout by interposing between them and the opinions of the world its inflexible teachings, its dogmatic opinions, which are a kind of peace or trade treaty and a customs barrier between religious certainty and worldly opinion.

Religious certainty cannot express itself in human society other than as opinion. It may be free, spontaneous opinion, subject to every worldly influence, or it may be protected and armed by the church or the state. We must assume, therefore, that language cannot transmit more of our certainty than mere opinion. It does not seem possible that religion can have a second specific medium in language other than opinion. And, indeed, religion depends only indirectly on language, not directly ; for music, architecture, painting, dancing, and gestures are of similar, and often even better service. It can frequently dispense with the mediation of language. The community of language and the community of religion can be, but are not necessarily the same, chiefly because religious certainty can only express itself through language as opinion. So it expresses itself sometimes in rigidly dogmatic forms, sometimes fluently and easily, using now a loquacious, now a mysterious and involved style. Indeed, the worshippers in a church can even feel themselves the more intimately in touch with their god if they do not understand the language used in their cult, a proof how much deeper that which is intended goes than that which is spoken and understood.[1]

Nevertheless, pious minds are always inclined to look

[1] *Saliorum carmina vix sacerdotibus suis satis intellecta.* Quintilian, I, 6, 40.

upon language, like everything else, as the special gift and tool of divinity.[1]

But if one points out that language is also used for evil, and that it can give rise to fraud, misunderstandings and confusions, the sinfulness and blindness of man are held responsible, or some particular sin that has brought with it the curse of God. See what Dante says in *De vulgari eloquentia*, I, 6 : " Since men pursue their business in many very different languages, so that they can frequently understand each other with words no better than without, let us endeavour to discover that language which the first man probably used." Everyone's national pride would like to make him believe that his own mother tongue was also that of mankind, " but we maintain that with the first human soul, God also created a particular language, a primal language form for the naming of things, and the structure of sentences and speech. All human language would be using this form, had it not been destroyed by our pride. Adam and all his descendants up to the building of the tower of Babel, the tower of language confusion, spoke in this primal form. The sons of Heber, whom we call Hebrews, inherited it. They alone kept it after the fall of the tower, so that the Saviour, who was to come from among them as a man, should be able to use the language of Grace and not that of confusion. Hebrew, therefore, is the language that was formed on the lips of the first speaker." Dante's style gets more excited as he continues by describing the instigation of the building of the tower by Nimrod as an act of criminal rebellion against God ; how all the peoples of the earth with the exception of the Israelites took part

---

[1] In the following pages I have made use of an essay, " Über das Verhältnis von Sprache und Religion ", *Neuere Sprachen*, XXVIII, 1920, p. 97 ff. It has been amplified by the numerous examples quoted by Leo Spitzer in his review of my article that appeared in the *Literaturblatt für germanische und romanische Philologie*, XLII, 1921, especially p. 81 ff. A rich material from our point of view is to be found in Hermann Güntert, *Von der Sprache der Götter und Geister*, Halle, 1921.

in it, and how, according to the magnitude of their sin, their language got cruder and more barbaric ; how they had spread over the earth, and how the curse continues, dividing the languages from generation to generation into trunks, branches and twigs, that is, into language families and dialects, and so by continual modifications driving them ever further apart. In order to stop some of this unending destruction, the grammarians had invented Latin as a written language with fixed rules, as an artificial island in the stream of language degradation.

If, then, God is the author of human language, he must have had his own language as well.[1] And we find, in fact, that the word of God, *mēmrā*, plays a tremendous part in the Bible. " And God said, Let there be light : and there was light ".—" By the word of the LORD were the heavens made ; and all the host of them by the breath of his mouth " (33rd Psalm, 6). Not only did this word of God create the whole world ; it also cares for the world and makes it fruitful. " For as the rain cometh down, and the snow from heaven, and returneth not thither, but watereth the earth, and maketh it bring forth and bud, that it may give seed to the sower, and bread to the eater : So shall my word be that goeth forth out of my mouth : it shall not return unto me void, but it shall accomplish that which I please, and it shall prosper in the thing whereto I send it " (Isaiah lv. 10–11). The word of God is also full of destructive force. " Is not my word like as a fire ? saith the LORD ; and like a hammer that breaketh the rock in pieces ? " (Jeremiah xxiii. 29). Later the Greek concept of universal reason is added to the Israelitic conception of the word of God. Logos and *mēmrā* merge, and in the Gospel according to St. John, Christ appears as the incarnation of the word of God. " In the beginning was the Word, and the Word was with God, and the Word was God. . . . And the Word was made flesh, and dwelt among us (and we beheld his glory, the glory as of the only begotten of the

[1] Cf. Güntert, *op. cit.*, p. 20 ff.

Father), full of grace and truth" (St. John i. 1 and 14).[1]

It would be easy, but careless, to discard as unimportant inventions the ideas of a divine language, the word of God, and of a language given by God to man. For with an insistence that almost seems to be a necessity, such ideas recur in many other religions, even if only in the primitive form of a supernatural power attributed to language. Deeply implanted in all of us is the belief in the power of magic formulæ, blessings, curses, oracles, prophecies and prayers, and in some cases at any rate the belief that language is the link between man and superhuman agencies, be they divine or Satanic. The most intense labour is necessary to convince men that language is of use only for speaking, that is, as a means of communication.

It was soon discovered and generally recognized that not every language and not every man was capable of exorcizing the supernatural through words. This led to a distinction between religious and profane speaking, which became more or less rigid. For the purpose of conversing with the deity, the language can remain grammatically the same as that of daily intercourse, or it can become different. It depends on a number of factors, all of which we cannot as yet appreciate. But we can at least say that the more completely a religious community segregates itself from the outside world, the stronger will be the tendency to keep a special ' Sunday ' language for religious purposes. The Jews did this while they were dispersed through an alien world. Hebrew has become for them the language of religious ceremonies. In the Catholic Occident, Latin remained the language of religion and of all church and theological matters for a very long time after the national languages, German, French, Spanish, and Italian had established themselves

---

[1] The Indians seem to have worshipped the word *vāc* almost as a god. Cf. Güntert, p. 49, and E. Cassirer, *Philosophie der symbolischen Formen*, vol. I, p. 57 (Berlin, 1923).

in mundane affairs.   Even to-day the Russians use church
Slavonic when they pray, and the Mohammedans use the
Arabic of their prophet, though in everyday life they
may be using Turkish or Slavonic or some other language.
They believe that the Koran is efficacious only in its
original language, and that it loses its effect by being
translated.   Religious people very often cling to those
languages or even to the actual words in which they
first received religious instructions or revelations.   This
respect for authority can become a terror of holy syllables
and letters, which reaches its height in magic, where a
single mispronounced name or sound, the omission of a
word, a wrong gesture, can destroy the whole effect.

We ought not to smile even at that ; for such half-
childish, half-superstitious reverence for the divine word
and magical incantations is the mother of philosophic
exactitude and the technique of editing.   To take a few
examples : inverted commas have developed from the
small strokes or lines with which the sanctity of quotations
from the Bible used to be marked in the theological
writings of the Middle Ages.   Contraction as a means
of abbreviating writing was first practised by learned
Jews in ancient Egypt.   The sacred name of God was
written in golden letters, in the form of a seal, and in this
way it could be emphasized and concealed at the same
time.   This religious ceremony was gradually extended
to other sacred names, and eventually to ordinary words,
thus becoming a practical aid to quick writing.[1]   If the
belief had not existed that the Bible was God's word,
we should hardly have developed such exact, unswervingly
conscientious textual criticism as is our pride and sometimes our bane to-day.   And beyond that our whole
consciousness of style has been developed and schooled
by the difference between sacred and profane.   All peoples
and times have felt that a solemn style was particularly
suited to religious things.   This ceremonial style can
only extend to profane spheres when a certain degree of

[1] Ludwig Traube, *Nomina Sacra*, Munich, 1907.

religious sentiment is transferred to mundane affairs, to the state, to law, or to art.[1] For this reason ceremonial Latin, at first used only for religious purposes, could develop into a written language and finally crystallize once more into church Latin, while vulgar Latin continued to develop into Italian, Spanish, French, Roumanian, etc. In the course of centuries differences of style have become differences of language.[2]

Many historians and students of comparative religion are of opinion that in the beginning all cultures were dominated by and rooted in religion. As human endeavour begins to be specialized and emerges from the unity of religion, and as special fields of knowledge become more worldly and independent, so a civilization splits up into a number of separate, non-religious spheres. Law, science, art, they think, become more and more superficial, technical, and disconnected, the more they recede from religion. Culture then dries up and degenerates into ' civilization ', which knows only technical problems and must finally perish from inner sterility. This line of thought has been most emphatically developed by Oswald Spengler in *Der Untergang des Abendlandes*.

If this is so, it should also be true for language ; and, indeed, where their historical origins are still recognizable, it would seem that language and religion were once closely interwoven. This was the theory held by Max Müller, the Anglo-German scholar of languages and religions. He tried to construct a genealogical tree of religions like that of languages. " If," he says, " there is a truly genetic relation between languages, the same tie that binds and separates the main languages of

---

[1] Cf. the investigations on the history of the style of prayers and predicatory formulæ, by Ed. Norden, *Agnostos Theos*, Berlin and Leipzig, 1913, p. 140 ff.

[2] Cf. H. Schuchardt, *Der Vokalismus des Vulgärlateins*, vol. I, Leipzig, 1866, particularly p. 44 ff. Some observers have reported that the Dyaks in the Dutch East Indies have two different languages, an everyday one, and one for ritual, which consists only of taboo words. Cf. Güntert, *op. cit.*, p. 16 f.

humanity should also bring back the religions, at any rate the oldest, into their true mutual relation, both separately and as a whole." [1] Müller believed he could prove " that before the first breaking up of the Aryans there was an Aryan, before the first breaking up of the Semites a Semitic religion, and that there are traces of a Turanian belief in God, which goes beyond the separation of the agglutinative north Turanian languages and has its roots in the monosyllabic Chinese languages." [2]

We have become more cautious to-day, for numerous examples have taught us that we cannot assume similarity in the contents of faiths from the similarity or equivalence of the names of deities.[3] Sometimes the name remains while the belief changes, sometimes it is the other way round ; and sometimes—but who knows where and for how long ?—they remain together. The most significant religious concepts are continually being renewed. A man can be a truly pious believer without clinging to the actual letter of his holy books and teachings. For, as we have seen, language is not an immediate, but only a secondary medium for religious certainty. In contrast to the fearful, anxious, and largely magical attitude to which the formal aspects are of such great importance, there is, thank God, also a freer, more courageous, more inward kind of belief, an essentially mystical attitude towards religion, which breaks through forms, is independent of words, and rejects the mere letter. For " the letter kills, but the spirit gives life ".[4] Above all, the leading and creative minds of religious communities feel themselves forced to break through the structure of traditional forms and modes of expression. Thus the

[1] F. Max Müller, *Einleitung in die vergleichende Religionswissenschaft*, 2nd. edn., Strassburg, 1876, p. 138.

[2] P. 193.

[3] O. Gruppe, in *Die griechischen Kulte und Mythen*, 1887, has shown that not a single religious concept of the Greeks can with certainty be proved to have an Indo-Germanic origin.

[4] How powerful the belief in letters and formulæ can be, is shown in Güntert, *op. cit.*, p. 39 ff.

prophets continued to interpret the Mosaic laws ever more widely and deeply, until the Christian movement poured them into the mould of the heathen languages of the Greeks, Syrians, and Romans. Luther banished Latin from the cult and made German the means of Protestant intercession. A similar task was undertaken before him by the Waldensians and after him by the Calvinists. What happened in such great ' reformations ' is still taking place every day. The deeper true piety is, the less can it bear to be bound by words.

When the Holy Ghost came upon the apostles on the day of Pentecost, we are told that " there appeared unto them cloven tongues like as of fire, and it sat upon each of them. And they were all filled with the Holy Ghost, and began to speak with other tongues, as the Spirit gave them utterance. . . . Now when this was noised abroad, the multitude came together, and were confounded, because that every man heard them speak in his own language. And they were all amazed and marvelled, saying one to another, Behold, are not all these which speak Galileans ? and how hear we every man in our own tongue, wherein we were born ? Parthians, and Medes, and Elamites, and the dwellers in Mesopotamia, and in Judæa, and Cappadocia, in Pontus, and Asia, Phrygia, and Pamphilia, in Egypt, and in the parts of Lybia about Cyrene, and strangers of Rome, Jews and proselytes, Cretes and Arabians, we do hear them speak in our tongues the wonderful works of God. . . . What meaneth this ? "

This fine myth expresses the thought that religious truth lies beyond, or rather before, all human speech. It is therefore bound to no one language, but can unfold itself in each—only partially, it is true, since it cannot be fully expressed in any.

One final mystery remains, which is unattainable by language. When Dante wrote the *Paradiso*, he realized that here *no* language could be adequate. The blessed spirits and the angels in his heaven communicate with one another without language ; for they read each other's thoughts mirrored in the divine light. In the *Paradiso* Dante also corrects the view he put forward in his *de vulgari eloquentia*. Even Hebrew, he says, was not created by God, but was the product of human nature ; and the language of Adam perished long before the tower of Babel.[1] Dante has, therefore, progressed from an essentially magical philosophy of language to a more mystical and naturalistic conception.

Extreme mystics, finally, see in language only the earthly obstacle that prevents us from attaining an immediate perception of religious truth and certainty.

> Denkst Du den Namen Gotts zu sprechen in der Zeit ?
> Man spricht ihn auch nicht aus in einer Ewigkeit,

we are told in *Der Cherubinische Wandersmann*.

Dionysius the Areopagite, father of Christian mystics, wrote a treatise on the names of God in the fifth century A.D. One of his main contentions is that no name fits God, because he stands above all things that have names ; but since he is the creator of all things, all names of all things could be applied to him. In short, God is ἀνώνυμος and πολυώνυμος at once.[2] Ever since then, mystics have never tired of glorifying God as the highest and the lowest, the greatest and the smallest, the day and the night, all and nothing ; they have surrounded him with a wild dance of words where each negates the one before it.

---

[1] Opera naturale è ch'uom favella ;
    Ma, così o così, natura lascia
    Poi fare a voi secondo che v'abbella.
                    (Parad. XXVI, 130 ff.)

[2] Dionysius Areopagita, " De divinis nominibus ", *Patrol. Graeca*, III, Cap. II, § 7. Οὕτως οὖν τῇ πάντων αἰτίᾳ καὶ ὑπὲρ πάντα οὔσῃ καὶ τὸ ἀνώνυμον ἐφαρμόσει, καθ' ὃ ὑπὲρ πάντα ἐστί, καὶ οὐδὲν τούτων καὶ πάλιν πάντα ἐφαρμόσει τὰ τῶν ὄντων ὀνόματα, καθ' ὃ αἰτία πάντων ἐστί, καὶ μετέχουσιν αὐτῆς ἀναλόγως τὰ πάντα, ἀκριβῶς οὔσης ἁπάντων βασιλείας, ὡς τῷ μὲν ἀξιώματι ὑπεξῃρημένης, καὶ μὴ ἀπό τινος ὀνομαζομένης, τῇ δὲ προνοίᾳ καὶ τῇ συνοχῇ ἐντὸς οὔσης, καὶ ἀπ' αὐτῶν ὀνομαζομένης.

C

Wo ist der Schönste, den ich liebe?
Wo ist mein Seelenbräutigam?
Wo ist mein Hirt und auch mein Lamm,
Um den ich mich so sehr betrübe? . . .

Wo ist mein Brunn, ihr kühlen Brünne?
Ihr Bäche, sagt, wo ist mein Bach?
Mein Ursprung, dem ich gehe nach?
Mein Quell', auf den ich immer sinne?

Wo ist mein Lustwald, o ihr Wälder?
Ihr Ebenen, wo ist mein Plan?
Wo ist mein grünes Feld, ihr Felder?
Ach zeigt mir doch zu ihm die Bahn!

Wo ist mein Täublein, ihr Gefieder?
Wo ist mein treuer Pelikan,
der mich lebendig machen kann?
Ach dass ich ihn doch finde wieder!

Ihr Berge, wo ist meine Höhe?
Ihr Täler, sagt, wo ist mein Tal?
Schaut, wie ich hin und wieder gehe
Und ihn gesucht hab überall.

.   .   .   .   .

Ach Gott, wo soll ich weiter fragen!
Er ist bei keiner Kreatur.—

(Angelus Silesius.)

And Rainer Maria Rilke writes in his *Stundenbuch* :

Du bist die Zukunft, grosses Morgenrot
Über den Ebenen der Ewigkeit.
Du bist der Hahnschrei nach der Nacht der Zeit,
Der Tau, die Morgenmette und die Maid,
Der fremde Mann, die Mutter und der Tod.

.   .   .   .   .

Du bist der Dinge tiefer Inbegriff,
Der seines Wesens letztes Wort verschweigt—
Und sich den andern immer anders zeigt :
Dem Schiff als Küste und dem Land als Schiff.[1]

We have come to know many different attitudes of the
religious man towards language. Some cling to the word,

[1] Cf. August Faust, " Der dichterische Ausdruck mystischer
Religiosität bei R. M. Rilke ", in *Logos*, XI, 1922, p. 235 ff.

the syllable, the letter, even the accent. Among the ancient Greeks and Romans, for instance, praying aloud was the rule ; people who muttered or prayed silently were regarded as magicians. *Tacitas preces in templo dis allegasti, igitur magus est*, it is said in the *Apologia* of Apuleius.[1] Others, again, do not attempt to clothe divinity in words or to reach it through language ; they dematerialize and reject language as a mere veil, an obstacle, a snare and a delusion, that interposes itself between the world of eternity and the world of sense.

Here in religious life we find repeated those attitudes and mental types, which, as we pointed out in the first chapter, are the most general starting-points for the study of language.

But language itself behaves equivocally and unpredictably with regard to the contents of religion. In Spanish, for instance, the word for ' God ' has become watered down to a mere superlative. *Llueve de Dios*, " it is raining hard " ; *pegáronlle de Dios*, " he was thoroughly beaten " ; one can say *fulano es más rico*, or even *más feo, más cobarde que Dios*, without in the least feeling that it is blasphemous. In Mallorka *tot-deu* has the meaning " everyone ", " all ". The Sardinian *ite*, " what ? ", has been formalized from *quid deo*.[2] The French phrases, *il n'est pas Dieu possible, Dieu croyable, Dieu permis*,[3] the Old Italian conjunctions *quamvisdeo, eziandio, avvegnia Iddio che*, show how unscrupulously language uses the emphatic power of the divine name. The saints are no better off, as we see in the Catalonian ; *¿ en nom di quin sant ?* meaning " in what way ? ", or the Spanish ; *¿ a santo de qué ?*, " what for ? ", " why ? ".[4]

---

[1] Cf. Siegfr. Sudhaus, " Lautes und leises Beten ", *Archiv für Religionswissenschaft*, IX, 1906, p. 185 ff.

[2] Cf. Meyer-Lübke, " Zur Kenntnis des Altloguduresischen ", *Sitzungsber. d. Akad. d. Wissensch. in Wien*, CXLV, 1902, p. 35 ff.

[3] Cf. A. Tobler, *Vermischte Beiträge zur französischen Grammatik*, 3rd. series, 2nd. edn., Leipzig, 1908, p. 122 ff.

[4] Cf. Leo Spitzer, *Aufsätze zur romanischen Syntax und Stilistik*, Halle, 1918, p. 262 ff.

On the other hand, a religious heritage is often so faithfully preserved by language, and the smallest, most superficial detail so carefully embalmed, that this very faithfulness is a proof of a somewhat unthinking, absent-minded participation. The attitude of language towards religious things resembles that of an absent-minded professor, in whose capacious pockets all sorts of irrelevant objects jostle each other, while the most important have been lost. In Bosnia, for instance, where Orthodox, Mohammedans, and Catholics live together, the different confessions can be recognized by several peculiarities of dialect. In foreign words the Catholics avoid the *f* and use a *p* instead ; thus they say *Stjepan* and *Josip*, where the Orthodox say *Stjefan* and *Josif* because they feel that the *p* is something Roman Catholic. The Mohammedans and Catholics, again, cling to archaic forms of the so-called *êa* dialect, which is foreign to the other Bosnians.[1] The written form of Obwaldic Rhaeto-Romance is, as we know, differentiated into Protestant and Catholic forms. In Catholic Bavaria of the eighteenth century there was strong opposition against the new form of the creed, " *Ich glaube* AN *Gott Vater* " instead of " IN *Gott Vater* " as it had been. The *an* was hated as being Lutheran, as was the final -*e* in words like *Liebe, Sonne, Blume.* In France the Protestants say *jesykrist*, the Catholics *jesykri*. The Spaniards say *Dios*, the Spanish Jews *Dio*. In writing, religious differences are even more carefully preserved than in common speech.[2]

This double-faced, faithlessly-faithful attitude of languages towards every kind of religious value is due to the fact that language is by nature symbolic. ' Symbolic ' is the theological term for ' mediate '. Everything that functions as a medium and is not taken in and for itself as absolute, be it an opinion, a dogma, a church, a con-

---

[1] Cf. Matthias Miese, *Die Entstehungsursache der jüdischen Dialekte*, Vienna, 1915.

[2] *Idem, Die Gesetze der Schriftgeschichte. Konfession und Schrift im Leben der Völker*, Vienna, 1919.

versation, a deed, or a person, is regarded as a symbol
by the religious mind, which tries to penetrate the veils
hiding reality.

That is the reason why there are as many differences
of opinion in the philosophy of religion about the value
of symbolism as about the value of language. Sometimes
these differences are accentuated to such a degree that
they give rise to the bitterest religious wars. Think of
the battles that were fought about the divine or human
nature of Christ ; how much blood and ink has been spilt
over the question whether Christ was a man and represented the divine only symbolically, or whether he really
was God and only symbolically a man. Or think of the
fight over Holy Communion between Luther and Zwingli ;
for the former, wine *is* the blood of Christ, for the
latter, wine merely represents it. One can therefore only
say that, if a symbol is to acquire and retain religious
value, it has to be believed. For the decisive factor in
any religious attitude is certainty, a certainty of belief
that is as personal as it is absolute, as mysterious as it is
obvious. As long as a symbol is understood merely
symbolically, it is valueless, and remains an appearance,
an illusion, a veil, and an obstacle, like language with its
empty, sounding words. Only that symbol is alive for
religion, in which the godhead is thought and believed to
be active and immanent. Literally and in fact, here and
now, the symbol must *be* God, and not merely *mean*
God, just as in a magic word of power, in a benediction,
in a prophecy, in holy writ, God lives and has his being,
God becomes language or even the letters of a text.

There are not only church and cult symbols, but also
political, moral, scientific, and artistic symbols. The
red flag is a political symbol, for which the revolutionary
will go through fire and die, because here and now, at
this decisive moment, it not only represents but *is* the
revolution in its general aspect as well as in its immediate
and concrete manifestation of the will to revolt. The
man who raises the red flag on the king's palace has a

definite political belief, he wants the revolution, and wants it through the hoisting of the flag. The idle spectator, who wants nothing, and has no belief, sees in the same flag merely a stick with a cloth tied to it, a sign for something that does not concern him. The hat can become a moral symbol, when, overcoming myself, I respectfully raise it to my opponent. Then, in so far as he has reverence and moral religion, he will see virtue radiating from my bared head. A scientific symbol may be a mathematical formula ; for, provided I take it seriously in a scientific sense, the formula as it stands is a vehicle of knowledge, that is, of the particular science with which I am concerned.

The questions relevant to all symbols are, have they validity or not ? have they the value of certainty ? are they the thing itself, or only the appearance ? If we keep these in mind, we are able to resolve the peculiar contradiction of the statement that a merely symbolic symbol is no symbol. If the appearance of a thing is merely appearance, and not a real manifestation, it is not the thing itself.

Symbols are like persons. Everything depends on whether a person is true or false, whether he is merely acting his part, whether he is a mask or a personality. As it is with a personal spokesman, so it is with impersonal language. No sooner has the divine appeared in language, than it again recedes. This unreliability of language contaminates its relation to all aspects of life.

Language is sometimes politically active, and sometimes not. Hence there are statesmen, the great orators, the Demosthenes and Ciceros, who lean entirely on the might of words. Others place no value on language and demand deeds only ; these are the great silent men, soldiers like Moltke and Charlemagne.

> Der König Karl am Steuer sass,
> Der hat kein Wort gesprochen,
> Er lenkt das Schiff mit festem Mass,
> Bis sich der Sturm gebrochen.—

To some, a science like philosophy consists of words and their meaning, as the word ' Logic ' indicates ; to others all explanations in terms of words are as empty as they were to the man who defined philosophy as *Umwortung der Worte*—rewording words—instead of *Umwertung der Werte*—revaluing values. These antagonistic conceptions appear even in poetry, which to most people would appear to be language, and language only. There are classical word-artists like Virgil, Racine, and Flaubert ; and there are destroyers of the art of words, those who are consciously primitive and clumsy, who deny form and regard it ironically, the romantics, ultra-symbolists, expressionists, to whom the essence of poetry is the dionysian intoxication of phantasy, and not the apollinic creation of language.

Which of these is right, and is it possible to find a compromise between them ? I believe we shall be safest if we return to our original example of religion, and consider the first and simplest forms of religious thought. The oldest gods were solitary, and were gods of the moment. That, at any rate, is what we believe we know at the present time. An example of this is *Kurche*, a god of the ancient Prussians. They believed that a deity lived in every harvest field. When they began to reap, the god retreated step by step before the mowing sickle or scythe to the end of the field. But in the last ears of wheat he might be caught and bound. Hence the last sheaf was looked upon as sacred, as that *Kurche* in which the corn god lived. Every peasant who reaped his field in this belief, had, every time he reaped, and every year, his particular corn daimon whom he could capture, and who died on the threshing floor, to rise again on the fields in spring.[1] The whole world used to be full of such transient gods, gods of certain lightnings, winds, hail-storms, of spears that found their mark, of protective shields, of bubbling springs, gods that suddenly appeared and vanished again, who lived a flickering life like that

[1] H. Usener, *Götternamen*, Bonn, 1896, p. 279 ff.

symbol, the red flag, which lives only while the revolutionary flaunts it, and again becomes a stick with a piece of cloth attached ; or like the doll that is an animate being while the child plays with it, and then again lies inanimate in the corner.

We can now understand why the manifestations of the gods, and of religious thought itself in language, are partly denied and partly affirmed by the pious. In this conflict of opinions we see the ghost of the old transient gods, who live only when one needs them and believes in them.

If we wish to understand how a permanent and personal god arises out of these momentary appearances, we have to go to the history of language. Hermann Usener believed that Apollo was a transient god. In the Doric form his name is ʼΑπέλλων, a compound of the preposition ἀπὸ away from, and the verb πέλειν or πέλεσθαι to move, to drive. ʼΑπέλλων would therefore have meant, ' the driver-away ', and would have been an indeterminate, improvised god who was only invoked when an evil had to be driven off, or a danger forestalled. For purely fortuitous, phonetic reasons, it is assumed, the later Greeks no longer understood the origin and meaning of the term Apollon. The word became unintelligible, dark, and so mysterious. Finally it crystallized into the name of a person, just as one is apt to forget that Saviour means one who saves, or that *Heiland* (Christ) means ' the healer '. As a personal name the word Apollon then became the staff to which the tendrils of myths and cults could cling. Usener's derivation of the word Apollon is probably wrong ; [1] but the fact remains that there are transient gods who, through phonetic accidents, become permanent gods. The word then resembles a block of marble, out of which the religious imagination carves a clear statue of the personified deity.

---

[1] Cf. O. Gruppe, *Bericht über die Literatur zur antiken Mythologie und Religionsgeschichte aus den Jahren* 1898–1905, Leipzig, 1908, p. 401 ff. All the philological derivations of Apollon from the Greek are rejected in this book.

This process is continually repeating itself. As long as the word has a perfectly clear meaning, it does not stimulate the imagination to any extent. That is the reason why Gaia, ' the earth ', Uranos, ' the sky ', Chronos, ' time ', and Helios, ' the sun ', never became real, concrete gods in Greek religion.[1] Such objective nouns and concepts of common speech could at most become the allegorical shadow of a personal god, never his flesh and bone. To do that, the word must first itself become ossified into a personal pronoun. Linguistic forms that are no longer analysable by reason can always become holy vessels, provided our minds are already thinking along religious lines. In this way a number of saints were born from misunderstood words, like the armed soldiers from the dragon's teeth sown by Jason. Thus in a Bernese *Martyrologium* a Saint Cuminia figures, who is no more than the misinterpreted name of a place in Phrygia called Eumenia ; Saint Tibulus or Tripus was made out of the name Tripolis ; the town Massa Candida gave rise to a crowd of three hundred martyrs, about whose massacre an involved and uplifting tale has been written.[2] The peasants have gained a Saint Gétorix from the monument to Vercingetorix, which was erected in 1865 at Alise-Sainte-Reine (Auxois).[3] But the maddest invention was reserved for a Frenchman, Radulfus, who lived at the end of the thirteenth century. This man had the idea—whether in earnest or in jest is hard to decide—that the Latin word for no one, *nemo*, was the name of a person. He hunted for passages in the Bible and other authorities in which this Nemo was mentioned, and actually discovered that Nemo was the true son of God. He preached sermons about him, attracted believers, and founded a sect of worshippers of Nemo, *Neminiana*

---

[1] Usener, *loc. cit.*

[2] Cf. Heinrich Günter, *Legenden-Studien*, Cologne, 1906, p. 70 ; and Hippolyte Delehaye, *Les légendes hagiographiques*, Brussels, 1905, p. 91.

[3] Heinrich Günter, *Die christliche Legende des Abendlandes*, Heidelberg, 1910, p. 123.

secta. Unintentionally, or intentionally, Radulfus became a laughing-stock,[1] like the German traveller in Holland, who is said to have imagined a moving story about Mr. Kannitverstaan. In the year 1435 the body of an unknown girl was discovered in the Spanish village of Jaca, and henceforth worshipped as a saint under the name Eurosia.[2]

From belief to foolishness is but a step, for the world of religion and of the gods is not hedged in, but is open to life on all sides. Also it would be a romantic error to seek true religion only at the beginning of cultures. It is to be found wherever mental life is fresh and active. For what is religion but the certainty of the individual spirit about the spirit of the whole? Only temporarily, spasmodically, in the form of an occasional experience can this certainty break through the sensuous atmosphere with which the daily life of our bodies surrounds us. Only in some who are born as Sunday children can this certainty become a permanent state. I do not know. At any rate it only shows itself fitfully in language, which is, after all, the medium of everyday intercourse. Every attempt to hold it fast in language fails. There are, it is true, sacred words, sentences, formulæ, writings, and, if you like, even sacred secret languages; but they have become so only because they have been set aside and are preserved for this special purpose. In themselves, that is, by their linguistic nature, they are by no means guarded against profanation; on the contrary, they are dependent on it.

Sacred words are no whit better off than any other word. They bloom and die like the transient gods, like symbols, like catchwords. The catchwords of democracy, or the cry, " equal opportunities for talent ", may

---

[1] H. Denifle, in the *Archiv für Lit. und Kirchengeschichte d. Mittelalters*, Freiburg i. Br., IV (1888), p. 330 ff.; and Paul Lehmann, *Die Parodie im Mittelalter*, Munich, 1922, p. 240 ff.

[2] E. A. Stückelberg, " Eine apokryphe Heilige des späten Mittelalters ", *Archiv für Religionswissenschaft*, XVII, 1914, p. 159 ff.

work wonders to-day and lift the world off its hinges;
but some day, in the degree to which democratic
spirit and belief leave them, these rallying cries will
become mechanized, an empty shell for babblers and
children.

Between the times when it is fully alive and completely
dead, the catchword goes through a trance-like phase in
which it is particularly dangerous; for it is only half
believed and so serves to delude both the people and one's
own conscience. This intermediate phase of half truth, half
sacredness and hypocrisy has made such an impression
on philologists like Fritz Mauthner and Leo Spitzer, that
they tend to regard the whole of language as an illusion
of the mind from which there is no escape.

Language, doubtless, is inadequate in some respects;
for at bottom all words are merely bad substitutes for
feelings, actions, and activities of the mind. Man would
probably never have thought of speaking, had he been
all-loving, omnipotent, and omniscient. There is some
truth in the belief that our tongues were loosened by the
feeling of our helplessness, our inner and outer need. But
has language really mitigated our troubles? It seems to
me that the modes of expression, both in creatures who
possess speech and in dumb creatures, are inadequate. And
yet not in the same way; for need has found an expression in language. To this extent, therefore, the motive and
content of speech is the inadequacy of man, and all his
languages bear this stigma. Measured by themselves,
however, as an expression of human inadequacy, our
languages are perfectly reliable and efficient; for they
express what we want them to: our needs and desires.
Indeed they express these things doubly, mediately and
immediately. Immediately, our language is concerned
with all those situations and needs that are agitating us
at the moment; and in this sense language fulfils its
purpose by being " a sociable noise " that we can emit,
and in so doing forget " the thousand ills that flesh is
heir to ". Mediately, however, and in an undercurrent,

all our words express a feeling of weakness and a longing for other things.

In this mediate aspect of language the truly religious element has its being, the element of opinion, which, it is true, is not exclusively religious, but is common to all forms of psychic life. Though hidden, and only occasionally shining forth, it is somehow always present, if not as certainty, at any rate as an unexpressed but self-evident longing for certainty; if not as religion, then certainly as a natural desire of the soul for religion. How could it otherwise, like a transient god of the moment, suddenly emerge from language, as we have seen, had it not been active underground all the time? How could catchwords arise, if languages were not full of psychic tensions or currents? Their hidden fluid usually only makes itself felt as a feeling tone, be it in the colours of hope, fear, or anxiety, in those of doubt and uncertainty, or of love, hate, desire, and trustfulness, of joy or pain. In whatever key we are speaking to someone; about whatever subject or circumstance; whether we are speaking intimately or in anger; there need be no syllable of intimacy or anger in our whole talk. Nevertheless these feelings are present as the fundamental basis of our speech, and are recognized in voice, accent, and facial expression by everyone who has any sense for that key signature. It corresponds more or less to that which poets lift out of human nature and temperament—in the last resort out of their own individuality—into art; that which actors embody in a part; in short, the psychic life in our speaking. It is the heart's blood of words, by virtue of which a confidential talk is the expression of confidence, an angry one the expression of anger through language, without anger or confidence having been called by name at all.

This vital fluid appears always as something special, something purely individual, in the speech of the moment; in speaking, therefore, not in language. " Appears " for the time being merely means that it betrays itself and is capable of being understood, not that it expressly reveals itself, portrays, or creates. To express the feeling and meaning behind words is the work of the poet ; it is something artistic, which not everyone is capable or desirous of expressing.

The difference between the spontaneous appearance of our feelings in speech, and their artistic expression by means of speech, can best be seen in the case of the speaker who consciously tries to avoid their expression. Take the most inartistic, untheatrical man, one who through shame or shyness keeps his feelings out of his words as much as possible, without, however, consciously trying to act the opposite way. In spite of the poverty of his language, sometimes even because of it, by his very stammering and grunting, we can still detect his repressed feelings. They trickle through between the words, which finally betray him. Instead of the dam they are intended to be, they become a filter, which distils the most hidden and intimate of his inner states. The fire of the soul gnaws through language. If I may say so, this impersonal treachery of language constitutes its religious aspect. It is a marvellous, yet natural coalescing of words with the soul, a defenceless and spontaneous surrender of the voice and of all the organs of speech and the nerve paths to our feelings, an involuntary truthfulness, naturalness, and spontaneity, without which all our speaking would be but an empty jingle.

The artists of realism and naturalism, Flaubert, Mérimée, Maupassant, Hauptmann, Verga, and others, systematically made use of this natural spirituality and warmth of language in their attempts at impersonalness and *impassibilité*. They stylized the inartistic and untheatrical part of humanity in their characters and in themselves, in order to achieve stronger artistic effects. They implied a soberness and frugality in their emotional life, from which, in fact, they were far removed ; for fundamentally it was exuberant and romantic. In order to portray and fashion their inner life, they relied on the natural warmth and religious transparency of their apparently stony and cold words. They even made use of scientific terms and of expressions taken from various dialects—the most clumsy and most virginal literary material—the more surely to allow the hidden and modest spiritual forces of language to express themselves. But the discipline and calculation of their diplomatic art of language has no more in common with the natural behaviour of the man we described above, with his inability to express himself, his lack of artistic talent, and his modesty, than my reflexion has in common with me. So wide is the difference, and so close is the resemblance between one and the same word in its spiritual bondage and its artistic freedom, between the natural or religious, and the artistic or æsthetic spontaneity of our speech.

Glossolalia or ' speaking in tongues ', is religious speaking in a narrow, crude, strictly theological, sectarian sense.[1] Unintelligible voices and sounds burst from the overstimulated mind and organs of speech of the ecstatic. There is no doubt that he is then particularly strongly under the influence of the emotional value of sounds, rhythms, melodies, rhymes, alliterations, etc., in short, of the whole sensual character of speech. But this stammering ebullition is not language, for the simple reason that it remains unintelligible both to himself and to an impartial audience. However spiritual, or however profound the emotional emphasis of his effusion may be, as an act of speech it remains below the threshold of human language because it cannot be understood. It is religious expression, but not language, for the element of imparting is absent.

It may be doubted whether the designation ' religious ' is applicable to the psychic emphasis of our common speech. But that is a quibble in words. ' The soul ' is, after all, a religious concept, which Psychology has appropriated, but which it can neither create nor resolve

[1] Cf. Güntert, *op. cit.*, p. 23 ff., and p. 73 ff.

with its own methods. If Psychology is satisfied with the definition of the soul as " the totality of inner experiences " (W. Wundt), it is again using a concept taken from religious life, that of experience. The worldly man, at the door of whose consciousness only the chance experiences of the day knock in the form of impressions, encounters and so on, would never have arrived through his thinking at the concept of ' inner experience ', of *Erlebnis*. To grasp this concept at its real, not etymological, source, we have to seek that unique, miraculous experience, the decisive psychic event through which Saul became Paul, Augustine a Christian, and Luther a reformer. The more general and apparently rationalized concept of experience, which includes all those frequent and more common experiences to which mankind is subject, is without doubt a derived one, wider in scope, but emptier in essence. It is the hat which is raised to the other.

Soul, psychic experience, inner knowledge, inner opinion are all religious concepts, since to begin with the processes that lie behind them have a personal and immediate meaning only for one who has religion. The interest of the psychologist in such mental phenomena is only secondary. Churches and temples were built ages before laboratories. For ages men were sacrificed and slaughtered because of the unique power of religion, before we learnt to analyse and understand its generalities. If, then, we wish to fathom the hidden, psychic meaning of the speech of man, we need the inquisitorial spirit, which has been developed to a higher degree in the confessional than in the lecture rooms of psychology.

The question now remains whether this permanent spiritual marriage of meaning and speaking is detectable in language, and whether we can prove that languages also have something akin to a soul and an individuality. To begin with, an undercurrent of psychic meaning can be grasped and interpreted only in the speech of an individual—provided it makes sense—and even then only according to the context and at the opportune moment. But within the dominant usage of a whole language, among the individuals that make up the language community of a people many millions in number, the speeches and conversations of the day, of the years and centuries, cross and recross with infinite variety, contradictions, and changes. One despairs of ever being able to listen to the growth of the spirit among the turmoil of the highways of grammar, syntax and phonetics, that lead in all directions. In the individual's meaning as it has been expressed through language, the numberless tones, colours, moods and attitudes are interwoven to such an extent, that the result of their continuous succession, mixing, overlaying and fusion can at most be a neutral characterless gray.

Nevertheless the obvious fact that each of the languages of peoples and of millennia had their peculiar psychic physiognomy cannot be overlooked. Latin differs from Greek, or Chinese, or German not only in respect of grammar and diction, but above all in its psychic aspect. Even languages whose structure is as related and as similar as that of Portuguese, Spanish, Catalan, Provençal, French, and Italian, have psychic differences that we may not be able to define, but can immediately feel. If we go with open minds from Munich to Ulm, we shall hear and feel something that can be called the transition from the Bavarian to the Suavian language spirit.

The empiricists never tire of assuring us that languages, peoples, and herds have no souls. Nevertheless we find that psychic attitudes or habits are formed within the individuals that belong to this herd, or people, or language. When we spoke a moment ago of passing from the Bavarian to the Suavian language spirit, we naturally did not mean more than that a different psychic attitude speaks in the two dialects. Indeed, the collective psychic attitudes develop more quickly and easily than the individualistic. Many years pass before man achieves an all-round consciousness of the ego ; [1] and in the history of culture the so-called discovery of the individual is a late and dangerous fruit. In this sense we must even say that language is earlier than style.

The psychic attitude or tone of a language or dialect can hardly be anything else but the total result of all the individual meanings that are expressed in it. It would be a desperate undertaking to attempt to enumerate them singly. Fortunately the dynamic interplay of speaking and listening fuses them into such a manifold unity, that every member of a language community develops a feeling for the habits and possibilities of psychic expression. For only those things can be meant and expressed in a language that are allowed by common use.

General Psychology, abstract Logic, and comparative, formalistic Grammar, have, with their wide-meshed casuistry, bred in us the prejudice that everyone can at all times mean, think, and say all possible things. But this is a gross intellectualistic error. Man cannot even turn a longing, a vague intuition, or an emotion this way or that as he desires. The structure of the language to which he is heir, the stream of language on which even his dreams—indeed, above all his dreams—are borne and rocked, only allow him psychic vision and freedom in those directions in which his times and his people expect their salvation or fear their undoing.

This dependence of the spirit on those things that have been realized, handed down, brought into common use, and so made possible in language, is due to the continuous contact between our beliefs and opinions and our speaking. In this respect we may say that every language develops its own particular psychic aspect, and although it does not force its members into some definite religious certainty, it at any rate points out the way to them. Languages do not contain or realize religious values, or scientific knowledge, or ethical advice, or specific artistic ideals.

[1] Cf. Cl. and W. Stern, *Die Kindersprache*, Leipzig, 1907, p. 243. K. Bühler, *The Mental Development of the Child*, Kegan Paul, 1930.

D

They are neither specially equipped nor called upon to do so. A language can never do this, a personality only under favourable circumstances. Languages are not personalities. Nevertheless in every language a peculiar upward urge manifests itself, which, in its ultimate orientation, is religious. It bears the spiritual endeavour of personalities, as the air with its pressure and currents bears an airman. This upward urge, naturally, is not exclusively religious, but is religious in the widest sense of the spiritual. It can therefore be of equal service to logical, or ethical, or æsthetic aspirations.

The examples that follow in the next chapter may serve to make these delicate aspects clearer than is possible in such generalized treatment as we have adopted here.

We do not flatter ourselves that we have said anything newer or even better than Goethe in the beautiful verses of the *Westöstliche Diwan* :

> Was auch in irdischer Luft und Art
> Für Töne lauten,
> Die wollen alle herauf,
> Viele verklingen da unten zuhauf ;
> Andere mit Geistes Flug und Lauf,
> Wie das Flügelpferd des Propheten,
> Steigen empor und flöten
> Draussen an dem Tor.

CHAPTER IV

AN EXAMPLE :

NEW FORMS OF THOUGHT IN VULGAR LATIN [1]

By 'Vulgar Latin' we mean those Latin language forms
that were current in daily and immediate—and thus
chiefly oral—intercourse. They were forms of thinking
that had not been schooled in literature, or had been
rejected by and relieved of this schooling. We are therefore not concerned very much with the educational level
of those who spoke Latin, still less with their social
standing or hierarchy, but chiefly with their occasional
attitude. The deciding characteristic according to which
we assign an expression to high literary Latin or to Vulgar
Latin, which has no literary pretensions, is the extent to
which the speaker makes demands on his own thinking or
that of others. It is a question of differences of degree or
tension. Naturally even the mode of speech that is laziest
in thought or word makes some demand, however small,
on the human mind, on body and soul. Vulgar Latin
is the easier, more modest and therefore poorer kind,
merely with regard to specific literary strain, literary
discipline and habit, not with reference to the mode of
speaking or emotional power. Since literary discipline
and education were something that had been brought to
the Romans from outside, from Greece, we might call
Vulgar Latin 'unhellenized' Latin. However much it
may have filled itself with borrowed Greek words and
other hellenisms in the course of centuries, particularly
in the Christian era, it was nevertheless foreign to the

[1] This chapter first appeared in the *Festschrift für Ph. A. Becker,*
" *Hauptfragen der Romanistik,*" Heidelberg, 1922, p. 170 ff.

spirit of Greek antiquity from the very beginning and later its path lay not from Roman to Catholic, but from Latin to Romance. In other words, it never was and never became the language of a state, school, or church, but has always belonged to the people and later the nations that to-day are called Italian, Spanish, French, and Roumanian.

On the other hand, thanks to its literary mummification, hellenized Latin could neither die nor live after the downfall of the Roman state. As ' Middle Latin ' it led a supernatural existence in the church, the school, on paper, on the tongues and in the ears of scholars. ￢ Ludwig Traube has compared it to a dead man, whose hair and nails continue to grow. But if we remember the forceful poetry in which it is sometimes resurrected—the hymns and sequences, the joyful, blunt, happy lyrics of the Goliards, the melting poetry of Pontanus, or even in the twentieth century that of Giovanni Pascoli—we feel like comparing this school-Latin to one of those timeless elemental spirits, perhaps a gnome under the earth, or even an Undine, who, in secret intercourse with a chosen mortal, conceives real living children and herself receives a human soul in his fructifying embrace. But, as everyone knows, he has to be careful not to venture on the waters of everyday talk, or the beautiful Undine will vanish in anger. So unbearably foreign has Vulgar Latin at length become to school-Latin.[1]

The literary modesty of Vulgar Latin can best be appreciated by considering the *sequence* of words.

The involved sequences that Cicero, Virgil, Horace, Ovid, etc., liked to employ in their serious works of art were naturally never popular and were not used in every-day conversation even by these authors. The order of words is employed as a stylistic tool to make speech impressive, intense, exciting, etc. As a grammatical

---

[1] " Volkslatein, Schriftlatein, Kirchenlatein," by Josef Martin, *Histor. Jahrbuch der Görres-Gesellschaft*, 41, 1922, pp. 201–214, is an instructive review.

usage it is an aid to intelligibility. The attempts of the stylist to be emphatic are limited by the desire of everyday practical speech to remain intelligible. If intelligibility is endangered by too bold and free a word order, the possibility of being emphatic and finally of expressing anything at all by means of language, vanishes. The poorer a language is in those grammatical forms with which the ordinary relations between object, subject, predicate, etc., are expressed, the less freedom there is for stylistic word-inversion. The more the order of words is encumbered with syntactic and inflexional functions, and made subservient to the desire for intelligibility, the less can the desire for emphatic expression be gratified. We know that the great freedom of word sequence in Greek and Latin is due to the wealth of inflexional and syntactic forms. It does not follow that this wealth is the immediate result of such freedom. Rather is the freedom of style a concomitant of the wealth of inflexions, and this again only a condition or limit of freedom. The inflexional and syntactic forms that facilitate under-standing are like a garden fence, beyond which the land is no longer arable. A fence has never yet forced a gardener to use the whole area included by it. In archaic times Vulgar Latin doubtless had in its inflexions the same theoretical potentialities for creating involved word sequences as literary Latin had ; it had the same area of garden, but, modest as it was, it only cultivated this in part. To begin with, the only difference between literary and Vulgar Latin, as far as the order of words is concerned, is that the former uses it to its fullest extent, whilst the latter is satisfied with a modest mean.[1]

[1] Since there are as few Vulgar Latin authors as there are of literary Latin, one can only get an idea of the word order of the ordinary language of intercourse by roundabout methods, such as by a comparison of ' high ' and late Latin types, as Elise Richter has done (*Zur Entwick-lung der romanischen Wortstellung*, Halle, 1903), or by a critical analysis of the style of various clumsy, half-educated authors, such as Gregory of Tours. Cf. Max Bonnet, *Le Latin de Grégor de Tours*, Paris thesis, 1890, p. 716 ff.

Now the more completely and the longer Vulgar Latin renounced the full exercise of its grammatical rights, and voluntarily, from a lack of literary initiative, limited itself to a middle course, the more possibilities of word inversion it lost. Thus a flexible body averse to taking exercise atrophies, grows stiff and clumsy, until its habitual stiffness becomes constitutional. The grammatical fence, weary of protecting a bleak soil, shrinks until it encloses only the space that has been cultivated. A number of signs of inflexion is lost, until finally certain types of word order are no longer possible, since they have been too long neglected. But this state of a ˙ ˙rs only began to make itself felt in late Vulgar Latin, when the separate development of the Romance languages began.

During this period of increasing poverty, of descent from stylistic freedom into average intelligibility, Vulgar Latin, as far as one knows, hardly created any new type of word order, unless we hail the group " preposition + infinitive " as a new achievement. *C'est difficile à faire ; il est injuste de croire ;* and finally *je lui ai dit de venir.* This is the Romance continuation of the Vulgar Latin type " preposition + gerund " : *loca grata ad videndum ; difficile ad dicendum ; media nocte surgebam ad confitendum tibi ; dat illos majordomus ad laborandum,* etc.[1]

The most important innovation lies in the increase of poverty, in the renunciation by the speaker of a stylistic will of his own in favour of a better understanding on the part of the listener. In high Latin, the word order shows that the mental and spiritual interests of the speaker take first place, in Vulgar Latin those of the listener. In the former, representation and emphasis are of greater importance ; in the latter, communication and facility of thinking. That is why, compared to a page from Livy, Tacitus, or Virgil, all modern Romance, and

---

[1] Elise Richter, *loc. cit.*, p. 156, footnote. This type is already foreshadowed in high Latin, *e.g. oppidum magnam ad ducendum bellum dabat facultatem ; Archias Ciceroni princeps exstitit ad ingrediendam optimarum artium rationem.*

in particular French poetry and prose, seem like a pamphlet compared to a bronze tablet. That is why, too, whenever the French, Italians, or Spaniards aim at a higher and more monumental form of art, they invariably go back to the models of Latin and Greek antiquity.

When the speaker of Vulgar Latin begins to attune his sentences to the ear of his listener rather than to his own natural inclination, he begins to forsake the naïve egocentricity, individualism, and anthropomorphism of the classics. In his language he gradually develops the capacity for brushing aside the atmosphere of his personal feelings and entering that of others. Certain forms of speech that chiefly serve the expression of personal feeling become of less importance, until finally they are superfluous and vanish from the language.

The same is true of the *passive* verb form. Objectively speaking, one can only suffer in one's own feelings. Indeed, all suffering is feeling and nothing more.[1] When we say the earth is irradiated by the sun and express this in such a way that the earth appears as the bearer of a passive voice of irradiate, we are attributing human characteristics to her. For as a matter of fact she neither suffers nor enjoys the kiss of Helios. When the reeds were moved by the wind, antiquity, which had a passive verb form, took up an attitude the loss of which is bewailed by Schiller in *Die Götter Griechenlands* :

> Syrinx' Klage tönt aus jenem Schilfe,
> Philomelens Schmerz aus diesem Hain,
> Jener Busch empfing Demeters Zähre,
> Die sie um Persephonen geweint,
> Und von diesem Hügel rief Cythere,
> Ach vergebens ! ihren schönen Freund.

---

[1] Hugo Schuchardt is quite right when he says : " If the sole concern of man had been the true reproduction of reality, he would always have represented the agent as subject, wherever the agent was recognisable as such, and would not have admitted the passive at all ; but, in the formation of language, personal interests were his chief guide." " Excurs zu Sprachursprung, III," in the *Sitzungsber. d. preuss. Akad. d. Wissensch.*, VII, 1921, p. 200.

While the passive voice, and with it the middle in so far as it continues to exist in the passive, vanish from Vulgar Latin, the indicative function of the active is necessarily also modified : it becomes wider, more neutral, and, as it were, more soulless. For natural events, for psychic experience,[1] for emotional suffering, and for purposive action there is only one verbal genus. From now on logical thought must abstract, distinguish and divide what language used to keep apart and classify into active, passive, and middle forms, so that they stood ready to hand for each individual speaker. Now that these conveniences are no longer there, the individual has to take trouble himself every time : in order to describe them, he has to think the relations of activity, passivity, and mediality in some other way than through the schematism of language. So the loss of forms becomes a stimulus for replacing them, and that is a stimulus towards a new way of looking at things. Natural events are more and more sharply distinguished from human acts, personal from impersonal. A new *Weltanschauung*, one that is in the main dualistic, is coming into being.

The grammatical circumstances that occasioned the downfall of the passive in Vulgar Latin have no immediate connection with this *Weltanschauung*, it is true ; but mediately, that is, as far as the psychological concomitants are concerned, they have as much to do with it as the tail coat, the bouquet and the patent leather shoes of a loving suitor have to do with his proposal of marriage,

---

[1] Moritz Geiger, in his beautifully acute " Fragment über den Begriff des Unbewussten und die psychische Realität " (*Husserls Jahrbuch für Philosophie*, IV, 1921, p. 43) says : " The grammatical structure of language is such that it cannot allow for the fact that that which is experienced is not an external object of experience, but its *content.*" He can only be thinking of modern European languages, and forgets that the old middle voice was the grammatical form for this circumstance. λούεται τὰς χεῖρας does not mean " he is washing his hands for himself " (er wäscht *sich* die Hände) still less " he is washing his hands ", but really, " he has, he experiences, his washing in his hands ", " it is happening to him that he is washing his hands ".

which he places at the feet of his beloved according to the customary traditions of his country. Historical grammars note and give account of the ceremonial or the language customs that regulate the aspirations and the wooing of linguistic thinking ; but they are silent about the thought itself. Certainly external circumstances are also of importance ; and if we examine those that contributed specially to the loss of the passive, we are confirmed in our assertion that the whole movement expresses a striving towards impersonal forms of expression. Impersonal verbs such as *piget, taedet, poenitet* became more and more frequent, and others were added : *horret, solet, habet, potest, debet.*[1] These quite often got mixed up with their passive. *Pugnari debetur* and *pugnare debet* became equivalent for the language sense, the more so since in later times the endings of the infinitive, *-re* and *-ri* sounded alike. An impersonal passive was often combined with an accusative of the object. Even Plautus wrote : *mi advenienti hac noctu agitandumst vigilias.* Furthermore, since the meaning of the passive was not original, but had been deduced from the medium, it probably from the very beginning had no broad basis in the colloquial language. Its roots were logical more than emotional, although it does express something that is felt. This weakness within the language can be recognized from the fact that in many verbs, namely in the deponents, the formal mode of passive inflexion—*amor, amaris, amabar, amabor*—has no passive significance at all. Hence we find that vacillation and change to the active in so many passively declined deponents, while on the other hand many active verbs, particularly if they had an intransitive, middle, neutral, or reflex sense, change into the passive form. This is noticeable in archaic Latin and

---

[1] The first instance for the impersonal use of *debet* in the sense of *opportet* is found in the year A.D. 114. It occurs in the *Corp. Inscr. lat.* XI, 3614. Cf. Einar Löfstedt, *Spätlateinische Studien*, Upsala, 1908, p. 59 ff. ; *Philolog. Kommentar zur Peregrinatio Aetheriae*, Upsala, 1911, p. 45 ff. and p. 290 ff.

then again in later times, a sign that it was a colloquial rather than a literary process.[1]

Finally that form of the verb in which active and passive processes are confused, in which activity and passivity, being and becoming, merge in an indistinguishable resultant, became the starting-point for the final, complete inundation of the decrepit barrier between active and passive : I mean the *participium perfecti*. This is a sort of adjective, which takes part in verbal indicative functions, a true ' active-passive '. What we ' wished ', ' wanted ', ' undertook ', ' experienced ', and ' suffered ', is our ' wishes ', ' wants ', ' undertakings ', ' experiences ' and ' sufferings ' ; something complete, in which nevertheless the past is still continually and timelessly active and therefore capable of again appearing in time. Hence *scriptum* does not merely connote what one has written once and for all, but also that which one always writes ; the written as well as the being-written, or writing ; *dictum* that which is spoken as well as the saying. Because of these double implications Vulgar Latin becomes able to rewrite the uncolloquial passive constructions and to say *littera scribitur*, instead of *littera scripta est*. This shows up the double sense even more clearly, for the expression in no way distinguishes between the being and the becoming of what has been written. *Les chevaux sont attelés* even in present-day French can mean that the horses are harnessed, or that they are being harnessed, according to whether the sentence is spoken in connection with a quiet statement or a dramatic narrative. The practical attitude of the man who is using the colloquial language is generally only concerned with what is actually present and complete. He is only interested in the passive forms in so far as they yield results, and these are sufficiently clearly indicated by the perfect participle. Further than that he does not need passive inflexions. His word thinking has left the sphere of his personal

---

[1] Cf. Stolz und Schmalz, *Lat. Grammatik*, 4th. edn. Munich, 1910, p. 490 ff. and Max Bonnet, *loc. cit.*, p. 400 ff.

feelings and has become matter-of-fact, purposive, and in a certain sense soulless.

When the language sense turned away from the passive and from the idea of ' becoming ' in time, the indicative of the imperfect tense lost much of its significance in Vulgar Latin and received a modal tinge.[1] Also the inchoative suffixes, -asco, -esco, -isco, almost completely lost their specific meaning. In most of the Romance languages they only remain as a purely inflexional formative, and can therefore no longer indicate a ' beginning ' and ' becoming ', or a ' causing '.[2]

The Latin future, the supine, the gerundive, and the future participle went much the same way. In all these forms as in the passive and the inchoatives, there resides a piece of natural superstition. They all express an immanent destiny, a natural fate, which is at work in the processes of the universe, in human activity, in organic life, and in events as such. *Moriturus* means a man whose fate it is to die, whether it is his will or his destiny ; and it makes no difference whether we adopt a stoical, epicurean, academic, or any other attitude. The use of the participle in -*urus* was inclined to increase in post-classical times rather than decrease, and is found far into late Latin literature. Greek influence probably had a good deal to do with this. Its entire absence in the Romance languages is all the more surprising. Italian forms such as *venturo, passuro, fatturo*, which are used by Dante, are obviously learned ones. It is impossible to discover any reason for the loss of this form either from the history of phonetics, or on syntactical and grammatical grounds in general. It only remains to presume that it did not suit the Vulgar Latin way of thinking, either from the very beginning, or, what is

[1] E. Gamillscheg, " Studium zur Vorgeschichte einer romanischen Tempuslehre ", *Sitzungsber. d. Akad. d. Wiss., Wien, philos.-hist. Kl.,* 172, 1913, §§ 25, 32, 168, 183 ff.

[2] The inchoative sense has been kept in a few isolated cases, such as the OF *iraistre (irascere)*, to become angry or " to make angry ". Otherwise it is occasionally taken over by prefixes, *in-, ad-, ex-, re-*, etc., but it is no longer systematically organized.

more probable, in later times, when more emphatic and unequivocal expressions for will, should, and must were sought after, and when the concept of immanent destiny began to be evolved from the verb and to be represented by means of prepositions: *les choses à venir; une chose à faire; las casas vendidas; y por vender.*

From a phonetic point of view the supine, which expresses the direction or intention of a motion, an act, or an event, might have held its own for a long time in the *-u*, or, better still, in the *-ui* form. The form in *-um* was liable to be confused with the perfect participle or with verb substantives, from which it had proceeded, such as *reditu(s)*, *sensu(s)*, etc. The *-u* form, or the second supine, is still quite often found in Lactantius and Macrobius. Gregory of Tours († 594) only uses it as a formula.[1] Usually he paraphrases it by *ad* with the gerund, the infinitive, a verb substantive or by other means. The supine can never have been very popular.

The case of the gerundive is similar and its implications are similar too. It indicates a purpose, an aim or object, a necessity or a need inherent in the verb concept. *Censores locant statuam faciendam.* Löfstedt thinks that the gerundive was never popular in colloquial speech.[2] Its oracular multiple meanings were probably felt to be a hindrance in everyday intercourse. In addition its phonetic quality was such that it might easily be confused with the gerund, most easily, moreover, in those constructions in which the gerund acted as a popular substitute for the gerundive, when a preposition preceded it. It was only a small step from *ad oblationem faciendam* to *ad faciendum oblationem.*

The downfall of the future tense was fraught with the gravest consequences. The conditions under which it occurred were manifold. I can only indicate the most important here. To begin with, the future as an inflexional schema was not unequivocally laid down. Because of its

---

[1] Bonnet, *loc. cit.*, p. 414.

[2] *Philolog. Kommentar zur Peregrinatio*, p. 156 f.

relation to the present conjunctive, it oscillated between a modal and a temporal orientation; between *amabo* and *delebo* on the one hand, *legam* and *audiam* on the other; *-bo* and *-am* were equally balanced and began to contest each other's position. So we find all kinds of confusions in later Latin : *floriet* for *florebit, respondeam* for *respondebo; audibo* and *dormibo* for *audiam* and *dormiam*, etc. In addition there was the similarity in sound between *amabit* and *amavit, amabunt* and *amabant*, of *leges* and *leget* with the conjunctive of the first conjugation : *am-es, am-et*, etc. Nevertheless, the form impulse of the language could very well have found a way out by means of analogous transpositions, and could have constructed a coherent future declension, provided the thinking impulse really set store by it. But the whole temporal conception of the future was weak and it broke down. There is hardly a language in which it is regularly used by the common people. The concept of the future, like the prophet in his own land, is usually neglected, or in some way misused and obscured by colloquial speech. For the ordinary man's attitude towards things is always that of willing, wishing, hoping and fearing rather than that of imagination, thought or knowledge. Probably the surest measure of the extent and depth of our education is the degree of calm and self-possession that we preserve in view of the future. Continuous collectedness and self-possession, in short, a philosophic temperament and attitude of mind are needed if the temporal outlook on the future is not to deviate into the modal spheres of fear and hope, of the wish, and of uncertainty. If we could survey all the uses of expressions for the future current at the beginning of antiquity, and with this in mind could compare, say, the language used in the intercourse of the masses with the style of the most outstanding literary personalities, we should, I believe, have before us in all its philological depth and nuances the great gulf that separated the *ataraxia* of the great from the feverish religious hallucinations and the passionate dullness of the plebs.

After the meaning of the future in Vulgar Latin had been deflected into the more practical and emotional directions of willing, wishing, demanding, fearing, etc., the old forms of inflexion could be dispensed with. For there were several other fresher and stronger means of expressing the new meaning : conjunctive, imperative, indicative, the simple infinitive,[1] periphrasis with *velle, posse, debere* and others, and finally the periphrasis with infinitive + *habere*, which in most Romance languages has become grammaticized into a new future.[2]

This by no means exhausts the list of grammatical losses in Vulgar Latin. I shall touch on the others only in so far as they throw light on the new attitudes of thought that induced these losses or were induced by them.

After we have seen how strong the tendency of Vulgar Latin was towards impersonal, practical, objective, and neutral forms of expression, the loss of the neuter is very surprising. But it is not the idea of the neuter that was lost, only its inflexional form. The neuter that was expelled from the grammatical category lived on, and even lived more independently, in the psychological category.[3] In historical grammars we usually find the matter represented in this way : most of the neuter nouns were by way of analogy assimilated to the masculine, and some to the feminine nouns ; in this way the whole stock of Latin neuters was divided among the two surviving genders of the Romance languages. But not even

---

[1] For the use of the infinitive in demands see Löfstedt, *Spätlat. Studien*, p. 85.

[2] Concerning the substitute for the future see Leo Spitzer, *Aufsätze zur romanischen Syntax und Stilistik*, Halle, 1918, p. 173 ff. ; concerning the new modal use of the Romance future tense as an expression of moral obligation, cf. Eugen Lerch, *Die Verwendung des romanischen Futurums als Ausdruck eines sittlichen Sollens*, Leipzig, 1919 ; concerning the origin of the Romance future, cf. Gerhard Rohlfs, " Das romanische Habeo-Futurum und Konditionalis ", *Archivum Romanicum*, VI, 1922, p. 105 ff.

[3] Cf. the author's investigation, " Über grammatische u. psychologische Sprachformen," *Logos*, VIII, 1919, p. 1 ff. ; and *Gesammelte Aufsätze zur Sprachphilosophie*, Munich, 1923, p. 105 ff.

the lowest colloquial language works in this way. The neuter form was thrown out of circulation by so-called ' sense constructions '. It is hardly possible to represent sufficiently strongly the hankering of Vulgar Latin for achieving congruence through sense and not through grammatical tendency. The grammatical differences in gender were undermined by an unconscious antiformalistic stream. The gender of substantives was more and more frequently determined according to their fundamental nature instead of their external characteristics. Hence it came about that those substantives, which represented something—whatever their grammatical gender—were preferably thought of as *objects*, in contrast to those indicating persons, which were preferably given the subjective case. A sensibility was developed in language, which saw in persons and living things generally the true vehicles of action, while things, that is, conceptual neuters, were the objects of action. It was felt that a true neuter could not have a *casus rectus*, but only a *casus obliquus*. Now since the nominative of the neuter looks exactly like the accusative, we may say that the neuter has not really been lost, but has merged into the oblique of Vulgar Latin. It has retreated to this as the essentially objective case in the degree to which the other cases dropped out of use. Seen from this angle, the ' downfall of the neuter ' is connected with that of the case declension. This is most clearly seen in Spanish, where the oblique case has to such an extent become the case of ' objectivity ', that persons and things had to be given a special, personal accusative : *este hombre ama el juego*, but *este hombre ama á sus hijos*.

But this is only one side of the process ; for the neuter does not only denominate some purely objective thing, it also has a collective sense that brings it close to the plural. The Latin neuter is the expression of the individual thing as well as of the generality of things ; it can mean either the thing itself or its generalized abstraction. *gaudia, responsa, nubila* and many similar plurals were thought of as collective units in Vulgar Latin and construed with the feminine singular, to which they had been related of old.[1] If it is correct that Gregory of Tours uses the neuter *diabolum* instead of *diabolus*, if this indicates a common use and is not merely a mistake, it must have some collective sense like ' the devil people ', perhaps in analogy to *daemonium*, as my colleague Carl Weyman thinks.[2] With the well-substantiated neuter *populum* of the same Gregory this is certainly the case. In Roumanian, as we know, *populus* is treated as a neuter : *popor popoare*, which could be due to other reasons than the purely external one of inflexion. Here as elsewhere Spanish is particularly instructive. It has most completely cleared away the remnants of old neuter plural forms, while Italian and Old French, not to mention Roumanian, have kept many of them (*le frutta, legna*, etc., *cinquante carre, deus doie*). Spanish, on the other hand, has worked out the collective *idea* of the neuter all the more exactly and clearly. The neuter Spanish definite article *lo* is the sign of this idea. Many people have puzzled their heads as to its meaning.[3] It seems to me that it has above all a collective significance ; but we must not forget that there is nearly always of necessity some idealization when things or attributes are generalized. Anything that is looked at as a totality, be it things or attributes, easily receives a taint of value or non-value, unless it is raised to the purely abstract ; *por lo puro y correcto de sus facciones* is about equivalent to *por la pureza y corrección de sus facciones; el pasado* is " that which is past ",

---

[1] Cf. Löfstedt, *Philolog. Komm. z. Peregr.*, p. 134 ff. ; and Meyer-Lübke, *Einführung in d. Stud. d. rom. Sprachw.*, 3rd. edn., Heidelberg, 1920, § 176.

[2] Bonnet, *loc. cit.*, only gives *one* example from the text, p. 349.

[3] Cf. Friedr. Hanssen, *Spanische Grammatik*, Halle, 1910, p. 139 ; Ad. Tobler, *Vermischte Beiträge z. franz. Gramm.*, 2nd. series, 2nd. edn., Leipzig, 1906, p. 204 ff. Concerning the meaning of neuter pronouns in French, cf. the instructive investigation of Leo Spitzer, " Idealistische Neuphilologie," in the *Festschrift für Karl Vossler*, Heidelberg, 1922, p. 120 ff.

lo pasado is "the past", the whole past thought of collectively ; that is why *todo* is so frequently put before *lo*. It can even accompany masculine or feminine nouns and adjectives : *á representármelas todo lo bellas, todo lo seductoras que pueden ser* (Juan Valera, *Pepita Jimènez*), "when I think of them as all the beauty, all the seductiveness of which they are capable". This *todo lo*, "so wholly something", is the Spanish neuter. It points to the ideal universal. In Spanish there is apparently no difference between saying *en el blanco de los ojos* and *en lo blanco de los ojos* ; but in the first case one thinks of the white of the eye as an empirical particular, in the second as an ideal particular, with a suspicion of metaphysical emphasis or even irony.

As the inflexional forms of the neuter vanished from Vulgar Latin in later times, the form in which it expressed itself in thought became purified, and began to differentiate itself towards its two historical poles : on the one hand towards objectivity, in so far as it became a case ; on the other towards the abstract, in so far as it became a pronoun or an article. The loss of inflexional forms always stirs up the independence and responsibility of thought. From the ruins of the objective in language the objectivity of thought arises. Indeed, the predilection for the abstract ideal, which Plato had been the first to cultivate, becomes stronger and stronger at the end of classical antiquity and during the Middle Ages. It was not only the educated who were seized by neo-platonic conceptual realism, according to which true reality lies not in appearances, but in concepts ; not in things, but in ideas ; in objectivity, not in objects. Even to the lower classes the world of the senses began to be suspect, strange, or angry ; even they began to think transcendentally and, if not philo-sophically, at any rate in terms of Christianity. The sense - constructions of their common language of intercourse, and the consequent loss of the sign for individual neuter objects, are a modest, partial proof

E

of this. The cruder Germanic peoples kept their neuter.

It will be objected that connections like these are very doubtful, and that the Greeks, in whom the tendency towards the ideal and the abstract arose far earlier and far more definitely than among the Latin speaking peoples, kept their neuters. But the Greeks had the article ; they had τό, which was so particularly well suited for philosophizing. In any case a single linguistic illustration is never sufficient to prove that the mode of thinking has changed. Only when it is considered in connection with the whole expression of language in a whole people and their times, can it become significant.

We shall therefore amplify the discussion of the neuter by indicating the collective suffixes. From the neuter plural of the adjectives in -alis, -ilis, -ulis, Vulgar Latin obtained the collective nouns in -alia, -ilia, -ulia, of which the first is particularly strongly represented : victualia, mirabilia, fundululia (sediment, Sardinian funduludza). The suffix -ata also to a large extent contains the collective plural of the neuter,[1] similarly -anea (interanea, entrails ; montanea, mountain range),[2] -aria (arenaria, sandpit),[3] -eta, -atica, -menta, to which correspond the singular forms in -etum, -aticum, -mentum, which in themselves already tend to have a collective meaning.[4] From -aceus and -icius neuter plurals with a collective sense are also formed.[5] Next to these, old collective nouns in -amen, -tura, -erium remain and flourish. Since the suffixes have no meaning in themselves, a collective sense can be given by numerous other suffixes as well. The abstract nouns are particularly exposed to this influx. Colloquial speech is not abstract ; that is why the abstract nouns of literary Latin, in -tudo, -tus, -tas, -itia never became popular, as

[1] For further details cf. Carl S. R. Collin, *Étude sur le développement de sens du suffixe* -ATA, Lund, 1918.

[2] Meyer-Lübke, *Gramm. d. roman. Sprach.*, II, § 460.

[3] *Idem*, § 469.

[4] *Idem*, §§ 447 f., 479, 482.

[5] *Idem*, § 414 ff.

their fate in the Romance languages shows. Collective nouns are the popular substitute for abstract nouns. In the Latin of the *Vitae Patrum*, for instance, a strong tendency towards collective plurals has been noticed : *desideria* instead of *desiderium*, *voluntates*, *sanitates*, *languores*, *flectus*, *stridores*, *timores*, *tormenta*, *supplicia*, etc. The vulgar tendency towards the collective singular instead of the plural is also seen in : *civis*, *hostis*, etc., instead of *cives*, *hostes*.[1] Doubtless Greek influence is also at work. But that does not alter the fact that in everyday speech a whole world of concrete images lies behind each concept expressed by a word. As soon as something of this is poured out on the abstract noun, it becomes collective ; as soon as it evaporates again, the collective noun once more becomes abstract.[2] In the language of the people, collective nouns are the forerunners as well as the degenerate variants of abstract nouns. The predilection for collective nouns is also evident in *totus* and *toti* for *omnis* and *omnes*, which grew after the time of Apuleius, so that we find *toti illi montes*. In addition *totus* is also fond of taking on an idealistic meaning, somewhat in the sense of *summus: totius ingeniositatis ac sapientiae puero* (*Corp. Inscr. lat.*, VI, 33,929) ; *virgo totius bonitatis* (*ibid.*, X, 4538).[3]

We shall not enter into the question whether the mass-production of collective nouns in Vulgar Latin was due to the need for expressing the new order in the state, the churches, in the new society of later imperial times ; or whether it is connected with the rise of the world

---

[1] A. H. Salonius, *Vitae Patrum, Kritische Untersuchung*, Lund, 1920, p. 76 ff., p. 73 ff. ; Löfstedt, *Philolog. Kommentar*, p. 178.

[2] Concerning the late Latin change in meaning from abstract to concrete, cf. Löfstedt, *Phil. Komm.*, p. 111 ff. We find there, for instance, *venatio* meaning ' venison ', *offizia* meaning ' the servants', *ministeria*=' the hosts of heaven ', *virtutes*=' miracle-working objects ', *vires*=' means (money) ', further *testimonia*=testes, *ibid.*, p. 332. Cf. also Gamillscheg, in *Bericht über die 19. Tagung des Neuphilologenverbandes*, Berlin, 1925, p. 123 ff.

[3] Cf. Löfstedt, *Phil. Komm.*, p. 69.

empire with its great cities, popular spectacles, mass amusements and feeding, its new time reckoning, coins, measures, etc. The purely internal evidence from the facts of language is sufficient to show us how its vision became more acute for practical, objective, impersonal, super-individual, typical, ideal, and universal things.

Our picture is enriched by a further line if we look at the verb suffixes, which were very much in favour in Vulgar Latin. To begin with we find the Greek -ίζειν, which must have spread very widely, as -idjare in Vulgar Latin, -izare in Middle Latin. It may have spread from ecclesiastical words like baptizare, catechizare, ¬and was able to conjure up a lot of new verbs from substantives and adjectives and to censure or emphasize any action as fussy; cf. the Italian bamboleggiare, cristianeggiare, manzoneggiare. There is no lack in Vulgar Latin of verb suffixes having an iterative, frequentive, diminutive, and pejorative shade of meaning: -aceare, -aculare, -iculare, -uculare, -ulare, -inare, -onare, -ittare, -illare, -ellare, -ottare: -antare and -entare, which are formed from the present participle, are particularly characteristic: crepantem facere = crepantare. Literary Latin knew praesentare, but the universal practice of the Romance languages shows how popular this suffix was in Vulgar Latin.[1] Its factual, dynamic sense is obvious and indicates a striving towards increasing the stock of verbs as well as giving weight to its active meaning. (Cf. the Spanish levantar, huyentar, amedrentar, etc.) It is well known how much colloquial speech prefers a verb that is stronger both in sound and meaning. Thus it uses tollere for sumere; auferre or portare for ferre; vadere or salire for ire; ambulare for vadere; eicere for ducere; clamare for vocare; quiritare for clamare; tremere for timere, etc. Often it uses a compound instead of a simple verb. If we further consider how in Vulgar Latin the verb velle is lifted out of its close relation to nolle and malle, and posse out of its close companionship with esse, and how both are completely

---

[1] Meyer-Lübke, loc. cit., II, § 592.

reorganized into a new temporal auxiliary ; if we consider how *facere* is dissected into strongly and weakly toned form and sense groups,[1] we shall realize, I believe, how important the will aspect and the force of human action have become for the speaker. Again, action that is only half or insufficiently done, or that is mere dilettantism—for this is what the above-named iterative and diminutive suffixes imply—can only be adequately expressed by a language that can equally well express unique, final, strong, and valuable action.

The appreciation of the strength and weakness of will, shall, and must awakens in the degree to which the ' I ' becomes estranged from the ' not-I '. It is only when anthropomorphic faith breaks, the faith by which antiquity saw in God and nature something human and familiar, that Man can show what he is able to accomplish in the face of a dumb and hostile nature. As long as man looks upon himself as the measure of all things and does not recognize natural events that are hostile to him ; as long as he does not even faintly suspect the existence of natural science in the modern sense ; as long as the *lex naturalis* seems to him merely the precept or the image of the *lex gentium* : so long will he see mechanical causality through the medium of human will and wish, and will obscure it affectively or teleologically. To illustrate this by a special example from language : he will use the subjunctive, which is a mode of wishing, intending, hoping, fearing, doubting, even where it is absolutely out of place according to the modern way of thinking. Classical Latin said : *Agesilaus, cum ex Aegypto* REVERTERETUR, *in morbum implicitus, decessit.* Because of the subjunctive after *cum*, the language implies a connection, which we can hardly understand to-day, between the return of Agesilaus from Egypt and his death. It is not a causal, and also not a final connection ; and yet an inner relationship is suggested between the return

---

[1] Concerning the periphrases and extensions of the expressive power of verbs see Löfstedt, *Philolog. Komm.*, pp. 162 ff., 245 ff., and 207 ff.

and the death, as though fate had allowed Agesilaus to return in order to lead him to his death. In later and in Vulgar Latin this subjunctive of situation or of immanent meaning is no longer understood, at any rate no longer used with a sure intuition of its import. On the one hand it is exaggerated and carried over to *dum* (during), and even to the purely temporal *ut*,[1] on the other abandoned altogether. Most of the things that in classical Latin depend on expressions of saying, meaning, asserting, knowing, apprehending, are thought of in a mythical way, that is, they have no meaning or validity of their own ; and those of saying, meaning, etc., are thought into, suggested, attributed, imparted to them. Hence the subjunctive of indirect speech, hence above all the classical literary accusative with infinitive. *Traditum est Homerum caecum fuisse—fertur Homerus caecus fuisse.* It is the tradition, the belief, the myth, which will have it that Homer was blind. *Cæsar existimabat se victum esse* : it was the belief or the judgment of Cæsar himself that made him the vanquished. But Vulgar and late Latin prefer the expression with *quod : traditum est quod Homerus caecus fuit* or *erat* or *fuerit* or *esset* or even *fuisset*, according to the context. *Cæsar existimabat quod ipse victus erat* or *esset*, according to whether he really was vanquished or only believed himself to be. The mode of thinking is now no longer mythical. What is asserted in the *quod* sentence has its own meaning in itself and no longer receives its deciding direction or validity from the ruling verb of saying, asserting, meaning ; it merely has its origin in the latter as far as speech is concerned, and its dependence is merely formal. *Quod* can take the indicative as well as the subjunctive after it.[2] To say or to believe something does not mean that it exists. If Vulgar Latin threw overboard so many subordinating conjunctions, especially

---

[1] Cf. Bonnet, p. 681 ; Löfstedt, *Beiträge zur Kenntnis der späteren Latinität*, Stockholm, 1907, p. 1 ff., and *Philol. Komm. z. Peregr.*, p. 97 ff.

[2] Cf. Josef Svennung, *Orosiana*, Upsala, 1922 (dissertation), p. 86 ff.

those that demand the subjunctive, it indicates not only that the ordinary language of intercourse did not employ many subordinate clauses, but certainly also that the interconnections of things and events were no longer felt anthropomorphically and mystically.

At the end of classical antiquity the mythical habit of thinking becomes symbolical. This is a profound and revolutionary change, probably the greatest of the changes in mental outlook, and from which we are somewhat better able to understand the innovations of Vulgar Latin in their totality. If I may be allowed to define the difference between mythical and symbolical ways of thinking from a philological standpoint, I should say that the former tells us how the divine is called, what names, forms and embodiments it assumes for our senses ; symbolical thought, on the other hand, disembodies the mythical divinities and inquires into their connotation, not their denotation. Mythical thought and speech give to the eternal things their names, symbolical thought and speech give them meaning. The relations of mythology and symbology to one another in theology are similar to those of onomasiology and semasiology in philology. As every denotation has its connotation, every name its meaning, so every myth contains something symbolic. In mythical thought the divine is called Neptune, Vulcan, Jupiter, Minerva, according to what it does in the spheres of water, fire, heaven, and the arts ; according as it is now water, now fire, etc. In symbolical thought Neptune, Vulcan, etc., *all* mean the same, namely, the divine, however and wherever it may manifest itself. The myth assumes that God here and now is Neptune, to which symbolism replies : " That which you call Neptune, and as such are imagining and creating here and now, is God, *also* God, the only God." In its exaggerated form mythical thinking leads to anecdote and fable, symbolical thinking to colourless and formless nebulous speculation. But language is at once *fabula* and *speculum*. When we speak, we are describing, creating, and fabling ; when we wish to understand what has been spoken, we cannot do without interpretation, disembodiment, and speculation. The science of names (onomasiology) stands in the service of speech, where mythical thought is at home and the children receive their names ; the science of meanings (semasiology) is on the side of the hearing and understanding aspect of language, where symbolical thinking operates and apprehends the meaning of those names and the implication of the myths.

Since Vulgar Latin is a language of every day, it favours, as we have seen, the mental interests of those who hear and understand, and therefore quite naturally it leans more on the symbolic than on the mythical leg of its forms of thought and speech.

The *adverb* is particularly called to interpret and to indicate the sense and meaning of events, and the way in which they happen. Here Vulgar Latin has created something new, in which the strengthening of symbolic forms is strikingly manifested : the adverbial suffix *-mente*. The chief stimulus for this new creation arises from phrases like *dubia mente proprius accessi* (Apuleius, Metam., I, 6), or *saucia mente fluctuat* (*idem*, V, 2), or *religionem devota mente suscipere* (Le Blant, Inscript. chrét., 436). It is a kind of Latin *ablativus modi*, which was very much favoured by African authors, perhaps through semitic influence : [1] *hoc, illo, nullo, modo ; hac lege ; nullo pacto ; illo consilio, ordine, animo ; illa ratione, via, condicione, consuetudine*, and : *mente*.[2] From this *mente* all the Romance languages, with the exception of Roumanian,[3] made an adverbial suffix. Therefore, although it must have been common in Vulgar Latin, it can only have come into general use after the connection between Rome and the eastern provinces, Dacia and

---

[1] Schmalz and Stolz, *loc. cit.*, § 96, footnote.

[2] R. Kühner, *Ausführliche Gramm. d. lat. Spr.*, 2nd. edn., Part I (" Satzlehre ", by K. Stegmann), Hannover, 1912, § 81, note 32.

[3] Roumanian only knows *dimintre(a)=alia* or *altera mente*. Cf. Pusçariu, *Etymol. Wörterbuch d. rumän. Spr.*, Heidelberg, 1905, No. 44.

Moesia, had been severed. Even in the Middle Ages this suffix had not yet become a permanent part of grammar in the western Romance languages, including Old Italian ; [1] and Spanish does not contain it to-day. One says, *clara, concisa y elegantemente*, indicating that *-mente* is still felt to be a more or less independent word. This slow, reluctant development of the suffix is not evidence of the weakness of symbolical thinking, but on the contrary of its strength and freshness. For as long as the meaning of *mente* is fully understood it cannot be worn down to a mere form. If we read the late Latin authors of the sixth to tenth centuries, we are struck by the fact that they very rarely form an adverbial expression with *mente*. There may be two reasons for this. In the first place, they had stronger methods of describing the way in which something happened. In the Merovingian and Carolingian formularies, for instance, we find *quieto ordine* substituted for, or making more emphatic, *quiete ; malo ordine* for *male* or *iniuste ; cum integritate* for *diligenter ; in veritate* for *vere ; per legem et iustitiam* for *legitime ; per ingenia mala adque volontate pessima* (sic) for *malitiose*.[2] In the Alexander fragments at Bamberg I have noticed phrases like the following : *per patientiam supportare ; nos enim talem voluntatem cum placido animo suscipimus ; per simplicitatem omnia dicimus*,[3] etc., which sound as though the Italian editor of the tenth century wanted to find some stronger expressions than the modern *pazientemente, placidamente, semplicemente*. But it was not only the occurrence of such individualizing stylistic adverbial expressions that prevented the *-mente* forms from becoming general. The second cause for this retardation is the fact that even in late Latin *mens* kept the literary meaning of ' mind ', or ' organ of thought ', whereas the meanings

---

[1] Cf. A. Tobler, *Vermischte Beiträge*, I, 3rd. edn., p. 104 ff., and p. 96 ff.

[2] Ed. by Jul. Pirson, Heidelberg, 1913, *passim*.

[3] *Kleine Texte zum Alexanderroman*, ed. by Fr. Pfister, Heidelberg, 1910, pp. 6, 7, 14.

' disposition ', ' attitude ', ' sentiment ' seem gradually to
have dropped out of popular use. The bookword *mens*
split off from the root *mente* in a similar fashion to that
in which the literary *pensare* = ' think ', ' cogitate ',
developed from the common *pesare* = ' weigh '. The
language of the common people took over the feeling,
willing, and practical aspects of the meaning of *mens*, so
that bookish late Latin only retained the intellectualistic
side. Thus we see the evolution of the suffix -*mente* as
a gradual process taking place in the speech of the people ;
it may have been slowed down by reflexion, but was
by no means hindered by it.

Once one's inner eye has been sharpened for and attuned
to the symbolic tendencies of thought, which are directed
towards meanings and feelings, towards those secret, inner
relationships of things that can only be defined in parables,
surmised and felt rather than clearly apprehended, one
begins to recognize these symbolic tendencies in many other
neologisms of Vulgar Latin as well. Only occasionally do
they show themselves clearly ; they have to be analysed
and uncovered step by step. Consider how much symbolism there is in the numberless diminutives and
augmentatives of late Vulgar Latin. *Soliculus,* ' the dear
sun ',[1] is the sun thought no longer mythically as God,
but symbolically, *i.e.* as the sign of a cosmic Love, be it
that of God for mankind, or of mankind for God *through*

---

[1] Of course not ' the little sun ', as Gilliéron and Meyer-Lübke
assume (*Histor. Gramm. d. franz. Sprache*, II, Heidelberg, 1921, §§ 13
and 153). One only has to remember how frequent the diminutive of
sun is in the Slavonic language. Leo Spitzer (Gamillschegg und Spitzer,
Beiträge zur romanischen Wortbildungslehre, Geneva, 1921) has given
very interesting proofs of the emotional character of the diminutives
and augmentatives. Ed. Wölfflin (*Philologus*, 34, 153 ff.) had already
recognized that *auricula* and *ocellus* originally meant not the ' small ',
but the ' dear ' ear and eye of a loved person. Vitruvius even uses
a number of technical terms diminutively : *axilla, buccula, canaliculus,
modiolus, securicula, denticulus, torulus, verticula, tubulus.* We see in
that not only the attempt to give a more exact definition of size, but
just as much the pleasure that his products and tools give to the
workman. Cf. also Löfstedt, *Philolog. Komm.*, p. 310 ff.

the sun. *Filiolus, avicellus, pauperellus* ; the diminutives in *-itta* and *-ittus*, transferred from personal names (*suavitta*) ; those in *-inus*, which denote origin and similarity ; these and others show us the awakening of a cosmic love and an ethical exuberance that reminds us of those animal and stone books, in which the Middle Ages moralized about the whole of nature as an indication and demonstration of the divine will.

We do not wish to enter into more particulars, although what we mean can only be made clear by a wealth of detail. For languages do not set to work in a radical fashion ; they do not proceed straight ahead according to fixed principles ; they trace their trickling serpentines like water downhill, wherever opportunity offers. But the slope they descend, the urge that impels them, can remain the same for centuries and millennia on end.

We have only wished to sketch in outline the uniform inclination, or rather the effort, that manifested itself in Vulgar Latin from the decline of the period of classical Latin until the evolution of the Romance languages. The Latin of the common people moves and aspires from anthropomorphic, deterministic, intellectualistic forms of thought towards dualistic, concrete, practical, voluntaristic forms. From the mythical, pantheistic conception of the world it proceeds to the symbolic, the deeper, more psychic conception and presentation, thereby paving a way through language to the thought of the Middle Ages and of Christianity. Indeed, it *is* the road on which the Latin peoples progressed from antique to Christian ways of thinking.

CHAPTER V

LANGUAGE AND NATURE

THE examples of the previous chapter have revealed to us the mode of thought and the main directions of Vulgar Latin. We now feel the need, indeed the hope, of bringing the mode of speaking and its changes into relation with them. The sounds of speech have no living meaning apart from the thought behind speech. Thought form and sound form, like the kernel and rind of a fruit, soul and body of man, spirit and nature, have grown together and are intimately dependent on one another. If, as we believe we have shown, there is an intelligible history of thought in Vulgar Latin, an intelligible history of its speech ought also to be possible, at any rate theoretically.[1] Whether we can reconstruct it practically with convincing likeness is doubtful, for that depends not only on the sensitiveness to language forms and the linguistic training of the phonetic historian, but to a certain extent also on the richness and dependability of the documentary material. Vulgar Latin phonograms of earlier centuries are crude, incomplete, rare, and arbitrary. We possess accurate phonograms only of the Romance languages and dialects of the present times. This state of affairs is similar to that in portraiture. The spiritual personalities, the thoughts and feelings of Cicero or Plato are relatively clear and well defined ; but what the body looked like through which the soul acted, will probably remain a mystery for ever.

[1] The possibilities and difficulties of a phonetic history of French are discussed in the epilogue to the new edition of my book, *Frankreichs Kultur im Spiegel seiner Sprachentwicklung*, Heidelberg, 1921, pp. 375–379.

We shall leave out of consideration whether the desire to see the image of Plato may still be styled search after scientific knowledge, or whether it is merely the ridiculous, materialistic curiosity of the visitor to Madame Tussaud's. Nor do we wish to pass judgment on the desire that continually impels the artistic mind, in the absence of the real Plato, to dream and create a picture, memorial, or symbol of him in bronze or stone. In the same way, the religious sensuousness of the Christian never tires of demanding concrete, colourful, and ever more speaking likenesses of Jesus Christ and his mother, so often and so strongly that satiety, disappointment and doubt eventually intervene, and the mind, sick of the deceptive externality of its own divine essence, turns once more to the inner forms of this essence.

I believe we are not quite certain in our own minds whether the attempts to reconstruct the phonetic body of a vanished language or fix mechanically that of a living one are not tainted with something pseudo-scientific, with dilettantic curiosity, artistic greed, or naturalistic super-stition. Who has not yawned or laughed irrepressibly when he has sat over phonetic studies or experiments or even speculations ? Has not his reason faintly warned him that he is cultivating a frontier region, where scientific interest threatens to degenerate ? How often has science not been duped when, relying on a beautiful harmony between soul and body, mind and nature, it has attempted to read the inner meaning from the external appearance ! Graphology, Chiromantics, and Phrenology are suspect sciences ; and Phonetics has been able to hold an honour-able reputation only because it has maintained a discreet silence on the question as to the relations between the mode of speaking and the mode of thinking.

There is in fact no answer that completely satisfies us, while there are two that disappoint. The first is that speaking and thinking in terms of language are one and the same thing ; that the forms of linguistic thought and the sound forms are not merely like the difference between inner and outer, but the outer is the very innermost itself. The sound of the English language is so truly the English spirit, that all descriptions, enumerations, and analyses of English characteristics must seem pale and external as compared with the living language that has become sound. That which is English cannot be rendered more concretely obvious to the senses than in the sound of the English language. And the second answer maintains that, precisely because the sound of English is the true and whole English being, because the John Bull who speaks is the authentic John Bull, therefore no tension exists between him and his phonetic expression and no causal connection can be traced. If we take away the phonetic forms that are himself, they are no longer his forms, but, tangled and arbitrary chance facts, they fall about him as something strange, like the hair of the shorn Samson. Hegel has seen this when he says : " Language and work are expressions in which the individual no longer remains with himself or belongs to himself, but lets his inner nature come to the surface and surrenders it to other things. We can say with equal truth that the inner world is expressed too much, or that it is expressed too little. Too much, because it manifests itself even in these expressions, and so leaves no antithesis between itself and them ; they are not merely expressions of the inner, but the inner itself. Too little, because the inner becomes something else when it is expressed through language and action, thereby becoming subject to the force of transformations, which turn the spoken word and the completed action round and makes something different out of them than they are in themselves as actions of this particular individual." [1]

Those who are interested in phonetics, therefore, have these two aspects to choose from. They can look upon the phonetic history of a language as being identical with the history of its forms of thought, and allow the phonetic

[1] *Phänomenologie des Geistes*, ed. by G. Lasson, Leipzig, 1907, p. 205. [English translation, *The Phenomenology of the Spirit*, 2nd. edn., 1931.]

element to have no special position as compared to the element of thought. That is, they will extend, deepen, and remodel their interest in phonetics in such a way that all explanations of phonetic changes are understood and interpreted in terms of changes in the forms of thought. Or they must take aside the shorn locks of Samson, and attempt to discover what meaning these dead growths can have.

But they can no longer talk of the meaning of phonetics within the history of language, after the life-giving force has departed and is at most recognizable through some change in the ' nature ' of the estranged object.

It is time that we should bring some clarity into the glittering concept of nature.

Nature is that which was born, became, and grew to perfection, which, in its further bearing and becoming, remains true to itself, so that the mind with its discontinuities and flights appears characterless beside it. Nature remains docile, and does not, like the mind, retreat from the perception of our senses or the concepts of our reason. The whole universe, therefore, can be thought of as nature, from inanimate stones and human beings, to whatever processes take place in this infinite realm and are causally or teleologically determined and explicable. The narrower concept of nature, which comprises only the mechanical world of causal events, has long been transcended. All organic life and even the mental and material products of man, have something of nature about them. The scholastics talked of the nature of the angels and even of God. In the same way the present-day conception of nature offers no logical obstacle towards its extension to the highest efforts and creations of mental life. All existence, life, and work, whether it fulfils its purpose or not, as long as it has an adequate cause and is bound up in some such way that it can be understood as permanent, subject to law, normal, functional or at least habitual, belongs to nature—more or less. In its widest form, the concept of nature is an activity, in its narrowest, a mechanism. Through this concept our thinking is able to compare things ; it measures, calculates, standardizes, and orders them. It is impossible to see what object, because of its ' nature ', can be excluded from this activity. The universe can be circled by these comparisons ; and even those things that transcend it in a unique way, as pure quality, are nevertheless still bound to the hierarchy of nature by being termed ' super-natural '.

The limits of the concept of nature are to be found not in things, but in the concept itself, when thought tires of its unsuccessful efforts at comparing things and their appearances, and begins to doubt the truth of the laws, classifications, and rules it has discovered, when it becomes aware that it is producing a more fundamental norm out of itself than the norms established by the processes of deduction and application and verified by observation. These norms are not abstracted by comparative processes, but spring ever afresh out of the uniqueness of the mental impulse and the upward urge of the personality. They are the religious, ethical, æsthetic and scientific ideals, and to transfer them from one to the other would be senseless, since, infinitely variable, they establish themselves in each case only where the capacity, will and strength for fulfilling them are already at work. They are norms of thought, urgent norms, whose thirst for life must be satisfied by the creation of reality. Natural laws, on the other hand, are norms that have been thought. They are overloaded and over-run with reality. They do not attract, or hold, or create the stream of existence. The most they can do is to canalize it in those regions where it is already flowing quietly and slowly, shallow enough for our explanations, tamable and usable for everyday human life.

Now if we regard language as nature, *i.e.* as canal and not as spring, the main difficulty is that although there is a continuous transition between its natural application and its nascent mental force according as the speakers let themselves go or make greater or smaller efforts, our scientific thought always has to take a leap in order to keep up with these transitions, and has to oscillate between naturalistic and philosophic or historic concepts. For there is no uniform transition between these concepts. The spiritual aspects of language live naturally and closely together; but our thoughts and concepts about them collide harshly in the sphere of method.

We have, then, two classes of concepts and a changing order of thought for *one* thing; but it is this that makes philology so complicated and so attractive. The greater the danger becomes that the desire for knowledge will split on this rock and lose itself in a multitude of scattered aims, the more strongly we ought to insist that in the conflict of scientific concepts about language no specialist should lose sight of the main philosophic direction.

Language is embedded so deeply and in so many ways in the tissue of nature, that the illusion of its being a piece of nature constantly arises anew, and as constantly has to be dissipated.

No further proof is needed that language in the form of dialect seems to be bound to its environment and to have a natural home, but that it can transcend these limits and range across mountains and valleys, rivers and oceans, through human migrations, economic intercourse, political expansion, etc. The successful researches of recent years into the geographical distribution of languages do not need further confirmation as regards fundamentals, and the cultural, or rather spiritual nature of the so-called language frontiers, even where they coincide with natural landscapes and economic barriers, is beyond question.

In the light of modern science no one dares to believe that climate and the nature of the soil have any influence on the speech of man. Nor has it ever been proved that there is a necessary natural connection between races and

F

their language forms.[1]   The centre of gravity of a language does not lie in countries and climates, nor in houses and settlements, nor in the animal groupings and species of man.   It has to be sought for in the *use* of the language itself.   It is in being used that a language has its only true natural element, in which it is immediately and effectively confined.   Other natural factors can affect it for good or ill only by penetrating through the wrappings of usage.   Thus Italian, for example, is bound to the country and the people that are called Italian through no other natural power than its usage.   By virtue of their usage languages take root and migrate.   Usage resembles the arms of a polyp, with which languages attach, nourish, and move themselves.

The speaker or the scientific inquirer who disregards the instances of usage, misses the essence of a language and does poor work.   If we offend against German usage, it means that we are speaking incorrectly, that is, in an un-German fashion.   In a linguistic sense this is un-national, even unnatural, in so far as the usage of a language is its nature.

It is frequently assumed that German, Italian, etc., have a further first or second nature beyond their German-ness or Italianness, something that might be called a general language nature ; but that is an illusion arising from the abstractions of reason.   Linguists have compared a number of languages with each other and have found a number of common traits, which they have generalized into the rules and laws of phonetics, word economy, psychology, sociology, or even logic ; these rules seemed to hold for wide groups and even for the totality of human languages.   They have even demanded that no language process should fall out of the systematic conceptual framework, the phonetic, grammatical and psychological keyboards that are called phonetic change, analogy,

---

[1] Cf. the *Hugo Schuchardt-Brevier*, ed. by Leo Spitzer, Halle, 1922, under the index word " *Rasse* ", pp. 131, 203, 272, 277, 279.

change of meaning, contamination, etc., and that depend on a mechanical to-and-fro between differentiation and uniformization of language forms.[1] But this to-and-fro is nothing more than the continuity of language usage, and does not imply that something is added to the concept of usage from outside, from above or below. Usage is the to-and-fro of speaking and listening, a synthesis and analysis, a constant change of linguistic expressions and impressions. It therefore contains within itself this system of psychic mechanics, or keyboards. The machine-like rhythm between uniformization and differentiation is inherent in every language, be it German, or Chinese, or Esperanto. There is therefore no sense in searching for natural elements or laws of language as such beyond the usage of the historically present languages. Apart from the individual language usages that are continually being modified in space and time, there is no general norm or ' nature of language ', except in the minds and textbooks of philological enthusiasts ; just as ' the nose ' is to be found only in books, not among the multitude of human noses.

Many philologists are still incapable of appreciating this simple fact. They believe that they are establishing something scientifically exact and final when they reduce the individual phenomena of language to laws of nature. How little really is achieved in this way may be made clear by a few examples.

Although the belief that phonetic and analogical mutations are due to the operation of natural law may be regarded as exploded, and although all purely mechanical explanations have been discredited, naturalistic thinking still tries to fool us in the guise of biology. There has been a tendency recently to think of the living and the dying out of certain words in a language as a kind of Darwinian struggle for existence. For instance, the gradual extinction of the important French word *ouïr* =

[1] Cf. K. Vossler, *Gesammelte Aufsätze zur Sprachphilosophie*, Munich, 1923, chapter on " Das System der Grammatik ".

Latin *audire* has been explained in this way.[1] Since it was thought impossible or useless to search for cultural, that is, mental or spiritual causes for the gradual extinction of *ouïr*, it was hoped that the general biological law of competition would provide a solution for the problem. A search was made for word-rivals that could have strangled the poor *ouïr* and the murderer was soon discovered. Who else could it have been but *entendre*, Latin *intendere*, since it occupies the field of the suppressed *ouïr* and must therefore have had the strongest interest in the extinction of its predecessor? The task that remained for the investigator was now merely to find out when and how, with what allies, advances and reverses the types *audire* and *intendere* conducted their protracted campaigns on the language atlases of Gilliéron and in the memory cells of the French. This language drama, tirelessly pieced together from reliable documents and reports, is doubtless exciting; but it is merely a myth, and the most devoted textual criticisms cannot raise it to the dignity of a history of language. For the heroes of the fight are hollow masks, and the whole war of words is a didactic holiday of the linguists. Even if all the data were correct, the actual process was nevertheless quite different. *Entendre* and its relatives never settled in the cerebral or geographical sites of *ouïr*, for there is no lack of living-room in language. But *ouïr* always had a different, more sensual and spiritually less penetrating meaning than *entendre*, in which even to-day the old Latin meaning of *intendere aures et animum* is occasionally felt. Now it has been established that in the course of the seventeenth and eighteenth centuries French began to prefer *entendre* and gradually to neglect *ouïr*; and we also know that this movement proceeded from the cultural centres of the towns. We may therefore look upon the whole process as a result of the tremendous work accomplished by the Frenchmen of that time, by

[1] W. Gottschalk, *Lateinisch* AUDIRE *im Französischen*, Dissertation Giessen, 1921.

which they spread the new 'spiritual Renaissance' through Europe. French went far ahead of its Romance sister languages in the use of '*intendere*-hearing', at a time, moreover, when it helped to establish the spirit of analysis, of intellectualism and rationalism in many other language forms and in almost every department of life. In the centuries of Descartes and Voltaire the whole language was intellectually refined and trained to that type of hearing for which *entendre*, and no longer *ouïr* was the correct term. Vaugelas, the great master of language of that time, says : that it is much better *satisfaire l'entendement que l'oreille*,[1] wherever the demands of the ear do not coincide with those of the rational intelligence. So the driving forces behind the decay of *ouïr* and the growth of *entendre* are not the biological laws of language, but the peculiar and historically memorable efforts and achievements of French thought. This change did not come about in a day, like a discovery. It established itself hesitatingly, in a round-about way, imperfectly and with difficulty, during the course of centuries, somewhat as an institution does. For this we must blame the *nature* of language, the interminably dragging to-and-fro of habitual usage.

If we follow the function of a word habit in a special case like that of *ouïr* and *entendre*, it seems to be partly mechanical and somewhat thoughtless, partly exceedingly meaningful and purposive in the economic system of words. It is evident from the numerous geographical and historical monographs on words that have been written by students of the Romance and Germanic languages in the last twenty years, that accidental and mechanical causes, teleological instinct, and semi-conscious as well as perfectly clear thinking are all concerned in the formation of the habits and functions of words. Sometimes

[1] For further details cf. my review of Gottschalk's work in *Die Neueren Sprachen*, June–July, 1921 ; and my book, *Frankreichs Kultur im Spiegel seiner Sprachentwicklung*, 3rd. edn., Heidelberg, 1921, pp. 365–370 and 401.

one feels inclined to compare this growth of words with the wild vegetation of a primeval forest ; sometimes it reminds one of the wily moves of the hunted fox ; and then again of the rigid exactitude of a clockwork or even of the bureaucratic functioning of an administration, a bank, or an insurance company. So many-sided are the movements of this entity we have called the usage or the nature of language. All types of growth, from the mechanical to the consciously regulated are represented here and interwoven with one another. Every simile limps, every picture is inadequate, every rationalizing theory destroys the texture of the facts. Unless he wishes to become dogmatic, every philosopher of language is left with nothing more than the modest but important realization that the nature of a language is identical with its active-passive, that is, medial usage. All forms and turns of speech that are in use in our mother tongue are natural to it and, conversely, the more natural they are, the more they are used. There are as many language natures as there are usages, and conversely. There is no 'natural' language ; at most there are only natural sounds, and even these have to be sanctified by use before they are allowed an entrance into the language. Two anecdotes will serve to illustrate the limits of the natural and the habitual within a language.

An Alsatian woman, of German parentage but French 'education' came to give birth to a child. As long as she vented her anguish in the cry ai! ai! the doctor did not take the matter seriously ; only when she gave forth the German cry au! au! did he feel that her time had come. The experienced man obviously knew, first, that even the so-called 'natural' sounds are subject to language habits, secondly, that of two different language habits the more deeply rooted is the more 'natural', though it need not be the most frequent.

The second example is taken from "The Railway Accident", by Thomas Mann. "The guard: "Oh, Sir, I was stuck in between, it was against my chest, I escaped by way of the roof. Oh dear, Oh dear ! " His " I escaped by way of the roof " smacked of the newspaper report. The man certainly did not use " escaped by way of " as a rule. He had experienced not so much his accident, as a newspaper report of it." . . .

The guard who, in his excitement, takes to a less natural form of expression, and the Alsatian woman who takes to the more natural one in hers, seem to show, each from a different angle, that there are cases in which the natural and the more usual fall apart, and are therefore not as identical as we had postulated.

It is in fact not a static, mathematical identity, but a conceptual, philosophic one, which is something quite different. Just because the usage and the nature of a language are completely identical conceptually, that is, as regards the way in which their real and ideal aspects are thought, they have the principle or tendency within themselves to come together in reality and in practice. Through the constant flux of speaking and hearing by which they are continually being separated, they try to revert to their original unity. Here, too, in the evanescent multiplicity of linguistic life, the ancient metaphysical spectacle of unity through differentiation manifests itself. The forms and words of a language that are being constantly used tend to become so deeply rooted in the way in which that language is experienced, that they rise from being third or second nature to being its first and true nature. Similarly an original, spontaneous expression tries more and more to achieve the general validity of accepted usage, instead of retaining its unique individuality. If we look upon naturalness as the individual exception, usage appears as the general rule, as in the case of the Alsatian woman ; if we regard it as something remarkable and irregular, as in the case of the guard, regularity seems to be the more natural. Usage and nature, if I may say so, are in love with each other ; that is, in every member of one and the same language community there is more or less strongly active the will to seek that expression which is *natural* (or usual) to his way of feeling and thinking, and it expresses itself through those forms that are *usual* (or natural) to him.   The more energetically we wrestle with the language of our people, the more pliant and amenable it becomes.   The greatest master is always the man whose own expression in language sounds most intrinsically German, if he is a German ; most intrinsically French, if he is a Frenchman.   The formula of the identity of linguistic nature and linguistic usage, therefore, means and defines logically nothing more than the spiritual energy through which a language develops, that is, grows to a more manifold harmony.

Wherever people speak, this energy is at work, and language is created.   It can only temporarily be arrested or blocked, disturbed or divided.   This happens whenever the usage of a language departs from the nature immanent in it, that is, when an old usage is disturbed by a new one, as when Latin stepped from the old world, in which it had been formed, into the new Christian and barbaric world.   Or it may happen when a language usage is dictatorially continued without taking into account the natural aspects of our thoughts, feelings, and present ways of speaking, as in Esperanto, or wherever an alien tongue is forced upon us.   But in spite of such moments and centuries of arrest, obstruction, division and decay, the energy of language will finally find a way out, and soon the language habits will once more dig their natural channels.   The division creates new languages, and those that have become dammed up and motionless become a reservoir from which the more vital rivers and streams are fed.   In this infinite system nothing is lost.   The ' dead ' languages are a thousand times more numerous than the living ones ; yet not one of them is so dead that it does not in some way continue to influence the languages of to-day.   For out of the dim past nature and usage, rules and exceptions weave innumerable language threads into the small circle of our consciousness.   In the mastery over language of even the greatest thinker, the forgotten stammerings of his childhood still lead a shadowy existence.

One feels inclined to think that there must be a beginning and an end to spoken language somewhere, to its practice if not to its nature—to which one likes to attribute an absolute infinitude. But as human beings we can know the beginning as little as the end of this human habit, and it is senseless to attempt to transcend one's human limitations. That which we call language and the usage of language, because of its interweaving with nature, goes far deeper than the specific language structures of words and sentences. Hugo Schuchardt and Hermann Paul, it is true, hold that the question as to the origin of language is at bottom the same as the question as to the origin of the sentence.[1] They may be right in so far as our problem can be solved by the technical methods of the historical grammarian only if it is put in this more pointed form. But the empirical concept, that the languages of peoples and nations are made up of words and sentences, rests on a metaphysical concept of speech. We saw in Chapter II that the vehicle of this speech is the human spirit considered as single person playing an infinite number of parts and involved in a colossal conversation with itself.

Is this universal conversation, is any conversation at all, even the slightest, dependent on and circumscribed by words and sentences and grammatical forms ? Anyone who asks this question must answer, no. Everyone is aware how strongly the gestures of the hands, expressions of the face and eyes and body reinforce the spoken exchange of thoughts and feelings. But not everyone is conscious how much the imitative and indicative gestures are subject to the various habits and usages of language communities. They, too, have a kind of historical grammar ; and the natural spontaneity of such movements

[1] H. Schuchardt, " *Sprachursprung* ", I, II, III, and " Exkurs zu Sprachursprung, III ", *Sitzungsber d. preussischen Akademie d. Wissenschaften*, Berlin, 1919–1921.

of expression, of communication and representation are deeply enmeshed in a system of rules that is continually developing and changing. Old French gestures differ from those of modern French; and if our powers of observation had been better trained, we should, merely from the attitudes of the faces and bodies of speakers and without hearing a single word, be able to tell their country and the nation by which their mimic language has been trained. An attempt has recently been made to regard even the permanent facial expression, the physiognomy in its typical form, as a product of the mimic and articulatory habits of language. Thus the Frankish face is different to the Suabian, not because of a difference of race, but because in it different language motor habits have become fossilized, as it were.[1] How far such examples take us, we shall not discuss. We merely wished to point at a lower world, where a silent shadow-language lives entirely on the play of gestures, and yet in accord with language usages, through which the natural movements are trained and formed into means of understanding one another.

But this by no means exhausts the dimensions of the concept of language. In a sense it includes all the fine arts: dancing as the language of gesture, music as a language of sound, painting as a language of colour and line, sculpture and architecture as a language of solid bodies, and poetry as the language of languages.

What do we mean by 'the language of languages'? In our discussion of the relation of religion to language we found there something that was not expressed in spoken language, something spiritual that at most showed itself as 'feeling tone'. This immanent inner nature of language is expressed as speech in poetry. Poets are artists to whom it has been given to distil the language

---

[1] Willy Hellpach, "Das fränkische Gesicht, Untersuchungen zur Physiognomik der deutschen Volksstämme, I. Folge", *Sitzungsber. d. Heidelberger Akad. d. Wissenschaften, Mathem.-naturwiss. Klasse*, 2nd. paper, Heidelberg, 1921.

of the heart from the languages of man. They speak twice or double, as it were ; and to understand them one needs a kind of second hearing. Nevertheless their best creations seem to us complete, unified wholes. Nothing is so untranslatable, so fundamentally German, as a poem of Goethe. Yet this Germanness is due not so much to the use of language according to accepted rules, as to the actual concrete and spiritual nature of the German language. The relation of usage and nature has here been inverted. In the language of everyday speech the natural forms of expression, sounds, voice, rhythm, are ruled by usage, and are the outer form that has to obey our intentions and needs. In poetry they become the inner and dominant part, to which the rules of syntax and word usage have to adapt themselves. This seems to me to be the hidden core of truth in the classical theory of art, that poetry is the imitation of nature, which is so often misunderstood in modern works on æsthetics. The particular ' nature ', in the ' imitation ' of which the poet takes such great delight, is the singing and sounding, the thundering and whispering, the rhythm and melody of his mother tongue, as he hears it a thousandfold in the human voices about him. In Flaubert this delight in language became an almost pathological hypersensitivity. He was possessed by it, and was therefore more a virtuoso and a Sadist of language than a great poet. For a great poet does not merely hear the vibration of the vocal cords like Flaubert ; he hears also the beating of men's hearts. When Flaubert once came across some full-sounding verses of Victor Hugo, he wrote to Feydeau : " What a man, what a poet ! I must immediately cry three thousand such inimitable verses. Cry ? no, shout. I don't know myself any longer. Bind me fast ! Ah, that does me good." Here we see what an effect the pure sounds of language can have, how they can, almost like naked flesh, excite and torture the desire of the artist ; how the outer sound—that which we have called the shorn hair of Samson—can become the most important.

Normally, however, no passion or rage or juggling tricks are needed to invert the ordinary relation of language nature and language usage. True, this inversion will always be a miracle, the miracle of Poetry. Through it nature is given a soul, is made inward and spiritual, a process that is accessible to abstract reason only from the outside, although, like Samson's hair, it grows from within.

We recognize poetical genius by the capacity to reconvert the nature of language to spirit, its outer forms to something inward, and to give back to it the soul which is destroyed by ordinary speech. And the ' poetability ' of any language rests on the possibility of allowing this reversion to take place. That is what we meant by the ' language of languages '. It is the natural spirit of poetry, which is inherent in all languages, and is their highest and only unity, their truly active and creative principle. In its name the speaker as artist and poet may transcend the rules of usage, and enjoy unpunished what we call poetic licence. The servant of the poetic spirit of nature may be familiar with emperors and kings ; he may call a lady ' woman ', or ' girl ', or ' maid ', a young horse ' steed ' ; he may revive lost words, change the word order, dislocate a sentence, break through the congruence of grammatical gender, time and mode. He is not even required to be intelligible to every man, as long as he remains true to the poetical inspiration of his nature—

> *ed a quel modo*
> *che ditta dentro, vo significando.*

The common language usage of the country is not thereby completely set aside ; but it descends from a ruling to a serving position. That is, in order to rejuvenate itself and to be able to assume new domains, it allows itself to be dethroned for the time being, like God in Lamartine's verse :

> *Il prête sa parole à la voix qui le nie.*

Grammarians, therefore, if they are concerned with a conscientious study of language usage, cannot be careful enough in using illustrations drawn from poetry. For there ' style ' as an artistic and spiritual fact always takes precedence over ' use ' as a grammatical and social fact.

What is common to all languages and therefore is at once their true nature and their being, the spirit of poetry, is the soul when seen from the side of religion. As there is no mind without a soul, so there can be no poetry and no art without a religious urge. Accordingly the unity of language is felt wherever the soul expresses itself in poetry and art. To the pious ear of the artist all things have their language. The whole being and becoming of the world, stars, stones, plants and animals speak to him, and not only human beings. They speak to him because, on the strength of his belief and his poetry he lends them a soul, his own, and interprets as language the behaviour of the things thus ensouled. Since the universe speaks to him, all reality takes on the form of language or saga for him ; he thinks mythically. The mystery of the origin of language is therefore wrapped up with the mythical thinking of primitive man, and not only with the birth of the syntactical sentence.[1]

Here, it is true, we are moving in a circle. For how could the world be thought as saga and the stars and stones have a language attributed to them if we ourselves had not first said and spoken, and, by virtue of our own activity, experienced the pleasure and the sorrow of speaking and hearing and understanding ? How, on the other hand, could the mother speak to her child, or the warrior to his weapon, or the lover to his maid, if they had not first heard the voice of nature within them and interpreted it with religious certainty ? It is true that nothing that can be called language has ever been evolved without executive activity ; but are not hearing, listening, seeing, interpreting and understanding activities, some- times even as difficult as the articulation of a sound in a language ? We can hardly remember the intense

[1] Cf. E. Cassirer, *Sprache und Mythos*, Leipzig, 1925.

expectancy and the first intuitions of primitive man, before his tongue was loosened.

When at last he began to speak, all those forces that to-day still form the warp and woof of the most modern civilized languages were active in him from the very first moment, the forces that constitute the whole of the natural and spiritual man, with all his feelings and potentialities. Linguistically, that is, from the standpoint of philosophy, the language of prehistoric times was no whit more naïve, not a particle more natural, neither more poetical, nor more pious, nor less logical, nor less practical than the most developed literary languages of art or intercourse of the present day. The opinion of sentimental Philistines, that the poetical and the natural are gradually dwindling away in favour of the intellectual and technical, should find no further encouragement in science. The only real thing about this romantic malady of positivism is that its exponents have neither the desire nor the capacity for appreciating present spiritual values. So they indulge a predilection for the twilight of pre-history and the so-called prehistoric sources, as though language had been truly creative, naïve, and poetical only in those times ; or they hope that in dialects and in the language of children they will meet with the true, un-adulterated genius of speech. But as a matter of fact it is there that the rigid, conventional, technical aspects are more in evidence, the struggle with the limitations of the material, the difficulties of articulation, the bondage of narrow social organizations.[1] These things doubtless are deeply interesting ; but we advise anyone who wishes to approach more closely to the freer life of language, its

[1] G. von der Gabelentz in *Die Sprachwissenschaft*, Leipzig, 1891, pp. 46 and 243 f., relates that among the Polynesians the dictum of a priest or chief can remove a word from current use and introduce another. The Javanese distinguish three uses of language : a respectful, a middle, and a common one. Ancient Japanese courtesy forbids the application of ordinary adjectives to the doings of highly placed per-sonages. The Koreans, finally, are said to use more than twenty verbal modes according to the social rank of speaker and listener.

more ultimate and natural originality—in the philosophic, not the chronological sense—and its mythical and poetical creativeness, to read an ultra-modern lyrical poet like Christian Morgenstern,[1] who knows how to give free rein to the most whimsical moods of the language spirit, and in whom the true nature of language is reincarnate.

' Phonetic symbolism ', ' word myths ', ' popular etymology ', ' false analogy ', ' primitive creation ', ' onomatopœia ', ' phonetic rhythm ', or whatever else we like to call the utterances of instinct and emotion in language, are all mixed together here with wit and humour. In Morgenstern, the humour for the reader and the instructive example for the investigator consist in the fact that an original spirit here frees himself from language usage, plays all kinds of tricks with it, and leads it into impossible situations that can only have a meaning as language phantasy, language myth, language symbolism, or language belief, and whose relation to the logic of facts is one of joyous negation. In poets like Morgenstern, or in Rabelais,[2] who takes such a delight in language, we see how the natural sense of language functions. They exhibit it, in a kind of biological pure culture, far more drastically than the primitive languages and dialects, which, slaves of need, serfs of the soil, and chained to social dogmas as they are in both the Old and the New worlds, can allow themselves only a minimum of natural freedom of movement.

Those, however, who wish to look upon natural influences as a minimum and what has been regulated by common use as a maximum, may be advised to take up the study of dialects. There they can follow, for instance, the excellent researches of J. Gilliéron, and study how the

---

[1] Cf. Leo Spitzer, " Die groteske Gestaltungs- und Sprachkunst Christian Morgensterns ", in the book by Spitzer and Sperber, *Motiv und Wort*, Leipzig, 1918.

[2] Rabelais, too, has been examined under the linguistic microscope by Leo Spitzer in *Die Wortbildung als stilistisches Mittel*, Halle, 1910.

usual word types *serrare, resecare, sectare, secare,* overlie
one another in a rational system ; how *secare* has been
able to gain a footing only in those parts of Southern and
Eastern France where *resecare,* and *resecare* only where
serrare has taken over a different meaning and by its
disappearance cleared the field for the newcomer.[1] Or
they can read in Ernst Gamillscheg's work how the
distribution of the names for whetstones and basins and
their changing use have been determined almost entirely by
a rational and unimaginative word economy throughout
the whole range of the Gallo-Romance languages.[2] For
whetstones and basins are articles with which peasants
and not poets have been concerned and in whose use and
description during the course of centuries the poets have
made even less change than the grinders and manufacturers.
The favourite working hypothesis of Gilliéron and his
pupils is that through the power of usage, every language
and dialect regulate their store of words and forms
according to a perfect and rational economy ; they do
not allow disorder, gaps, equivocalities, or *embarras de
richesse* for any length of time, and constantly endeavour
to eliminate, smooth down, and liquidate the complica-
tions of homonyms and synonyms, or of other hindrances
such as the isolation and unique meanings of half-forgotten
words. In how far this desire and compulsion to form a
system is really inherent in the various languages, or is
no more than a method, an " as if " postulated by the
investigator, is a delicate problem that has to be solved
afresh from case to case. The matter here is similar to
that of the phonetic laws, which Gilliéron flatters himself
he has solved ; but in fact he has merely substituted
other laws—his own.

For the more radically the phonetic mutations of a
language are rationalized, that is, explained purely on

---

[1] J. Gilliéron et J. Mongin, " *Scier* " *dans la Gaule romane du Sud
et de l'Est,* Paris, 1905.

[2] E. Gamillscheg, " Wetzstein und Kumpf im Galloromanischen,"
Biblioteca dell'Archivum Romanicum, vol. II, Florence, 1922.

the basis of phonetic laws, the more irrational the movements of grammatical and syntactic usage must appear,
and vice versa. Gilliéron announces the bankruptcy of
phonetic laws and etymologies ; but he forgets that long
before him, and with as much justification, the ' young
grammarians ' had announced the bankruptcy of closed
language systems, language customs, dialect and language
limits, and therefore had by implication announced in
advance the bankruptcy of his ' popular etymologies '.
For every ' popular etymology ' in Gilliéron's sense, that
is, every association or amalgamation of a word with a
particular word order can only be regarded as a rational
measure when it actually is felt and undertaken as such
within the closed circle of a unitary language purpose.
But it will always be impossible to prove the existence
of such a language purpose directly, since language usage
is not a personality. This purposiveness can therefore
only be deduced mediately, *ex eventu*, and is thus always
liable to evaporate. There is nothing more treacherous
than irresponsible sentiments.

But we wish to strangle neither causal phonetic etymology nor Gilliéron's etymologizing. Both methods have
their failures and successes. The one postulates rational
articulation, the other rational selection and classification
of word forms. Thus this purposiveness, which is no
more than the striving of the average speaker after
intelligibility, is doubtless to be found in every language ;
only we must beware of regarding it as something
mechanical or even absolute. Nor may we think that it
has a different nature or is opposed to the artistic
striving after objectivity, emphasis, individuality, colour,
beauty, etc.

It is an easy-going and common habit for empirical
research to explain the development of individual language
forms or even of language as such as a duel between two
hostile forces : understanding and feeling, intellect and
intuition, mind and nature, the striving after intelligibility
and the need for expression, laziness and the will to

G

clarity, and so on.[1] As long as this method is not regarded as binding and is used merely for the purpose of gaining preliminary insight, we may let it pass. But from a strictly philosophical point of view every dualistic theory of language must lead to grave contradictions, from which we can save ourselves only by retreating to the firm ground of science.

On the other hand, positivists, pragmatists, and the followers of Bergson, to whom the weakening of the will to knowledge appears a metaphysical gain, would encourage us to make such leaps into mystic darkness.

But once the connection between the customary and the natural, between thesis and physis has been torn asunder, the estranged forces can never again be reconciled. Custom will degenerate and run wild as caricature and fashionable excess, nature as caprice and sloth. Finally, a history of language that sees in the customs which it records merely the conventional and not the natural as well, will remain a senseless, learned chronicle of words— like that history of painting, which refuses to hear of a development of the sense of sight or the possibility of educating the eye, and against whose unphilosophic anecdotage and disconnected all-knowingness Heinrich Wölfflin fights with all the power of his will to achieve knowledge.

---

[1] This has recently been, or rather still is the method of Friedrich Schürr in his otherwise excellent book *Sprachwissenschaft und Zeitgeist*, Marburg, a.d. L, 1922. Cf. in particular p. 37 ; also my review in *Cultura*, Rome, 1923 ; and in another connection my book *Positivismus und Idealismus in der Sprachwissenschaft*, Heidelberg, 1904, p. 33 ff.

CHAPTER VI

THE dualistic theory of language finds its strongest support in the fact that outside all speaking, and apparently quite independent of it, there exists a Nature which we have hitherto consistently ignored. Beyond the walls and windows of our lecture rooms there are green trees and whistling winds that take no notice of our words. What is that little bit of nature which we have thought out in our languages, compared to the eternal nature of the cosmos ?

Caggiono i regni intanto,
Passan genti e linguaggi : ella nol vede. . . .[1]

It is infinitely larger, infinitely smaller, infinitely more durable, and infinitely more quick, flexible and evanescent in its manifestations than human words can ever grasp. Bergson, who, like Schelling, attempts to capture and to intuit the eternal force and rhythm of nature, finds that nothing in our languages, neither words nor sentences, nor poetry, nor thinking in terms of language, can keep pace with the uninterrupted waves in the ocean of nature within, above and below us. " Nous tendons instinctivement à solidifier nos impressions, pour les exprimer par le langage. De là vient que nous confondons le sentiment même, qui est dans un perpétuel devenir, avec son objet extérieur permannent, et surtout avec le mot qui exprime cet objet. . . ."[2] Ainsi chacun de nous a sa manière d'aimer et de haïr, et cet amour, cette haine, reflétent sa personnalité tout entière. Cependant le langage désigne

---

[1] *Leopardi, La Ginestra, o il Fiore del Deserto.*

[2] *Essai sur les données immédiates de la conscience,* 6th. edn., Paris, 1908, p. 99. [English translation, *Time and Free Will.*]

ces états par les mêmes mots chez tous les hommes ; aussi n'a-t-il pu fixer que l'aspect objectif et impersonnel de l'amour, de la haine et des mille sentiments qui agitent l'âme ? Nous jugeons du talent d'un romancier à la puissance avec laquelle il tire du domaine public, où le langage les avait ainsi fait descendre, des sentiments et des idées auxquels il essaie de rendre, par une multiplicité de détails qui se juxtaposent, leur primitive et vivante individualité. Mais de même qu'on pourra intercaler indéfiniment des points entre deux positions d'un mobile sans jamais combler l'espace parcouru, ainsi par cela seul que nous parlons, par cela seul que nous assoĉions des idées les unes aux autres et que ces idées se juxtaposent au lieu de se pénétrer, nous échouons à traduire entièrement ce que notre âme ressent : la pensée demeure incommensurable avec le langage." [1]

For a philosopher, Bergson is too partial in this controversy between words and nature, between language and the life of the mind. Why should not someone else, who is as much in love with language as Bergson is with life, be able to quote just as many advantages for the former ? In Thomas Mann's story " Enttäuschung ", a sophist of the *language* camp, who is tired of life, says the following : " Verzückte Personen haben mir vorgesungen, die Sprache sei arm, ach, sie sei so arm,—o nein, mein Herr ! Die Sprache, dünkt mich, ist reich, ist überschwänglich reich im Vergleich mit der Dürftigkeit und Begrenztheit des Lebens. Der Schmerz hat seine Grenzen : der körperliche in der Ohnmacht, der seelische im Stumpfsinn,—es ist mit dem Glück nicht anders ! Das menschliche Mitteilungsbedürfnis aber hat sich Laute erfunden, die über diese Grenzen hinweglügen.—Liegt es an mir ? Läuft nur mir die Wirkung gewisser Worte auf eine Weise das Rückenmark hinunter, dass sie mir Ahnungen von Erlebnissen erwecken, die es garnicht giebt ? " All people who are susceptible to poetry tremble when they hear certain words ; and the true, the creative master of language is

---

[1] *Idem*, p. 126.

recognized in that he does not, like the *romancier* of Bergson, take over finished feelings, concepts, ideas, etc., from customary usage, and, having trimmed them with a few additional ornaments, warm them up again. That is mere literary cookery. No, the expression of his hate and his love is just as unique, as swinging and as sounding as the hating and the loving themselves. In its way as immeasurable as the *élan vital* of natural events, a poetic word acts and grows into the future and resounds through a hundred generations of new hearers ever afresh and ever deeper. Similar to the processes of growth and of feeling, there is a fusion of the spiritual meanings of words, which are not words but the breath and voice of the heart. Wherever there are human hearts they find an echo ; and more than that : they demand the intenser continuation of their existence. The spiritual meaning of a poem, however closely it may be bound to the words, goes beyond itself ; and the words without changing outwardly, even when they become archaic, share in this transcendence. In this process effects come to light that are completely new, and were not foreseen by the poet. But mediately and by implication they were meant and designed by him ; so they are not due to chance and are not false, but maintain the individual sound of their origin and spread it in an alien air. The ancient words of Homer and Dante still say the same things to-day ; and yet it is something different, something fuller and deeper than what they meant when they were alive. For man grows not only as his aims become higher, but also as his understanding becomes deeper.

" All this," it may be said, " is merely the beauty of age and dignity, the patina of language, the attractiveness of ruins." Well, let it be so. For it is precisely by such and similar concepts that we learn how intimately art and life, and language and life, are interwoven. The ' ruin ' is a creation of the observer. Five thousand years ago it might have been any common and useful building ; it might even have been artistically worthless. A later generation sees the mouldering remains, and, if it is susceptible, enjoys the tragic spectacle of time and stress, which have filled the old memorial with fate and storm, and, since they could not vanquish or reduce it, have made it great and noble. Ruins of stone or of words : through them we feel bound to other, distant peoples that also built, also wrote and spoke. This feeling of the link between our lives beyond the limitations of space and time is something religious, and in its presence there is something æsthetic.

Other than with the devout eyes of the artist the inter-relations of life, of whatever kind they may be, cannot be seen at all. It is to Bergson's credit that he has renewed and justified this devout contemplation, which, in the modern man of reason, has atrophied through too many scientific abstractions. Bergson, whose finest talent is mystical contemplation, and even more the capacity for making the dumb processes of life speak, should have been the very last to question the only means we have for this purpose, the æsthetic, and in the philosophic sense, linguistic. But now, with his one-sided, intellectualistically polished philosophy of language, he has sawn off the very branch on which his philosophy of life could have flowered.[1]

If we contemplate life, see it through experience, or experience it through seeing, we shall have a belief or a vision, or both together in a myth : but we shall not have a philosophy. The concept of life, like that of death, is a dogmatic, or as Heinrich Rickert says, a prophetic, but not a philosophic structure ; and life itself, far from being " the highest good ", has no structure at all. It seems to have one only because it is our sole opportunity for creating values and finding enjoyment. The man who clings to bare life, weak-willed, and without the capacity to grasp his opportunities, is rightly regarded as a miserable being. Of all religions the mere clinging to

[1] For further criticism of Bergson cf. Benedetto Croce, *Estetica*, 3rd edn., Bari, 1909, p. 482.

life at any price, " *bloss lebendige Lebenszappelei* ", is the last and lowest ; and after all belief has fled, our fear of death remains as the last and most shameful awe of the absolute. Philosophy can have very little use for this soulless, purely emotional attitude of denial or affirmation of life or death. Whether we are emphatic about life or despise it ; whether we regard death as a blessing or a misfortune, depends on everything else but science. Science *knows* only that life as such, like nature, is neither good nor bad ; it is essentially neutral and relative, and can therefore receive its meaning only through mind. For this reason the concepts of life and nature must remain empty concepts of relation for the philosophic understanding.

If, as we have seen, nature is related to language in such a way that they combine in language *usage* but have otherwise no connection, then, from a philosophic point of view, there must be a place where language and *life* meet. It is not in usage, even though we talk of ' living ' usages, since by using the word ' living ' we admit that there are dead and dying language usages, which have been and are being forsaken by life. For, to put it accurately and paradoxically, customs die, while language lives on. All the details of language, even individual languages, are mortal—except language itself. The life of language flows through its usages, and in its passage lets them flower and fade. It is this constant flow that constitutes life and is perceived more as contrast than as contradiction to immobility and rigidity. The philosophy of language knows no gulf between the living and the dead, no contradiction or opposition, only a difference. The one can therefore not be severed from the other ; both must be regarded as a unity and differentiated from one another as a rising and falling, as progress and pause in a rhythmical process.

It follows from this that nothing completely dead or hopelessly static can ever be thought of or demonstrated as existing in a language. No form, no language, no single word is so dead and forgotten that the speaking mind cannot find it again some day, stir it up and thaw it out. Wherever we find the dead shell of a language, fossilized in Etruscan inscriptions, mouldering under the earth, dispersed through the winds, it can again be comprehended and brought to life. The facts, it is true, seem to be against this. In Lemnos, Crete, and Cyprus, for instance, inscriptions have been found which, although written in perfectly legible archaic Greek characters, speak an absolutely unintelligible language. "Until a surprising chance gives us the key to these mysterious texts," writes A. Meillet,[1] "it is hopeless to try to learn more from them than the fact that up to the threshold of historic times languages existed in Lemnos, Crete, and Cyprus that are neither Greek nor Semitic. It would be Love's labours lost to attempt to interpret the inscriptions directly. We cannot apprehend the sense of an unknown language intuitively. If we are to succeed in understanding the text of a language whose tradition has been lost, we must either have a faithful translation into a known language, that is, we must possess bilingual texts, or the language in question must be closely related to one or more languages with which we are familiar. In other words, we must already know it." True enough ; but chance reaches her hand only to the man who is ready to take it and who keeps the oil of hope in his lamp. It is a philosophic, and not an irrational hope ; it believes that what has been spoken and written by man, man can again understand and decipher, however endless and difficult the particular task. In a certain sense even forgotten and unknown words, language forms of the past and the future, partake of the language life of to-day. For whenever and wherever we become instinctively conscious of our language capacities, and analyse them critically, we do it in a different way each time, according to our present language customs and natures. The people of the Middle Ages or of the eighteenth

[1] A. Meillet, *Aperçu d'une histoire de la langue grecque*, Paris, 1913, p. 48.

century took a different view of the languages of the past
and the future, not only because they had different
knowledge, but also because they had different language
usages and conceptions. The most distant language plants
live by the same spiritual breath that to-day animates my
speaking. How otherwise could I hope to understand
them, or even to guess at their meaning ? Only in so far
as we make them present to our consciousness, make
them our own, revive their tradition and bring it down into
our times, can foreign, and dead, and future languages
come to ' life '. Whatever is spiritually alive is the
present, even though its nature, that is, its common usage,
belongs to the realm of the dead.

The present, therefore, is the place where language
and life meet, and it is always the present language usage
that is the living one. In the philosophic sense of the
term, linguists always deal with the language of the
present, since it is the only one there is. That is, the
numerous vanished and strange language usages are called
from their natural death into the life of the mind ; from
being accidentally bound in space and time, they are
lifted into the swiftly moving present. Complacent con-
servatives and pedants have never been able to realize
what a living and dynamic thing the study of ' dead ' and
' foreign ' languages is ; for their own words are dead and
foreign in their own mouths.

Unfortunately the present, and the contemporaneous
stream of life are so diluted by speakers no less than by
students of language, that in fact only the merest fraction
of the full vigour of their minds is ever aroused. The
subject of which we happen to be speaking, the meaning
we intend to convey, may be compressed into a single
word, or even into a stressed syllable. The investigator,
therefore, will frequently have to concentrate his whole
attention on some small formal aspect, a suffix, or the
quality of a single sound. The whole life of a language,
as immeasurable, infinite and mysterious as God, contracts
into the fleeting moment and flies as a minute spark

through our consciousness. But this is the very living form of the mind, that, like the moving mountain of a wave, it rears its dark, fluid form from depths and breadths that cannot be encompassed, and, by a fleck of foam, makes the whole visible and bright, giving it through a sound expression as language. The living power of language is seen in its particularization of the infinite unity of the spirit and making it the present, here and now, through the infinite variety of shining, sounding, speaking forms of expression.

We may be expressing an affair of the moment ; yet behind the unassuming forms of our speech a whole philosophy of life may be surging. We study the development of a word ; and we find that the mental life of all who have used it has been precipitated and crystallized in it. The great task of the language historian, which has as yet hardly been attempted, is to recognize in its language customs the deposits of the mental life of the whole of humanity. For only in this way will that interweaving of language and life, as it took place in the mind of peoples from moment to moment, again become alive and intelligible to us, become the present to our analytic and comprehending consciousness.

What the science of language has achieved up to now is still far from fulfilling the double demands we have been making, that, like all history, the history of language should include the totality of mental life and view it in the present from the particular standpoint of the activity of speech ; that it should integrate into the universality and actuality of our knowledge what is scattered in grammars and textbooks, or, quite simply, make it alive and whole.

CHAPTER VII

LANGUAGE COMMUNITIES

(a) *The metaphysical and the empirical language community*

WE showed before that a language community presupposes several persons. But every non-human object in nature can be personified by the imagination. So it must always happen that language communities will extend beyond exclusively human societies. Primitive people and children speak to their gods and dolls, to stones and tables, even to air and light, to everything that is present to their mind and senses.

The distinction between these super- and infra-human participants in a language community and its human members is only apparent and external, in so far as gods, dolls, and stones do not reply. But what if we attribute to them the understanding and the answers we expect of them, or even observe that an animal which has been called, or a god who has been invoked, does our bidding ? The difference, it will be said, consists in their not using any organs of speech, or using different ones to the common human organs ; that they do not speak with tongues and lungs. But even within human communities and conversations the so-called organs of speech can be circumvented, replaced, or ignored. Gesture, picture, and alphabet writing, all kinds of pictorial, musical, and plastic signs and signals, even certain involuntary expressive movements show us how numerous are the stratagems employed by the speaking mind if its mouth and ears are closed. When the ear fails, all our other senses combine and build temporary bridges for our understanding. So, when and wherever the will blazes new language trails by means of the senses, new and special language communities arise, according to the power and usefulness of the means employed. It does not matter, therefore, whether the speaking and understanding man addresses himself to dogs, gods, stars, or his own kind ; for by the potency of his capacity for language he makes the strange beings his equals. In this sense, of course, we may maintain that man communicates only with his own kind, even when he is speaking to dolls or blocks of wood, or to ' the unknown god ', and that the empirical science of language should therefore concern itself only with purely human language communities and behave as though there were no others.

But in truth no single language community is purely ' human ' in the social sense of the word. Through the power of the anthropomorphic imagination of speech, a part of the environment, the whole world even, is drawn into it and also made to speak. In each, nature, the world, God, play a part as speaking subject, not only as object about which we speak.

> La nature est un temple où de vivants piliers
> Laissent parfois sortir de confuses paroles ;
> L'homme y passe à travers des forêts de symboles,
> Qui l'observent avec des regards familiers . . .,

as Baudelaire says.[1]

It may be a fiction that nature speaks in the spring song of a poet, or God in the warnings and promises of an Old Testament prophet. How weak this relation is may be seen from the fact that we can regard the poet or the prophet as the mouthpiece through which nature or God let us hear their voices, just as conversely nature or the deity are the vehicles for expressing the poet's meaning.

---

[1] Ferdinand Ebner (*Das Wort und die geistigen Realitäten, pneumatologische Fragmente*, Innsbruck, 1921) has been completely dazzled by the fact of the metaphysical language community. His speculations about the human ' I ' and the divine ' thou ', the primordial word, the oblique case, and the meaning of the sound *m*, etc., have no scientific value, but are interesting as a passionate reaction against the rationalistic empiricism of the grammarians.

The poet speaks through nature by making himself her spokesman and she in her turn speaks for him. Through this mutual relation between speaker and subject, subject and speaker, a spiritual, artistic, and æsthetic community of language grows up, which is set aside as a figment of the imagination, as ephemeral and unreal by the sober, unimaginative man. He does not dream that the sociable language community, which grows up between himself, Smith, Brown and Robinson at the bridge table, would fall to pieces without that metaphysical community of language with the forces and the spirit of the universe.

It would become even physically impossible ; for the air which they disturb with their vocal cords also belongs to that community, not only as sound carrier, but actually as language. It is not a person as such, and therefore not an autonomous speaker ; but it is a mobile partner now of this, now of that speaker, and sometimes one can almost observe how it co-operates in inspiring and forming speech, how its physis becomes metaphysis.

If the air round the group at a table is disturbed by powerful noises from other people or from the rattle of glasses and plates, our guests will have to force their vocal organs in order to understand one another, and will soon fall into a manner of speaking they did not in the least desire, and whose coarseness is, after all, due to the disturbed transmission of the air, which will become language under these circumstances only on condition that no delicate phonetic or psychic forms are confided to it.[1]

[1] It might be profitable to examine the question how far the phonetic form of peasant dialects is determined by the fact that they are usually spoken or shouted in still air and at great distances. This point of view might become fruitful for the phonetic history of Vulgar Latin. We saw on pp. 55 and 72 that the speaker of Vulgar Latin more frequently takes up the attitude of listener than that of speaker. It may therefore be assumed that his phonetic expression is regulated more by the sensorial than the motor and articulatory aspects of his organs of speech. We must see the relation of Vulgar Latin to classical Latin somewhat as the relation of a dialect to the written language. Is it strange that in the course of centuries two different phonetic structures were evolved ? For in each case typical situations are

The stone, paper, or bronze on which we write, the air and wires through which we speak, the ears with which we hear, our larynxes and vocal cords, nerves and muscles, lungs and hands, even our brains, become language when the necessity arises, though in themselves they are something completely different. They allow language to be attributed to them, and in their turn give forth language whenever the circumstances demand it. But at other times they are as unresponsive and strange as a coin that is not in circulation. Because of their indifference to speaking or not speaking, they are the embodied medium. In them we see concretely and clearly that incidence and reciprocity of life and death, of egocentricity and heterocentricity, of thesis and heterothesis, about which we spoke above. They are the material

continually arising that require different adjustments. The man who speaks the written language, or reads it aloud, the educated society man, the teacher, the orator, the actor, all these are forced towards greater clarity, articulation, and suppleness in their language ; the speaker of Vulgar Latin, the peasant, the working, everyday man towards greater sound volume.

The diction of written language attempts to arrange the phonetic body objectively and plastically, as though there were an eye in the ear. The speaker of the written language seems in some respects to be deaf, the speaker of the dialect blind. For the former, language, even when articulated, seems like a gesture of thought ; for the latter, even when the voice is lowered, like a megaphone and an echo. It is therefore not a matter of greater or less clarity, intelligibility, or emphasis—for both types of speaker wish to be understood and believed ; but, to reach the same goal, the speaker of classical Latin prefers the visually more objective, the speaker of Vulgar Latin the acoustically more objective method. The person whose language is uneducated shouts ; the person whose language is educated articulates. Hence the phonetic manifestations of Vulgar Latin are concerned more with consonants than with vowels, and consonantal changes are usually induced by the expansion of neighbouring vocal sounds. How far the phonetic changes of Vulgar Latin can be explained by this assumption of a continuous striving towards greater sonority, can only be decided by detailed phonetic investigations. At first sight it would seem as though the most important events point naturally in this direction : the change of vowel quantities to qualities, the change from i and u to the more sonorous e and o, the loss of unemphasized vowels under certain conditions, the muting of h and others.

seat and the vehicle of language intercourse, the in-
attentively faithful, mechanical guardians of language
customs, the point at which the person of the hearer and
reader keeps its rendezvous with the person of the speaker
and writer. In the present life and nature of our restlessly
wandering, continually reborn, leaping, sparkling speech
they are the only permanence. Measured by speech, they
are the only rigid elements. For when stone breaks,
paper bleaches or burns, air diffuses, the vocal cords
become diseased, and senile decay creeps over the brain,
these are purely physical, and not language changes, and
are as far removed from language as it is possible to
conceive. The physical being of these material agents of
communication seems purely fortuitous as seen from the
side of language. Like everything accidental, like all
matter, they have to be moulded. In themselves our
tongues, nerves, and brains are no more language than a
stone or a piece of paper. The stone has to be hewn,
the page written on, the tongue must be practised in
articulation, the brain trained and educated for language.
As we mould through speech and understanding, put
ourselves into them and separate ourselves from them,
that is, unite with them and dissociate ourselves from
them, we pass from the metaphysical language community
into the various special, material communities that co-
operate through language. All empirical language communities depend on communal work on and with common
materials and tools. They consist of persons who are
working with and are concerned about objects that are
amenable to language, whether they gather round a book,
a violin or piano, a canvas, a telephone ; or whether
they are satisfied with the less artistic pursuits that are
grouped round the human voice, ear, eye, hand, etc., and
are concerned with developing and perfecting these
organs with which we are born. The empirical language
communities are distinguished from the metaphysical
communities by their acquired capacities, their specifically
linguistic concerns and work, the adaptation of their

tools to linguistic thought—be it the child's attempts at articulation or the mastery of an artist or orator. Through our feelings, through sacrifice, through our religious and æsthetic being, all of us naturally belong to the metaphysical language community. This needs no practice; for the inner work of the mind is sufficient. A mood, a mystical and phantastic anthropomorphism is enough to make us feel at one with the universe, and to sense what we might call its infinite language. But only the person who knows German has access to the German empirical language community; only the person who can read and write to that of the written languages; only the musically trained and cultured to that of music. And the greater and more certain the specific knowledge and achievements of the individual within such a language community, the more unquestioned his membership, and the more important his position in it.

To the degree in which the anthropomorphism of the person who merely feels without knowing emerges from its intuitive contemplation, becomes active, takes up a special material with special organs, and, through the exercise of will and activity, moulds it for the purpose of his being understood, a specific language capacity arises that gives him the right of citizenship in this or that empirical language community. All linguistic ability, therefore, anthropomorphizes. It is a kind of magic art, a curious mental faculty and facility for momentarily and continually giving a language to the brain, to air, stone, paper, lines, colours, and everything that nature and the environment offer, that is, assimilating them to the present forms of human thought and understanding.

So that unity which we sense and feel between our humanity and the whole of the universe, extends as a metaphysical principle through all the technical ramifications of our speech, and into the tongue with which we articulate, the pen with which we write, the phonographs we build and play. Even these machines, as far as their purpose goes, are anthropomorphic, since their mechanical sounds are meant to be an image of and an example to the vibrations of the human soul.

That is why the mechanical, causal analysis and interpretation of the sounds of language or the signs of writing can never escape the ambiguousness of phonetic, acoustic, and visual phenomena, any more than an intuitive or interpretive symbology can. For by virtue of their medial nature, these structures are always both language and non-language, personal and impersonal, meaningful and accidental, spiritual and mechanical, metaphysical and physical, living and dead. The most useful analogy is to compare them to the vassals or representatives of a personal ruler, who can have a private life apart from their duty of communicating language. Between these two lives all sorts of cross purposes, interferences, conflicts and compromises are possible, but they can never be an indistinguishable unity. There is not a single physical organ that is intended solely for expressing language, or is wholly identified with language. Our ears take in a multitude of noises and sounds other than those of language, and our vocal chords can be used for coughing as well as for speaking. The fact that these means of communication, instruments, and materials have their private life apart from language may be important for understanding the difficulties, resistances, and the many barriers and hindrances towards linguistic expression that grow out of them. The real meaning of linguistic expression can no more be explained by this than the dispositions of an autocrat can be explained by reference to the faithfulness or treachery of his servants. For the ruler has either taken the reliable unreliability of his subjects into account, that is, fused their will with his own—in which case we have to go to him as the sole, autonomous ruler, for an understanding of his government—or his will is broken by the weakness or caprice of his instruments, and then there arises a mixture of sense and nonsense, which it would be a cumbersome task to illuminate from all sides.

H

In empirical language communities both cases occur, though not in the exemplary purity of a rigid harmony, nor in that hopeless confusion between the speaking spirit and its organs, as we have just constructed it. The alternative between the absolutely unitary community of language, which is something metaphysical, and the absolutely anarchical, which would not be a community at all, exists nowhere in reality, where we shall always find the need for a compromise between the two extreme cases. This does not mean that the one has as much right and claim to reality as the other; for the unconditional surrender of the instruments to their master, and the spiritual unity and coherence of the language community that are achieved by it, are an *ideal*, a goal towards which the language will of all the people concerned is tending. Decay is merely a *danger* towards which we are forced by an individualism not in accord with the goal, by the inertia and the casual accidents of matter, by unintentional sounds in our speech, and the like.

From the point of view of method, mechanically causal research, which clings to the dangerous inflexibility of the physical and examines the separate corporeal existence of the organs of speech, the individual sounds and signs, the 'independent' forms of words and sentences, is certain but harmless, and essentially aimless; whilst interpretive and idealizing work becomes the more dangerous, the more purposefully it seeks after a unitary meaning in language. On the long march that leads from the multiplicity and disconnectedness of language phenomena to the apprehension of the unity of the spirit of language, the latter needs the mechanistic and positivistic attitude as advance and rear-guard, but must itself form the main body.

Present-day philology has many well-trained scouts, excellent positivistic comparative philologists on its flanks, and heavily laden transport in its centre—but what of the main body?

(b) *National language as experienced language*

An empirical language community, such as that of the Greeks, the Latins, the French, the Germans, is thus held together by the will to work at a common language material as the special instrument of mutual understanding. Since all men possess in their ears and tongue the natural organs of speech, the particular linguistic equipment that distinguishes these peoples from one another has to be sought elsewhere than in the human senses. It is to be found in the Latin, Greek, French, German tongue, not in the tongue as such; that is, not in the instruments, but in the instrumentation of language. Human language is instrumentated differently by the Frenchman and the German. For instance, the former will emphasize something syntactically, where the latter uses a gesture or an intonation; where the one uses the future, the other uses the present; where one needs the subjunctive or a partitive article, the other is content with the indicative, or will dispense with an article.[1] The Frenchman not only uses a different vocabulary, different syntactic and phonetic systems, but even allocates their parts to speaker and listener, writer and reader in a different way to ours, expecting the speaker or writer to analyse his thought in a manner which we leave to the listener or reader, and so on. All these differences are historically conditioned; but in the final instance they are connected with the type of mind predominating in that particular language community, that is, with ' the national character '.

That there is a connection between national character, mental disposition, and language is as yet questioned by most philologists, or at any rate dismissed as scientifically unprovable. As a matter of fact it is not a question of natural or even of historical causal connections, but of a

---

[1] Examples of such differences in instrumentation have been historically explained and didactically well chosen by Ferdinand Sommer in his book, *Vergleichende Syntax der Schulsprachen*, Leipzig, 1921. (German, English, French, Greek, and Latin.)

phenomenological relation. The French language, that is, the French instrumentation of linguistic thought, is not in any way the consequence of their mental disposition or their national character.

Between these two factors there is no connection, no causal chain, no mediation, because there is no separation, no tension between them ; they are one and the same thing. The French do not speak French because they have a French attitude, type of mind, or character, but simply because they *speak*. Their language becomes French, not because of some outside influence, but because of themselves ; and through their speech, whatever and however it be, their national character is embodied and realized in what we call the French language. The same national character manifests itself in other and essentially different ways as well, such as the economic political, judicial, moral, scientific attitudes of the French. It can take on as many forms of reality or aspects as there are departments of life. Each of these facets shows a different picture of one and the same thing, and each represents in its *own* way the whole thing, the whole Frenchman— from one specific side, of course, by limiting the point of view to that which is due to the observer and not to the object, except in so far as observation has to mould itself to the object. The French language, therefore, is the *whole* of the French mind ; but only in the light of language, that is, in the light of human language *as a whole*. The Frenchman says nothing that falls out of the framework of his language, nothing that is not significant for his mental disposition and his method of instrumentation, or that has not got a French form. Even when he incorporates foreign words they become French to him ; and when he learns English or Chinese, he does it on a French basis. Through practice and habituation he may achieve citizenship in any number of languages ; but his spiritual home remains French, which he may deny or forget, but which he can no more lose than he can lose the experiences of his childhood.

Many languages can be studied and acquired, but only that one can be immediately experienced which was used at the time at which one worked one's way from the state of an infant to that of a member of a language community. The concept of a national language as an experienced language, as opposed to a foreign language which has been learnt or a technical language which has been agreed upon, rests on the natural fact that this ascent occurs only once in the lifetime of each person.

In spiritual, supernatural reality, however, every time we have something special to say and open our mouths to speak, we have to achieve anew the ascent from a state of temporary speechlessness to the community that is to understand us. Even the adult, linguistically competent man has never yet achieved a significant word that he did not have to experience and to create with a similar effort to that of the infant in the decisive moments of his first speech. Indeed, the linguistic experiences and achievements of a mature man are usually of more importance to the community than those of a child, though these are all the more valuable to the child itself and to its mental growth.

' Experienced language ', therefore, on the one hand has the subjective, limited, and natural affective value of childhood : on the other, a value of achievement, which is objective, spiritual, and has a general human significance. In the concept of a national language these two values and aspects rival each other. We love the English language as the experience of our childhood and the gift of our fathers and mothers ; but we also value it as a cultural possession or capital, in which the achievements of the English spirit are invested and bear interest. Our natural predilection is for the dialect of our home ; our objective judgment is more partial to the written language. We look on the former with the fondness we have for a series of successful youthful escapades ; of the latter we are proud, as of the achievements of manhood.

National feeling, then, is dependent on national language,

and oscillates between love and pride. The value we attach to our national language is our national pride. It is our whole, undiminished, undivided, complete national pride, but concentrated on language only.

(c) *Language and the sense of nationality*

If an ancient Greek or Roman, or a Christian of the Middle Ages were to descend to our present vale of tears and observe that we destroy each other not only for the sake of wealth and power, but even for the sake of which languages are to predominate in this or that frontier state, our cultural ancestors would be considerably astonished.

Wars and laws and prohibitions about language, such as we have experienced in Alsace Lorraine, Belgium, Schleswig Holstein, Poland, Czecho Slovakia, and the Tirol—to mention only the immediate neighbourhood of Germany—were unknown in the past. In Naples, for instance, the Greek language was allowed to exist during the whole of the Roman world empire. Greek inscriptions are found there as late as the seventh century A.D. When the emperors came on a visit, they willingly deferred to the Greek style of life of the country. The emperor Claudius had Greek plays performed there. We know similar things about the other coastal towns of southern Italy. In the senate at Syracuse Cicero, a Roman official, spoke Greek ; and if his compatriots took this amiss, it was because of a proper regard for Roman dignity, and not through language intolerance. The Romans never made war on the languages of the countries conquered by them. Evidently they were not as childish and as childishly enamoured of their mother tongue as the nations of to-day ; but they felt all the more certain, proud, and untroubled about their cultural superiority. Once the sway of Roman law had been ruthlessly established in Spain and Gaul, the sway of the Latin tongue was allowed to establish itself peacefully and gently.

Hence Iberian in Spain and Celtic in Gaul died a natural and painless death. As far as we know there was no struggle and no complaint.

To-day, I suppose, no language in Europe will allow itself to be extinguished as quietly. Provincialisms and dialects at most can still occasionally dissolve in this sickly and consumptive manner—and even then sorrowful philologists will stand at the sick bed. They die peacefully and without resisting, like those ancient languages of the Iberians and Gauls, largely because their extinction brings with it the entrance into a higher, culturally superior language community. But even this is not always the case. In Ireland the old language of the country, which has sunk to the status of a dialect, still defends itself as well as it can against English; in Switzerland Rhæto-Romanic resists German, and, in its fight against its nordic assailant, borrows weapons from its southern neighbour, and so is becoming italianized. Why does Rhæto-Romanic, in so far as it makes the effort at all, defend itself only feebly against Italian, which is also a menace to its existence? Because Rhæto-Romanic knows or feels that it is related to Italian. That is the important point: the feeling of racial similarity, the sense of nationality.

A language is defended more obstinately the more alive the feeling and the clearer the consciousness that it is a matter of preserving one's own tribal, racial, and national characteristics.

Did the ancient Iberians and Gauls, who so easily and quickly succumbed to Latin, have no sense of, or pride in, their own nationhood? Certainly; but it was a simple kind of pride, and though sturdy, robust, thorough-bred, and of a passionate instinctiveness, it was an unintelligent pride. Once it had been broken by armed force it lay supine, incapable of deeper resistance or spiritual support. But language is something spiritual. A disarmed Iberian or Gaul was at most capable of personal vanity, but not of national pride. And it was his vanity that led him to learn the language of his victors, preen himself in the Latin art of speech, and feel ashamed of his mother tongue as something childish. Soon the most self-complacent and word-eager masters of Latin rhetoric arose no longer in Italy, but in Spain and Gaul: Seneca, Lucan, Martial, C. Cornelius Gallus, Ausonius, etc.

Since at the present time we mostly see national languages around us, we have become accustomed to think of race and language as being inseparably interwoven. When a census of the races inhabiting Austria was taken, language was the sole criterion; and, in fact, there was no other reliable characteristic. Those who spoke German, that is, professed to German as their usual language, belonged to the German race; those who spoke Italian or Polish were classified as Italians or Poles in the racial, not the national sense. In doubtful cases a national language is like a church— one can belong to it, and also change it. That language binds us into nations is a natural *historical* fact, but not a *law* of nature.

Not every language community is at the same time a community of peoples. A language can bring men together in a hundred different kinds of communities. Latin to begin with was the language of the Latin race. In the course of time it became the language of the Roman state, then the language of the Catholic church, and finally the paper language of scholars. Similarly there are trade languages, like English overseas, criminal languages like *Rotwelsch* (thieves' language), unnatural, artificial world languages like Volapük and Esperanto, and finally as many special languages as there are special interests that bind men into castes and professions. In the Spain of the Middle Ages an artificial Galicio-Portuguese language existed beside Castilian up to the fifteenth century, but was reserved exclusively for the love lyrics of the court. King Alfonso el Sabio wrote his prose works in Castilian, his love lyrics in Galician, and a specially noble kind of love song in Provençal, according to the interests of the readers to whom he was addressing himself. How many languages fill the air of a modern city like Vienna, Constantinople, Cairo, New York, or Chicago ! In such places men are bred who become as characterless in language intercourse as money is in trade. The Viennese plutocrat who hankers after money and ' culture ', will speak Czech with his maid, Hungarian with his coachman, French with his mistress, Italian with his music master, English with his governess, and, if he has time and is in the mood, German with his family. This would almost lead one to believe that it is the nature of language not to have a being of its own, with its own purpose and value, but to have value merely as a medium of exchange.

In a certain sense it is true that the predominance or victory of one language over another is determined by the interplay of forces of the practical factors that arise from time to time. Research has given us numerous examples that show how language frontiers are determined and shifted by military, political, ecclesiastical, and economic needs, and how the weaker interest must always give way to the stronger. In Switzerland, a free and peaceful country, in which attempts are no longer made to advance this or that language by military or administrative compulsion, the movement of languages is determined solely by economic factors. The routes of communication decide the matter. The Gotthard railway carries German into the Tessin, the Simplon line takes Romance to the North, the federal lines and the line Basle-Biel, again, are routes along which German advances against French. In Wallis, however, French enters from the West by means of the railway, whilst German, which has to come from the East by means of the stage-coach, can make hardly any progress.[1]

But once a people has had its sense of nationality awakened and stands guard over its national language, all trade routes, needs and necessities, and all compulsory

---

[1] Morf, *Aus Dichtung und Sprache der Romanen*, II, 1911, p. 258 ff.

measures of police, state, or church must fail. That was seen in Poland. When their civic freedom and unity had been taken from the Poles and shattered, they sang Polish songs. They clung to their language as the last sign, security, and symbol of their national character and unity. The more rigidly they were prohibited from using their language in public, the prouder, deeper, more war-like, and religious became their love for it. Now it showed to the full its spiritual value to the community, and it was spoken and tended for its own sake alone, for the sake of the Polish sentiment, in defiance of all external oppression. Since every word could now lead to prison or banishment, every Polish sound became part of the national fame ; to the brother a greeting from the soul, a gesture of defiance to the enemy. Here we see in divine nakedness what so many politicians—and not only politicians, but even philologists—do not see : the ideal form urge, and the instinct for self-preservation that are immanent in every language, in so far as it is in any way the expression of spiritual characteristics and a spiritual community. To many of our German brothers who have fallen under an iniquitous foreign yoke, their language has become the last, dearest, and tenderest pledge of national memories and hopes. Since its more concrete supports in every-day intercourse have been shattered or undermined, it no longer has any other value than that of focussing common hopes and aspirations. It retreats into private, family and social life ; and if it is no longer tended there, it has to die. Hence the request of the German nation to German society at home and abroad, that its language must be tended and protected. It is a purely political demand, not a moral or religious one. Nevertheless it is addressed to the moral and religious forces of our conscience and our metaphysical will ; for if it is to be achieved here and now, it must appeal to the forces beyond us. A demand that is made on our social behaviour without political pressure, but with metaphysical power, is called a debt of honour. The sense of honour is the spiritual instinct of self-preservation ; for in the communities of men and of peoples the man who is without honour is dead.

So there is in fact a national, linguistic sense of honour, or at any rate there should and must be one, since and as long as there are national wars about languages and attempts at throttling them. If a man is robbed of his earthly home, he finds a spiritual home in his mother tongue, which is everywhere and always present to his senses, and can therefore at some time again become concrete and have an earthly home. This is true of national and political, as well as of religious and sectarian communities. For example, the more the Jews were persecuted, the more closely they clung to the language of their synagogue, protected the lyrical soul and the ancient writings of Hebrew as the home of their beliefs, and barricaded themselves behind them. In a similar way a poet filled with his emotions, shuts himself off from the demands and the turmoil of the world, in order to become an inner ear to these emotions, and their purest and clearest voice. It is true of every feeling, and therefore also of national feeling, that, when it has been excluded from every other refuge, language will become the spiritual fortress from which it will break out and conquer its environment when the times are propitious. The man who denies or gives up this last refuge and sally-port of his home sentiments, is without honour ; he is dead to the community in which he received his first experience of human language.

The sense of nationality and honour in a language has, however, not always or everywhere been as active and jealous as it is in Europe to-day. The Italians were the first, the Germans the last, and the French the most zealous in sounding the alarm, whilst the peoples along the frontiers of eastern Europe are even to-day still the most indifferent, as their semi-civilized state would lead us to expect.

Throughout the Middle Ages the national feeling of the occidental peoples was weighed down by the universalism that had been transmitted by Rome : the empire, the Catholic church, the Latin language. With their laws, their power, and their ideal demands these three included the whole of Christendom under their sway. They were experienced as something mighty, wide, and deep ; something more valuable than the claims of any one people. Among the Christian nations none was as deeply imbued with this universalism as the German. For since the time of Charlemagne Germany had sheltered the imperial throne and had therefore been the chosen guardian of the world empire and of its international and conciliatory spirit. The German of the Middle Ages felt to a higher degree than anyone else that he was responsible for the brotherhood and unity of the Christian peoples ; and because of this exalted care he was unable to retain any very strong feeling for his own particular nationhood. Even in such a national poet as Walter von der Vogelweide the idea of the Roman empire was more vital than German pride. We still retain from those days of the German-Roman empire a streak of universalism and supernationalism in our political and cultural thought. In certain ideas, that, in spite of the political turmoil of the moment, are again being expressed at the present time, we can recognize the continuation of this heritage. No nation has been less concerned with rounding off the boundaries of its nationality than the German. No language is more disrupted, neglected, and scattered on the philological atlas than German. In Switzerland, in Austria, in northern Italy, in Hungary, and deep into Russia beyond the Volga—not to speak of America—there are brothers of our race and tongue who no longer belong to us politically. It is impossible to realize how much of our national unity and strength we have used and wasted for the ideal of a world empire. And yet it may not have been waste. At any rate *we* are not the discoverers of the modern sense of nationality.

The Italians were. Ever since the Roman emperor was a German, since the time of Charlemagne, there has been hardly one Italian heart that has beaten for the idea of a universal Christian empire. There is hardly a trace in Italy of legend or poetry about the empire of the Middle Ages.[1] Dante, with his universality, his *Divina Commedia*, and his Latin tract about the universal monarchy, was a unique, magnificent exception. He had to pay for his sentiments with banishment. Nevertheless the memory of ancient Rome and its greatness was nowhere more strong than in Italy. But it was republican Rome, not the Rome of the empire, to which the Italians of the Middle Ages with their city republics felt drawn. It was *their* Rome, not the world's. *Roma nostra.* By opposing the concept of republican Rome to that of imperial Rome and exalting it, they transcended the Middle Ages politically, and brought about the Renaissance. And in the same way the Italian Humanists praised the pagan Latin of Cicero, Virgil, and Horace as against that of the church—the Latin of Italy against that of the world. After tending the Latin of their home, the Italian Humanists proceeded to give as much consciously artistic attention and philological care to its daughter, Italian. The tending and cleansing of the Latin language was immediately responsible for the birth of an Italian language. The same men stood for both purisms : Petrarch, Alberti, Politian, Bembo, etc. In short, the consciousness of national character as a historic creation and heritage, in politics as well as in language, first awakened in Italy. It was essentially a particularistic defence and reaction against the universalist ideas of the Middle Ages ; a *sacro egoismo.* To-day this national egoism still looks with suspicion or indifference on the universalism of the Curia.

When the movement of Humanism and the Renaissance

[1] The special position of Italy in the Middle Ages is discussed at greater length in *Medieval Culture. An introduction to Dante and his times*, vol. II, by Karl Vossler, Constable, 1931.

spread from Italy to France at the end of the fifteenth century, a strong, practically absolute monarchy had been established there. The French were so proud of their ruler, that their feeling of nationality was almost entirely subordinated to their love of the dynasty. The man who in those times boasted of being a Frenchman, hardly thought of the French language, and still less of the great past and the mediæval civilization of his country, but above all of the might and magnificence of his king in Paris. It was the example of Italy that first stirred the French consciously to study the history of their country, and systematically to enrich, ennoble, and purify their language as a national heritage. But in Italy the sense of nationality found no support in the political situation ; and up to the *risorgimento* in the nineteenth century it remained an artistic love of the nation, and kept a thoughtful, sentimental, and almost lustful arcadian air. In France, however, which was already strong and united, it immediately became all the more realistic, practical, and aggressive. Even the intellectual activity in the study of national history, literature, and language became a desire for conquest, and was prosecuted in the spirit of competition with antiquity and with the Italians. From the days of the Renaissance to the present, ennobling the language, defining the usage of spoken and written language, classifying its vocabulary, and giving uniformity to French phonetic and written forms, have been regarded not only as a national, but even as a state and political concern. It was in this sense that the kings promulgated their language laws and gave commissions to philologists and artists, that Richelieu founded the *Académie Française*, and the greatest masters of language placed their genius at the service of the *Roi Soleil*. In France the state for the first time undertook the organization of a unified national language. The revolution continued what the monarchy had begun. In the year 1790 the national assembly conceived the plan of eradicating all dialects, provincialisms, patois and jargons in the country for the sake of unity, and published a manifesto to arouse in all districts " *une sainte émulation pour bannir les jargons, derniers lambeaux de la féodalité et monuments de l'esclavage* ". In this forcible, proud, sophisticated manner the French learned to love and cultivate their language. That is why there is no country in which language discipline is so rigid and general as in theirs, no country that worked so early, so emphatically and purposefully for the propagation of its language in other countries. As early as the year 1509 the Humanist, Claude de Seyssel, drew the attention of king Louis XII to the importance of permeating foreign countries with the French language. He wanted nothing less than to gallicize Italy. And to-day the inhabitants of Alsace, the Palatinate, and the Rhineland can tell many an indignant tale of how French imperialistic language zeal operates in fundamentally German territory.

Germany has learnt a very great deal from the French and the Italians with respect to the cultivation of language as a national possession. The numerous societies of the seventeenth century that, half playfully, half didactically fought against the foreign affectations and the coarseness of the German language, were imitations of the French and Italian language academies. But there never could be a sense of national unity, because, to begin with, the country was split into Protestants and Catholics. Compared to the community of belief and sentiment, that of language seemed merely external. So a man could be German to the marrow, like Leibniz or Frederick the Great, and yet use a foreign language in the most important questions of heart and mind. Since the sentiments and feelings of the nation were divided against themselves, to think German and to speak German had become two separate things. Through painfully overcoming this contradiction, the Germans have arrived at their particular conception of the relation between nation and language. We can express this epigrammatically by saying that the Romance nations are men of speech, the Germans men of things.[1] The former are always inclined to overestimate language. They believe that they can bring about events through the power of language, which can in reality be brought about only by deeds. Therefore they cultivate their language, measure the value of a culture by the power and polish of its language, seek and find the highest education in the education of language. To them it is given to use words like *la liberté, la gloire, la victoire, la justice* so effectively, and to express them with such a wealth of sound and meaning, that merely by speaking their names, they proclaim to the whole world and to themselves that they are the possessors of these things. The German, however, will allow only deeds, thoughts, and feelings to have validity; and when he meets these riches of fact in the dandified clothing of words, he easily becomes suspicious. He believes that if the will is strong, the thought pure and deep, the feeling true, language will only spoil everything. He will modestly hide the finest emotion, or, what is worse, will clothe it in a confusion of complicated rhetoric until it is unintelligible or unpalatable to others, so that he may find it again all the more deeply within himself.

The great war showed to the fullest extent that both parties underestimate one another, and both had unpleasant surprises enough. Who in Germany would have thought that through the mere word, through their speeches, their press, the sweeping power of a phrase, their manifestos, the French could have made so many enemies for Germany and done her so much harm; but that *her* speeches, *her* press, *her* manifestos, however honest in intention, could have raised no echo, and could have been so hopelessly misheard by the rest of the world? The French, the Italians, and the Slavs (for they, too, are a language race) for their part were not a little astonished by the German blows, and the deeds,

[1] In analogy with the concepts " words " and " objects ", Hugo Schuchardt distinguishes *Wortmenschen* and *Sachmenschen*.

which, prepared long ahead and in silence, were suddenly launched upon the world.

We are not magicians of language, and an educated language appears to us as a formalism of doubtful value. If our own desire leads us to cultivate our language, it must be aroused by an objective, deep, pressing, universal need, as in Luther, who perfected modern German and almost created it out of the chaos of provincial dialects, because his aim was to bring the word of God, the Bible, closer to us. Or, to set a small example beside this great one : those officials and clerks of imperial times, who, at the opening of the new era, were concerned with creating a unitary German, did so merely to bring about order and peace in the land, and not to build up something beautiful that should be a glorious monument to the nation. So the written German language has grown up, more useful than beautiful, and often disfigured by foreign and dialect intrusions. It has become deep and wide, and remarkably patient, but not very attractive. Our deepest thinkers, Kant and Hegel, suffered rather than mastered it ; and Goethe, its greatest creator and most successful lover, impatiently rejected it.

> Vieles hab' ich versucht, gezeichnet, in Kupfer gestochen,
> Oel gemalt, in Ton hab' ich auch manches gedruckt,
> Unbeständig jedoch, und nichts gelernt noch geleistet.
> Nur ein einzig Talent bracht ich der Meisterschaft nah :
> Deutsch zu schreiben, und so verderb' ich unglücklicher Dichter
> In dem schlechtesten Stoff leider nun Leben und Kunst.

What Romance or Slav poet would have said anything like that even in anger or in jest ? Listen to the words of the banished Turgenieff :

In days of doubt, in days of gloom and anxiety about the fate of my motherland, thou alone art my support and my stay, oh great, mighty, true and free Russian tongue ! But for thee, should I not have to despair in the sight of all that is happening at home ? But it is unthinkable that such a language has not also been given to a great people.[1]

[1] *Poems in Prose*, conclusion.

I

Even mediæval Dante, firmly believing as he did in the necessity and glory of a world state, and convinced that Latin was the most perfect and lasting of all the languages of humanity, called everyone who dared to question his passionate love of his Italian mother tongue a fool and a blasphemer :

Se manifestamente per le finestre d'una casa uscisse fiamma di fuoco, e alcuno domandasse se là entro fosse il fuoco, e un altro rispondesse a lui di sì, non saprei ben giudicare qual di costoro fosse da schernire di più. E non altrimenti sarebbe fatta la domanda e la risposta di colui e di me, che mi domandasse se amore alla mia loquela propria è in me e io gli rispondessi di sì appresso le sue proposte ragioni.[1]

Dante, the first world citizen, is also the author of the first attempt at a scientific and æsthetic appreciation of the Italian language : *De vulgari eloquentia.*

And indeed the man who could attain to such a far-sighted, wide, and philosophical conception of the nature of a national language, had to be a world citizen. None of the philologists of the Renaissance or the period of French enlightenment ever attained again to the depth of Dante's essay. It was not until the days of romanticism, when the great reaction against French formalism and intellectualism began, that *German* thinkers and scholars founded a truly philosophical conception and critical investigation of language. Here the fruits of our universalism ripened and proved their value. The whole of modern philology is essentially and almost exclusively a German creation : Herder, Wilhelm von Humboldt, the Schlegel brothers, the Grimm brothers, Bopp, Schleicher, Diez, and many others have, through their philosophic, historical, and grammatical researches interpreted and established the attitude of the German mind to the language of its own people and to other languages. They have discovered the linguistic relation of the Indo-European races, and have accustomed us to embracing the languages of all the tribes and nations of

[1] *Convivio*, I, 12.

the world with equal love as a great spiritual family, in which every member has his rightful and meaningful separate existence. They have taught us that in reality there is only *one* language, and that national languages are merely mutations, different instrumentations of this unity. They have transcended dogmatic formalism, the academic didacticism of the Romance mind, and intolerance in the judgment of languages. A purer, more intelligent, more tolerant and therefore deeper, less proud, and more childlike love of their own language was the finest reward of these endeavours. Only now does it become clear how each race fashions its own *Weltanschauung*, or rather the potentialities of a *Weltanschauung* ; how by their language and through their language nations unfold their spiritual characteristics into living relationships and interactions ; and how there rests in the lap of each language a kind of predestination, a gentle urge to this or that way of thinking.

It is natural that only very few minds were capable of such a universal and critical attitude. For the majority of educated and half-educated people the childhood of races and their linguistic interrelatedness, which German scholarship had pointed out, became merely a renewed stimulus to nationalistic jealousies. In particular those nations, the Slavs above all, which as yet could boast of no cultural achievements, began to be conscious of their value. Encouraged by the example of the brothers Grimm, Czech, Serbian, Polish, and Russian scholars began to investigate the history, the language, the folk-songs, and the fairy-tales of their nations. The original nature of each, and at the same time the unity of all the Slav peoples were recognized, cultivated, and preached. From reverencing the memory of the *national* past, they proceeded to proud hopes and political demands for the future. Calm thoughts, peaceful children of German philology, grew up, armed themselves, and raised the battle cry of Pan-Slavism. Naturally enough, the nationalism of the older civilized peoples who were already in the process of yielding quietly to an enlightened, supra-national consciousness of their humanity, again caught a spark from this roaring, youthful fire ; and only now did the passionate language wars of yesterday and to-day blaze up in the frontier countries.

They will have to be fought to a finish ; for the idea of tolerance has never yet entered the minds of the masses along peaceful channels. How much blood and misery were necessary before religious toleration became a habit with us ? And who can give a pledge that it is secure for ever ?

Tolerance of national languages is a still later, tenderer flower of human culture. Once that insight has been gained, therefore, intolerance on this point is an even greater idiocy. If I grudge my neighbour his religious beliefs, and hammer my own into his skull, I shall at any rate be able to excuse myself on the ground that I believe my own to be the only ones that lead to salvation, that his lead to damnation, and that I want to save his soul. But if I throttle my neighbour's mother tongue in order to impose my own on him, what excuse can I have except that of conceit, which is made no better by the fact that it is a national conceit ? For my neighbour's language is his inner eye, his form of thought, with all its poten-tialities of expression, his spiritual childhood and future. To everyone who has understood this, all repressive measures directed against a language must seem like crimes against the budding life of their spirit.

Compared to the devastating consequences of mental compulsion, the harm done by a change of language, or by bi- or multi-lingualism, is transient and superficial. Many make a virtue of necessity, and even hold it as gain to grow up bi-lingual and tri-lingual. The differences between experienced and learnt, between national and foreign language are glossed over by them—and, from a higher point of view, the transition is indeed a gradual one.

Whoever desires to experience only his own language

and refuses to know others, be he an individual or a nation, will find that his own, too, sinks to the level of a barbaric stammering.

There are no rigid language frontiers ; and where they are artificially erected, they bring more harm than protection.

To-day, when the egoistic love of the Germanic and Slavic peoples for their natural language has been added to the French and Italian national pride in the culture of language, European nationalism has probably reached its highest point, if it has not already passed it. At any rate it has exhausted its fundamental possibilities. Politicians are now faced by the question whether it is any longer profitable to insult the language sensibilities of the present-day races of Europe, which have become conscious to such an extent of their characteristics, their origins, their achievements, and their potentialities, that is, their languages. Since every race clings desperately to its mother tongue, language frontiers have become fluid to such an extent, that if political frontiers, which are much more brittle and can be changed only in jerks, are not to be continually torn asunder, they will have to adapt themselves as far as possible to language frontiers and imitate their supple calm.[1]

No other nation is like the German in having so many inner and outer incentives to labour, suffer, and fight with its whole strength for this ideal. The concept of tolerance for national languages is an achievement of German scholarship, born of love and pride of one's own and understanding of the other's strange and yet related spirit. If *we* do not defend this ideal and strive for its practical realization, if we allow ourselves to become Romance in the West and South, Danish in the North, and Slav in the East, it is lost. No other nation will honour this ideal from inner necessity.

[1] Cf. L. M. Hartmann, *Die nationale Grenze vom soziologischen Standpunkt* (Commemorative Volume for Max Weber), I, p. 181 ff., Munich and Leipzig, 1923.

(d) *National languages as styles*

The first effect of hearing a foreign language spoken is to give us a shock or make us laugh. " How can anyone use his organs of speech differently to *me* or to *us* ? " think primitive people and children. They mock the foreigner and quickly pick out some characteristic of his speech, usually something quite external, which they ape and exaggerate.

These outstanding characteristics that, like a waving plume, challenge or attract us from afar, I call the ornamentation of a language. It has all sorts of aspects, essentials as well as unessentials, tone of voice, level, accentuation, melody, rhythm, or some group of sounds whose recurrence strikes the ear. For everything we do not understand about a language repels us as a caricature, or, if we take up a more friendly attitude, attracts us as an ornament. In short, what we do not understand we think either ugly or beautiful.

Grammatical research therefore rejects all æsthetic judgments about individual languages as the talk of laymen. Questions as to whether Italian is more ' beautiful ' than French or English are not regarded as objective problems. It is also suspicious—and rightly so—of any explanation of language phenomena by means of a desire for beauty, or by euphonic, eurhythmic, or similar criteria. Since it attempts to understand the structure of languages as a causal system, or even as a mechanism of the means of expression, it cannot allow the slightest freedom to the caprice of tastes. The ornamentation of language is regarded as an illusion. And, indeed, the more one begins to understand and speak a foreign language, the more this illusory ugliness or beauty fades. The charm dies, and the plumes vanish, because the student now wears them himself, and can no longer see them. A language that becomes my second nature, and reflects my own thoughts and feelings, no longer looks strange to me—

unless I stand before a mirror and by reflexion make it seem strange once more.

Then I shall see the plumes again, but with understanding and critical eyes, as something that is of me and yet outside me. I can wear them as I please, straight or at an angle. I try their effect, comb them and brush them. What scientific grammar rejected has come back after all, and is consciously cultivated by academic grammarians, schools of rhetoric, artists of diction, and purists.

But what is this ornamental aspect of a language, this double nature, that, objectively apparent to the stranger, invisible to the native, is doubted and denied by the language expert and affirmed and tended by the language lover ? It is the particular aspect of language in general, its characteristic, individual, national, provincial, idiomatic nature, as opposed to its universal and personal nature. In its striving for unity and objectivity language is universal and personal, in its urge towards multiplicity and ornamentation it is individual. The so-called technical languages and the universal languages have a tendency towards the purposive, conventional, and artificial ; they flee from the æsthetic and neglect ornament. They are indifferent to what they look like, as long as they are intelligible. They prefer having validity and power to giving pleasure. They have special interests. Individual and national languages, on the other hand, are proud of their looks and seek after style and appearance. They consciously and unconsciously cultivate ornamentation, which is despised by the former. Everyone knows how lacking in taste, how un-English is the technical jargon of business men, doctors, judges and engineers, and how dull and dry are Esperanto and all its rivals.

In the sphere of language, therefore, what is specifically national is part of the concept of the ornamental. German or Italian as specific national, individual instrumentations of language thinking are identical with German or Italian language ornamentation.

In our analysis of the concept of individuality [1] we denied that individuals, pure individualities such as nations with their sense of nationality would like to be, can be the exclusive vehicles of language. To have a part in language, we said, one must be above all a person, that is, be capable of appreciating the different rôles of hearing, understanding, and answering. In order to save the concept of a national language and with it that of language ornamentation we do not need to abandon our previous thesis. But we shall have to limit and connect, distinguish and unite the concepts of individuality and personality, of ornamental and objective language. In order to ascend from being individuals to being persons, we have to transcend the rigidity of stone and the dumbness of animals and enter into an objective and higher unity than ourselves. So, on the other hand, a language that is merely individual, merely ornamental and national, and remains fixed in its particular provincialism, will degenerate into a mere dialect. Above all, in the iron grip with which the language would try to retain its national aspect, the language itself would crumble.

There is no national language that could be entirely national and nothing but ornamental. In some way or another it must always be concerned with some factual or technical aspects. The German language does not merely represent German characteristics, it also serves German business, and that has never been exclusively German. In the same way ornamentation that has no other purpose than to be ornamental will become too inflexible, and will crumble from the building it is meant to embellish.[2] In language as in architecture, all meaningful ornamentation has a utilitarian function. The more closely ornament and structure are interwoven, the more style a language will have. Hence the demand that in

---

[1] Cf. p. 9 ff

[2] The distinction between rigid and plastic ornamentation is discussed in greater detail in K. Vossler, *Gesammelte Aufsätze zur Sprachphilosophie*, Munich, 1923, pp. 249 ff.

a perfect national language the structure should be regarded as the ornamentation and vice versa. The more exactly this equation holds, the more compact the style of the national language will be. In other words, if we wish to do justice to the special character of national languages, they have to be judged rather as styles than as languages. Nations are individuals, and as such they can express themselves through language and style though they cannot speak. It is an illusion to think that the language of some particular nation is spoken by the nation as such. The speakers are the many persons that constitute it. The nation itself is dumb, and is therefore constantly subject to suspicion and misunderstanding by other nations. If it wants to express itself and say something to another nation, both have to constitute themselves as *persons*, and have to choose their representatives and the language in which they want to converse.

In the life process of the language of humanity, the national languages represent the specifically stylistic aspect, that phase of the activity of speech in which the mind creates the field or the tracks within or along which speaking takes place. The rules of usage then no longer appear as compulsion, but as chosen bonds and as a freedom that has been achieved, not even as something complete, but as directions and tendencies in the language will. If we wish to examine the national characteristics, that is, the style of a language, we must not, like the grammarians, inquire what *can be* allowed and what can be possible in it, but what *is* aimed at and willed through it and what its possibilities *are*. In a style it is the actual free interplay of these forces that is important ; not what it can mean, but what it actually does mean. In every national language there is an æsthetic will, a master builder. We do not attribute this force to a language or invent it ; it is the linguistic, individual unity of the language itself. The Romantics called it the spirit or the genius of a people ; the Positivists laughed at this, because in a science they did not want to believe in spirits. We must not fall into the error of personifying this genius ; for if the nation is great, thousands and millions of persons who are its representatives are in its service. The genius or language spirit of a nation is no mythological being ; it is a force, a talent, a temperament. Individual nations, like individual persons, also have their specific power, characteristic temperament and peculiar abilities by which they as units distinguish themselves from other individual nations. They therefore reject what they feel to be foreign and unpalatable, and absorb only what they regard as pleasant and useful. Thanks to this natural spiritual instinct, a nation maintains its individual unity and has its limits within itself. It *wants* to limit itself ; and whenever it becomes mindful of its individuality, its nature, its genius, it renounces that imperialism with which the state, but not the nation, is afflicted. For why should the genius of a nation set out to conquer new realms, when it is being continually supplied with new ideas, when all kinds of mental treasures present themselves in such numbers that it has to guard itself against them rather than pursue them ? Foreign words offer themselves and force themselves into the language ; it would be showing a lack of taste to run after them. It is not the nature of genius to make conquests, but to be true and genuine, to remain true to itself. When the Arabs had conquered Spain, the whole peninsula might have been dominated by their language, had Arabic not been so truly the language of the conquerors and so foreign to the vanquished. If German had not been so intrinsically German, and so determined to remain true to itself, it might have become the European world language in the times of the emperors of the Middle Ages. There was no lack of external opportunities. But the style of every national language has in itself a measure, which it cannot exceed unpunished ; a limit, beyond which self-alienation begins, where the will to power falsifies and destroys the style, and the genius gives way to a demon. A national genius is therefore not suitable for world empire without considerable qualifications. Compare, for example, the Greeks to the Romans. The true life of a national language is centripetal and inward, not centrifugal. Conflicts and wars between national languages arise only when they want to become languages of a state, or the world, or specialized technical and utilitarian languages.

Language wars do not arise through malice or stupidity ; nations are driven to them by that same national will to style that should warn them against war. They are in the same position as the artist, who would have to remain dumb if he did not dare to express his genius and confess his inmost thoughts. Languages that are filled with the lust of conquest have their counterpart and image in those bombastic and loud poets, who can express their feelings only with a forced voice.

But are we not indulging in unscientific similes and metaphors by comparing a nation, or, what is worse, a national language, to a living individual, an artist, and by imagining that a nation is possessed by a genius who can voluntarily mould its language style as a poet shapes his work ? Who is the artist here ? The whole nation ? We cannot seek the *tertium comparationis* in the measurable quantities ' artist ' and ' work ' ; but the mental process, the purposive act of creation by which the work of art emerges from the artist—or, what is in essence the same, by which the artist enters into his work—is not only comparable to the ' life ' of a national language, but is essentially identical with it. Both create equally, consciously and unconsciously, emotionally and objectively, concretely and abstractly ; both take delight in the senses. But, because he is shortlived, the artist tries to round off his work and give it his personal stamp, so that we see one or several ' works ', whilst the nation elaborates its theme or chisels its memorial through many centuries, and is in no hurry to complete it. But this difference is external ; for in reality the national language is complete at all times, ready for its daily tasks, as punctual and prompt as the work of a composer who has been commissioned to write the music for a festival. It is more true to say that the work of an individual is in some respects hurried and improvised, however pure and mature it may be. It is essential to the concept of style that every part, however small, be permeated by the same æsthetic will that animates the whole. The individual form is therefore fundamentally contemporaneous with the total system of a national language.

Another, purely external and apparent distinction between the creativeness of a national language and individual literary achievement is that the latter has a definite content, whilst the former has every possible content. In every work of art we can find a motif or a theme ; in language we can not. A poem is a text, a national language is a style. But is it not the essence of a poetic text that it should have style, indeed, that it should be the embodied style of the poet himself ? And should not the subject-matter of poetic style always treat only of that with which the poet is inwardly concerned, which he really has experienced and by which he is possessed ? Is not the man who sings of things that do not touch his own emotions a bad poet ? Can and may the true poet ever express and represent anything but *his* way of seeing the world, feeling life, experiencing reality ? As the *Divina Commedia* is the whole universe expressed in ' Dantean ', so the Italian national language is the whole universe expressed in Italian, the German in German, Faust in ' Goethian ', Hamlet in ' Shakespearian '. " Is ", means there is a necessity and a will.

In so far as a language is or tries to be something, it points in that direction. Poetry and national language are brought together by the capacity for indication, not by the capacity for action. In their subject-matter, in what they describe, in what they embrace, poetry and language differ widely. Each has its own exclusive concerns, and each treats immediately of something else. Only the mediate tendencies of their meanings are universal, as universal as they are individual.

Why should we waste any more words to prove the philosophic identity of language and poetry, when the innumerable phrases, similes, metaphors, proverbs, popular rhymes, songs and epics, the whole cornucopia out of which a language pours its poetic seeds and fruits into everyone's garden, are plain enough to our ears ? In the poesy of the people language itself becomes poetry.

On the other hand, if we seriously begin to search for the originator of this or that folk-song, proverb, or parable, we shall, if we find him at all, find only a single individual, perhaps two or three, or at most a small group of creative individuals ; a whole people, a complete language community, can never be the author. The many have always been the public, the few, author. A poem is not popular and national because its author disappears in the shadow of anonymity, but because he is more deeply immersed in the language of his people than the artificial poet, because he writes in the dialect, or at any rate in the most popular and most loved of the language styles of his country.

But if he consciously cultivates the style of his home, like the Humanist Leonardo Giustiniani in his Venetian ballads or Politian in his Tuscan Rispetti or the German Romantics in their songs, the poems that are created in this way are no longer true folk-poetry, but popular art grafted on to literary models. It is essential for folk-poetry that it should remain unliterary.

We must admit that the last statement contains a certain contradiction ; for all poetry, even the most naïve and modest, is somehow art, which tries to escape from the coarseness and sensuality of the moment and the transitoriness of animal passion to the more permanent, organized forms that are made possible by the rules of social games, the rhythm of dances, the order of common work, the pious customs of religion, the pictures and symbols of writing, and finally, by books and ' literature '. But while language seeks these supports and this regular order because of its transience and mutability, it finds

something permanent in itself, in its own fragileness—
the natural preservatives of language metre, rhythm,
consonance, rhyme, alliteration, acoustic symmetry, syntactic organization, and the like. These have arisen not
only through a psycho-physical need, a desire and the
joy that comes from satisfying it ; they have been equally
invented and cultivated to serve the purpose of maintaining, consolidating, and immortalizing linguistic forms
and works of art. For all mental pleasure " seeks after
immortality ", and thereby distinguishes itself from the
sensual pleasure of the moment, which at most desires to
be repeated. But eternity is not made by the repetition
of moments, and permanence cannot be achieved in this
way, nor anything that has the rhythm of life. That has
been particularly clearly proved by Bergson.

In every language a principle of symmetry is active,
by which it can oppose the interference and destruction
threatened by the world of the senses, and don a formal
armour under whose elastic pressure the most delicate
phonetic forms are kept so well and so pure, that oral
tradition can often hand them on unharmed to the most
distant generations. The greater part of our so-called
archaic language heritage is handed down from our
ancestors in the symmetrical packing of proverbs, parables,
and folk-songs. In many respects this popular form of
poetic tradition is more reliable than that of inscriptions
on stone or brass, since on the whole it is best capable
of maintaining over long periods the most transient
aspects of a language, the quality of its sounds.

Popular poetry, therefore, is mnemonic poetry. I know
of no other definition of this concept apart from the
variable and contradictory ones given by the Romantics.
It is thus an art which, out of a language sense acquired
chiefly orally, rises only to such a height and width and
complexity of its forms as can be mastered by memory,
without having to seek other aids than those contained
in the form order of the work itself. It is a quantitative
concept, which nevertheless is to a certain extent also

qualitative, in so far as in the realm of art the format as a rule also determines the character, or should determine it. Popular poetry is modest poetry in a handy format, in small units that are taken from immediate language intercourse and can easily be entrusted to it again for preservation. It grows and diminishes, rises and falls, according to the creative and retentive power of the every-day language of a people, generally in inverse proportion to the written language. Hence the reciprocal transitions between popular and literary poetry are as fluid, vital, and frequent as are transitions between the colloquial and the written language.

Fundamentally, a folk-poem stands closer to the language of its people than a literary one, not so much because the personality of the author, which interposes itself between them, is stronger in the one than in the other—for there are weak and mighty singers on both sides—but in the last resort because, in writing, the literary poem erects an aid to memory between the eye and the ear. There is something strange and inflexible in writing, which speech can overcome only by exceptional efforts. That self-estrangement, which, as we saw, is suffered by every linguistic thought and every meaning as soon as they are enunciated in speech, becomes enlarged through writing by a second sense dimension. A new obstacle is interposed ; and if the language sense wants to remove this obstacle, it has to practise and train itself continually in softening its rigidity. Though the transition from straw and mud to stone and steel in architecture brings with it many new difficulties, it also brings new forms and an increase of power. In a similar way the introduction of writing implies new difficulties and at the same time an increase of power in the language development of a people.

Language is one of the most important, though not the only means of artistically ennobling and co-ordinating linguistic intercourse and its creative powers. Apart from pictures and letters, many other things can serve as a conventional linguistic bridge, mnemonic aid, and material for artistic form ; for instance, the forms and ceremonies of religion, the invocation of spirits—as long as they are sufficiently closely bound to definite formulæ, words, verses, or other linguistic forms. Thus the Druids in Gaul possessed an unwritten sacred poetry and ' literature ' that was nevertheless far above the popular level of everyday speech. The forms of law and of regal courts, if they are strict and hieratic enough, suffice, even without the help of writing, to raise a court language and a courtly art of language above the common language and popular art. There were many analphabetes even among those Minnesingers of the Middle Ages who paid the strictest attention to style. In addition, dancing and music can obviously support the formative will of language so successfully, that it can work its way up from the crudest country dance to the most delicate ballad, and, in a many terraced ascent, transcend the shifting bounds of popular art.

We must not imagine that on one side of this boundary there is nothing that is popular, and on the other nothing that is artistic. There is, for instance, no such thing as a purely Vulgar Latin text, just as there is no purely literary Latin text. The whole of Greek classical poetry is coloured by dialect intrusions, and it is almost possible to maintain that every type of poetry in ancient Greece, up to the final pinnacles of literary perfection, drags behind it the dialect of the particular region in which it arose or was originally cultivated. Not the pure dialect as a whole, but certain outstanding characteristics of it, were so closely linked with those literary types that they were felt to be essential to the character of their style.[1] As long as the Old French *Chansons de geste* were believed to be folk-songs of the purest water, attempts were made to discover the dialects and therefore the regions in which they had originated. But in this way one almost never arrived at the centre of a dialect, but

[1] This relation has been investigated with particular care by A. Meillet, in his *Aperçu d'une histoire de la langue grecque*, Paris, 1913.

generally at its frontiers and transitional regions to other dialects, so that one might sit astride two or even three dialect fences, without knowing on which side to descend. There was no end to the leaping of geographical language fences, since everyone was of the opinion that dialect and folk-poetry rested in themselves and were at one, like the egg and its shell.[1] But we are gradually returning to the view already expressed by Dante in *de vulgari eloquentia*, that there is an upward literary urge in the dialects of a national language, as there is in their poets and writers, so that, starting from the most distant homes, they aim at and intuitively perceive a norm until they meet in the realization of a national language style. When Antonio Ive was collecting folk-songs in Velletri, he noticed that they were comparatively free from dialect and he remarked that even the common people, particularly when it wanted to express thoughts, feelings, and emotions of a higher order, tried to get as far away from ordinary usage as it possibly could.[2] Why should the common man not also have his precious vein ? In the old lyrics of Provence the beginnings of a cultivated style, the *trobar clus*, go back, significantly enough, to the Trobadors, who were not members of the knighthood and who attempted to replace their lack of a noble birthright by nobility in the art of language.[3]

Every poet, however close he stands to the common people, and every language, however split up into dialects it may be, strives after a norm. And, indeed, in those very conditions of association and dissociation, the common unity of the formative will is clearer on both sides than

---

[1] Cf. Gertrud Wacker, " Über das Verhältnis von Dialekt und Schriftsprache im Altfranzösischen ", *Berlin Dissertation*, 1916 ; and my review in the Literaturblatt für german. und roman. Philologie, 1917, especially p. 109 ff. ; also " Französische Philologie ", *Wissenschaftl. Forschungsberichte*, I, Gotha, 1919, p. 22 f.

[2] A. Ive, *Canti popolari Velletrani*, Rome, 1907, p. XXX.

[3] K. Vossler, " Der Trobador Marcabru und die Anfänge des gekünstelten Stiles ", *Sitzungsber. d. bayrischen Akad. d. Wissensch.*, 1913.

K

where that unity is actually achieved to perfection. For a national language comes to perfection in the strict and universal validity of its grammatical usage ; a poem in the personal characteristics of its creator. In a language we see the goal that has been attained as a collective system, in a poem as an individual personality. Nevertheless both are the result of one and the same effort, of one and the same concern.

At the level of folk-poetry, the individual artist is caught up to such an extent in the feelings and the tastes of his environment, that his formative will appears to aim at something generic. He seeks success and acclamation only within the small and narrow circle of his immediate and momentary environment. The song that is appreciated here and now, establishes itself ; the other, that finds no immediate echo, falls to the ground and is forgotten. At first, the whole of literary criticism consists of this rapid, fortuitous, spontaneous selection. It is an echo or refrain, somewhat similar to the answers, affirmations, and denials that we receive in the course of conversation. That is why the parts played by poet, public, and critic are sometimes as quickly and readily interchangeable as hearing, speaking and answering in conversation. The antiphonies in the Italian Ritornello or Rispetto, or in the Bavarian *Schnaderhüpfel*, may serve as concrete instances of this relation. The small linguistic object flies from hand to hand like a ball or an ungainly dumpling, and, in the to-and-fro of throwing and catching, it is formed, kneaded and pressed into a more or less finished artistic form or poetic genus by the hands that take part in the game. The process is so quick and lively that it generally escapes philosophic observation. Under favourable conditions, however, it may occur in the light of history and be preserved in writing, as in the following example.

When the tactless upstart, Le Franc de Pompignan, was admitted to the *Académie française*, where he made a boastful inaugural speech, Voltaire had a pamphlet against him distributed in Paris, called " *Les Quand*, notes utiles sur un discours prononcé devant l'Académie française ". Every sentence of this ironical advice began with *quand*. " When one is received into a learned society, one should hide the bumptious conceit peculiar to hot heads and mediocre intelligences by spreading the veil of modesty over one's speech," etc. A second opponent of Le Franc immediately wrote a similar pamphlet, *Les En cas que* ; the Abbé Morellet followed with *Les Pourquoi* ; and finally Voltaire went over from prose to verse and wrote *Les Pour*, a satirical poem in which each verse began with *Pour* :

> *Pour* vivre en paix joyeusement,
> Croyez-moi, n'offensez personne :
> C'est un petit avis qu'on donne
> Au Sieur Le Franc de Pompignan.

And at the end :

> *Pour* prix d'un discours impudent,
> Digne des bords de la Garonne,
> Paris offre cette couronne
> Au Sieur Le Franc de Pompignan.

Now the flood gates were open, a genus of satirical poetry had been created, and a hail of couplets descended on the unfortunate Le Franc de Pompignan : *Les Que, Les Qui, Les Quoi, Les Oui, Les Non, Les Car, Les Ah, Ah !* [1]

Although fundamentally different in particulars, the genesis of the Tuscan Rispetto must be thought of as having gone through essentially the same process. As those couplets against Le Franc are mockery in the form of advice, which in each case is introduced by the same formal word, so the Rispetto is a lover's greeting in the form of protestations or professions, which as a rule are repeated two or three times or more, at the same time being varied and continually intensified :

[1] Cf. Georg Brandes, *Voltaire*, vol. II, Berlin, 1923, p. 186 f.

O viso bianco quanto la farina,
Chi l'ha composte a voi tante bellezze ?
Dove passate voi l'aria s'inchina,
Tutte le stelle vi fanno carezze :
Dove passate voi l'aria si posa,
Voi siete del giardin la vaga rosa :
Dove passate voi l'aria si ferma,
Voi siete del giardin la vaga stella :
(Dove passate voi l'aria si priva,
Voi siete del giardin la vaga cima).

Quando tu passi dalla casa mia,
Mi par che passi la spera del sole.
Alluminar tu fai tutta la via,
Quando tu passi, lasci lo splendore :
Ma lo splendor che lasci per la via
È sempre meno della fiamma mia :
Ma lo splendor che lasci, scema e cala,
L'amor mio durerà fino alla bara.

Dimmi, bellino, com'i'ho da fare
Per poterla salvar l'anima mia ?
I'vado 'n chiesa e non ci posso stare,
Nemmen la posso dir l'Ave Maria :
I'vado 'n chiesa, e niente posso dire :
Ch'i'ho sempre il tuo bel nome da pensare ;
I'vado 'n chiesa, e non posso dir niente,
Ch'i'ho sempre il tuo bel nome nella mente.

This last Rispetto has been compared to a Sicilian Strambotto with the idea that the Tuscan may have been derived from it :

Amuri, amuri, chi m'hai fattu fari !
Li senzii mi l'hai misu'n fantasia,
Lu patrinnostru m'ha' fattu scurdari
E la mitati di la vimmaria ;
Lu creddu nun lu sacciu 'ncumincari,
Vaju a la missa, e mi scordu la via ;
Di novu mi voggh' jri a vattiari,
Ca turcu addivintai pri amari a tia.

But this and similar comparisons, of which Alessandro D'Ancona has made a great number,[1] do not so much

[1] A. D'Ancona, *La poesia popolare italiana*, 2nd. edn., Livorno, 1906.

prove the Sicilian origin of the Tuscan Rispetto, as the specifically Tuscan characteristic of repetitive, varying, and gradually more emphatic protestations.

Folk-songs do not travel about like finished literary goods, packed in paper and neatly bound ; they are propagated like a conversation, that is, they are born anew at each place under new conditions. A borrowed word, a group of sounds, a linguistic usage, travel in the same way. Using social methods of transport, they go from mouth to ear, from ear to mouth ; they adapt themselves to the formative will that happens to be current, acquire citizenship and become nationalized.

Popular poetry and the rules and categories of the ordinary language of intercourse are alike not only in the method by which they move about and are transmitted, but in their whole structure. The rules of rhyme, assonance, and synæresis, and the number of syllables, have the same rather loose kind of validity in the sphere of Italian folk-poetry as the rules of grammatical congruence or *oratio recta* have in the corresponding language of intercourse. It is a mistake to believe that the former are merely artistic devices or conventional ' rules of the game ' to further the cause of the beauty or harmony of a language, the latter, on the other hand, a fundamental natural necessity ; and that to break the rules of metre leads to forgivable artistic blemishes, whilst grammatical sins prevent and destroy all understanding of language. A formalistic school of artificial poets, Meistersingers, or Parnassians may believe this ; but Beckmesser's preoccupation with rules has nothing to do with poetic genius or the language necessities of the common daily round. The art of verse of a people is meaningful and unschematic. Whenever a verse form is brought from outside, whether from music, dancing, or communal rhythmical work, or from the poetry of a foreign language, indigenous verse rejects everything that is not in accord with the phonetic and acoustic nature of its own linguistic material. Strictly speaking, therefore, we ought to say that it builds up its verse only out of the spontaneity of its traditional language usage ; it does not seek for or invent rhythms, metres, cæsuras, consonances, that are not already in germ contained in the simple language of everyday speech, like a geological deposit of poetic metal. The phonetic, acoustic, rhythmic, in short, the sensual aspect of language usage, is raised to a mental category by the folk-poet. That is, he gives it sense and meaning, whilst in everyday language it always remains that fortuitously ornamental phantom about which the native does not bother his head but which, as we saw, often annoys the foreigner. The folk-poet renders a national service, not because he intones patriotic songs and belittles alien language communities, but because he makes the ornamentation of his mother tongue audible and a joy to the senses, and bears witness to its beauty. If we wish to say anything at all useful and convincing about the ' beauty ' of a language, we should do well to pay special attention to its folk-poetry, for only there is its beauty intelligible and original at the same time.

It is also present in ordinary prose, even in the grammatical structure ; only much more scattered and deeply hidden. Philosophically we can pick it out even there, but we cannot apprehend it empirically.[1] To understand the style and the beauty of a landscape from its geological structure, we need a kind of scientific speculation and philosophical imagination, lacking in the layman and regarded with suspicion by the expert.

One fact, however, is so obvious that it cannot be disregarded : although there may not be any poetry in grammar, no poetry is without some grammar. However natural or artificial, the language of no poet can be so free that grammatical structures, rules, and categories cannot be found in it. Even a playful, anarchical creator of language such as Teofilo Folengo, who has improvised his own ' gibberish ' out of Latin, Italian, and Mantuan,

---

[1] Cf. K. Vossler, *Gesammelte Aufsätze zur Sprachphilosophie*, Munich, 1923, pp. 249–258.

has to fit it into some kind of grammatical mould. And when modern Expressionists declare war on grammar, all they are really doing is to exalt their own grammar.[1] They protest in the name of experience and feeling against a language usage that has been learnt and has become inflexible ; they set *solitum* against *curatum*, and that which has become grammaticized against that which is grammaticable. That is, instead of freeing themselves from grammar, they are helping to renew it.

Every poetic expression, therefore, can be reduced to grammatical categories, if we know how to analyse its meaning. Literary criticism, if properly inderstood, in effect does no more than this. That is, it points to the experiences and feelings, the actions and passions that dominate a poet and become so strong in him that under *their* pressure language becomes *categorical*, that is, attains a binding validity for him and for all those who wish to understand his experiences, his feelings, and his passions. Indeed, for no one as for the poet is the language that he uses to a greater extent κατηγορική, that is, by virtue of its formal occurrence so conclusively the accuser and betrayer of his soul, an obligation and a burden to his innermost being. Every other man can dissociate himself, if not from the content, at any rate from the form of his speech. But the poet is inescapably bound by it.

And again, folk-song with its smaller and more easily handled dimensions, gives us the most useful examples and opportunities for passing from literary criticism to grammatical analysis.

We saw that a generic characteristic of the Tuscan Rispetto is the way in which protestations of affection are repeated, varied, and intensified. It is obvious to anyone who has examined a sufficient number of examples. There is no need to pile on the evidence, so I shall only add one more example to those given above :

[1] *Idem*, p. 128 ff.

> Vo' pianger tanto, che mi vo' finare,
> Come fece Maria Maddalena :
> E un gran fiume di lacrime vo' fare
> Che in ogni tempo cì colghi la piena.
> Che in ogni tempo ci colgano i sassi ;
> Così pianger vogl'io se tu mi lassi :
> E d'ogni tempo ci colgano i fiori ;
> Così vo' pianger io se m'abbandoni.

Is it not as though the grammatical category of the formation of degrees of comparison, as though a kind of positive, comparative, and superlative are here experienced under the pressure of feelings, felt as something new, and written down with a trembling hand for the first time ? The logical grammarian, no doubt, will shake his bald head over a form in which ' flood-water ' (*piena*), ' stones ' (*sassi*), and ' flowers ' (*fiori*) are supposed to have a similar relation amongst each other as ' full ', ' fuller ', ' fullest '. But this way of thinking and feeling is precisely what constitutes the charm of this little song, that at its intensest moments the stream of tears should be like a meadow of flowers. The degrees of comparison are ' irregular ', somewhat like the climax, lion, tiger, man, developed by Schiller in the verse :

> Gefährlich ist's, den Leu zu wecken,
> Verderblich ist des Tigers Zahn,
> Jedoch der schrecklichste der Schrecken,
> Das ist der Mensch in seinem Wahn.

We feel that there is a formal principle in these verses ; and that it is in some way connected with the principle of grammatical comparation must be evident to everyone whose language feeling is at all developed. But what is it that is common to both ? We cannot seek it in conceptual similarity ; for it is in this very respect that the poet, with his ' meadow of flowers ' and his ' tiger's tooth ', diverges from grammatical comparison, which clings to *one* concept through all the degrees of comparison. Nor have they anything in common in the purely formal, in external form ; for grammar only admits certain classes of words, preferably adjectives and adverbs, to the scale of degrees of comparison. And finally, the similarity cannot lie in ' inner form ' ; for grammar, as perfected language usage, does not admit it as a norm. We are thus driven back to a sphere that, as it were, lies below language, out of which both poetry and the linguistic forms of grammar arise, but for which we have as yet no technical terms at our command. That this linguistic nether world contains not only feelings and sensations, but even vision and creative activity, will have to be assumed if only for the reason that the poetical and grammatical formal principle we are seeking arises living and warm from it ; only in the light of the upper world does it divide and establish itself as flexions and rhythms, as grammatical and poetical formal categories.

This nether world might be called the metaphysical language community.[1] It is the region of dreams and magic, where even things other than human are spoken of and have speech, so that they are anthropomorphized in two respects : by being magically and mechanically endowed with language, and by receiving a mythical and symbolical soul. But let us leave this picture of another or nether world ; what we mean is that moment in the activity of language which precedes the specific act of actual speech, in other words, the potentiality of language as distinguished from its actuality. But even this distinction—that potentiality precedes actuality—must be understood in a logical, not a temporal sense ; for potentiality and actuality are so closely interdependent that the latter can only be the other side of the first and not a second or independent aspect.

The actual capacity of language, therefore, is the logical place or aspect in which—to return to our example—the grammatical comparative coincides with the protestations of the Rispetto ; and what is common to the grammatical and the poetic forms is in this case the special capacity

[1] Cf. Chapter VII (a) on " The metaphysical and the empirical language community ".

of language for arranging any given phenomena and processes in the world in an ascending series, establishing permanent connections between them and giving them a continuous motion above and beyond each other—in short, the capacity for introducing rhythm and order into things. If the Italian language did not have this capacity, it would possess neither the grammatical comparative, nor a form of poetry like the Tuscan Rispetto.

Poets and language customs, poetic and grammatical forms are therefore alike in so far as they weave rhythm and order, movement and harmony into the universe of man, of peoples and of individuals. For what we have established for the formal principle of the comparative is true, *mutatis mutandis*, of all grammatical forms. It is true, for instance, of the verbal modes, by which the Indo-Germanic languages divide and synthesize all events and actions as free or determined, voluntary or involuntary. What we are taught in *Die Weisheit des Brahmanen* is also true of all our modal forms :

> Sechs Wörtchen nehmen mich in Anspruch jeden Tag :
> Ich soll, ich muss, ich kann, ich will, ich darf, ich mag.

And since grammatical and stylistic usage are changing continuously, the forms, functions, and meanings of the modi are also continuously being regrouped, relieved, and made to complete each other, so that they finally request and warn each language, and each individual speaker :

> Nur wenn Du stets mich lehrst, weiss ich, was jeden Tag
> Ich soll, ich muss, ich kann, ich will, ich darf, ich mag.

What is important from our point of view is not so much the obvious fact that the grammatical categories are a principle of order in language, but the fact that they have movement and rhythm. It is sufficient to establish an order, to understand it, and to give it its due respect ; but a waltz has to be played and danced. The poetical and national value of the grammatical categories lies in this, that they are not only accepted, learned, and observed, but that they are experienced, executed, practised, danced, marched, breathed, played on flutes, trombones and drums, drawn, painted, and sung. And it is this that is achieved far more quickly and thoroughly, in a more intense and concentrated form by poets than by the slow, hesitating, partial, extensive work of national language communities, which has millennia at its disposal. Such communities are engaged in knitting an endless, colossal stocking—the Romance or the Slav languages, for instance—slowly and comfortably extending it in length and breadth. In this process the grammatical categories are like meshes, and they are adhered to as long as possible. But in poetry they are all the more vitally active ; and the dialectical law of self-estrangement or of unity in difference immediately begins to operate on them.

For, the greater the fire which a poet infuses into a grammatical category, the less that category can remain itself. If we dance a waltz to the rhythm of our own heart, and not to that of the dancing master, we are no longer dancing a waltz, but our own joy in life. Let us examine a well-known French folk-song, which consists of conditional clauses :

Par derrière chez mon père
il y a un étang.
je me mettrai anguille,
anguille dans l'étang.—

Si tu te mets anguille,
anguille dans l'étang,
je me mettrai pêcheur,
je t'aurai en pêchant.—

Si tu te mets pêcheur
pour m'avoir en pêchant,
je me mettrai alouette,
alouette dans les champs.—

Si tu te mets alouette,
alouette dans les champs,
je me mettrai chasseur,
je te aurai en chassant.—

Si tu te mets chasseur
pour m'avoir en chassant,
je me mettrai nonnette,
nonnett' dans un couvent.—

Si tu te mets nonnette,
nonnett' dans un couvent,
je me mettrai prêcheur
je t'aurai en prêchant.—

Si tu te mets prêcheur
pour m'avoir en prêchant,
je me donnerai à toi,
puisque tu m'aimes tant.

There is no doubt that these are true hypothetical constructions ; and yet they are not true, since the real meaning, the inspiration of the song, arises not from a conditional attitude, but from an attitude of wishing, loving, desiring. But once the poet—or the lovers—have succumbed to this fiction of grammatical hypothesis, they are enmeshed by it and cannot escape from it. This amusing game—for such it is and remains, as long as the conditional categories are not taken seriously—can be extended indefinitely in this rigid form. The content of the song is ended by a charming idea ; but the song as a whole is not resolved either formally or artistically. The category of conditional clauses follows the course of the emotions only externally, without having an inner rhythm of its own, on the strength of which it could and must become another category. The reader will better understand what I mean, if he examines the way in which a more serious poet concludes a similar motif with similar methods :

Ich denke dein, wenn mir der Sonne Schimmer
    Vom Meere strahlt ;
Ich denke dein, wenn sich des Mondes Flimmer
    In Quellen malt.

Ich sehe dich, wenn auf dem fernen Wege
    Der Staub sich hebt ;
In stiller Nacht, wenn auf dem schmalen Stege
    Der Wandrer bebt.

Ich höre dich, wenn dort in dumpfem Rauschen
  Die Welle steigt.
Im stillen Haine geh' ich oft zu lauschen,
  Wenn alles schweigt.

Ich bin bei dir ; du seist auch noch so ferne,
  Du bist mir nah !
Die Sonne sinkt, bald leuchten mir die Sterne.
  O, wärst du da !

Grammatically, the conditional clauses here are correct ;
for if temporal clauses had been intended, Goethe would
have written *wann* and not *wenn*. But it is an accidental,
external conditionality, which provides a starting-point,
but is not a *conditio sine qua non*. And these reasons for
thinking of the loved one are truly and inwardly experienced. Here the category is not a fiction. And since
it is taken so seriously, sung so lovingly, it develops its
own rhythm and passes over and back into that category,
from which it had really started in intention : " *O, wärst
du da !* " It is the category of wishing, from which to
a great extent the hypothetical and conditional sentence
forms are philologically derived. The formal philological
law of the poem as a song of longing and wishing is thereby
fulfilled, its tension resolved, its rhythm executed and
brought to rest, the conditional form of expression
modulated and followed back to that of the wish, during
which it even passes through the intermediate stage of
granting—" *du seist auch noch so ferne* ".

In every poem, provided the feeling and the workman-
ship are strong enough, the grammatical categories are
modulated in a different way. To take a final example :
in the following folk-song the restful certainty and trust
of love are arrived at by starting from a conditional
sentence expressing an unreal wish, and proceeding by
way of adversative statements to an absolute, unconditional statement that excludes all eventualities. Longing
and wishing here take refuge in memory, while in Goethe's
poem the latter arose out of the former.

Wenn ich ein Vöglein wär
Und auch zwei Flügel hätt,
Flög ich zu dir ;
Weil's aber nicht kann sein,
Bleib ich allhier.

Bin ich gleich weit von dir,
Bin ich doch im Schlaf bei dir
Und red mit dir ;
Wenn ich erwachen tu,
Bin ich allein.

Es geht keine Stund in der Nacht,
Da nicht mein Herz erwacht
Und dein gedenkt,
Dass du mir viel tausendmal
Dein Herz geschenkt.—

The grammatical categories are the same for a whole national language, indeed for great groups of historically linked languages. If one knows the inflexional forms and syntactic functions of the Latin subjunctive and has understood how they belong together and work together, what they achieve and for what they are used, one has a concept of this grammatical category which, when the French, Italian, or Spanish use of the subjunctive is examined, does not need to be broken and cast aside, but has merely to be enriched and ' developed '. As a concept the category does not remain the same, but it remains true to itself. It is not inflexible, but possesses a certain constant inertia. As a form of speech it is flexible and moves with a different rhythm and in a different direction not only in every language, but in the style of each individual and at each moment. Here it is individually defined as ' this ' subjunctive, there generically as ' a ' subjunctive. ' A ' subjunctive can be used, avoided, applied, circumvented, or chosen in daily talk ; but ' this ' individually determined subjunctive must be experienced and felt in *this* particular movement, rhythm, context and meaning, if it is to be used and sounded and sung so that it may appeal to the heart. Seen from this angle, national languages, in all their particulars as well as in their total systems, are seen to be experienced language, style, and poetry, and also the changeable, historically conditioned realization of the great and unique community of language of man and the universe.

(e) *The community of language as a community of interests*

Not long ago a protagonist of Catalan autonomy gave an address to the students at Barcelona in which he said : " Under the present conditions in Catalonia, how often are we not forced to use an idiom that is not ours ! The bad Catalan is he who in using it feels neither pain nor shame. But there is a way of speaking Castilian, which can redeem us. It consists in hanging a bell on it, which the professors must hear. If you do that, the Spanish textbooks, note books, and lectures can do you no harm." [1] What is this bell ? Obviously a prearranged sign to show that the Spanish of the lecture rooms was a language that had been imposed, not experienced, a language that was alien and abhorred. So it was to be spoken with a consciously Catalan accent and surrounded with Catalanisms, as one would hang a bell round a cat if one were a mouse. If at the university of Barcelona Spanish were felt to be simply a scientific or technical language, there would be no sense in prefixing a negative sign of sentiment, like that ' bell '.[2] The language of a science is used without prejudice *as far as possible.*

[1] Cf. *La Revista*, any IX. Gener. I–XVI, 1923, Barcelona, p. 25 " *En l'estat actual de Catalunya, quantes vegades hem d'usar per força un idioma que no es el nostre ! El mal català es el qui en usar-lo no sent dolor i vergonya. Hi ha una manera de parlar castellà que us en pot redimir. Es posar-hi un picarol, que el sentin els professors. Aleshores no us faran mal ni els llibres de text, ni els " apuntes ", ni la lliçó dita en espanyol.*"

[2] The idea that Spanish is a literary language and Catalan merely a dialect is expressly repudiated by the speaker : " *Tots els que us parlin del caracter antieuropeu i limitat de l'ideal català, van lamentablement errats. Són ells els limitats. L'universalisme madrileny que diu que el món camina cap a la unitat, no coneix el món. A l'Europa d'avui*

The question as to this possibility is the decisive point. Where there is no sentiment, there can be no language. There is no thing, no subject, no cause that speaks for itself. When great philosophers like Hegel or Spinoza assert that truth or an idea will win through and realize itself, whether anyone has any feeling about them and fights for them by word and deed or not, they are commuting a necessary warning to maintain the highest possible objectivity, into a superhuman philosophy, in which language no longer has a place. The demand that one should be quiet and modest is turned by them into a metaphysical fact.

When the human language takes up the tendency to quiet and modest objectivity and tries to conform to it, it creates a number of more or less pure ' objective ' or technical languages. It thus imposes a discipline on itself, which can become a danger to its existence, the more strictly it is used. It would be curious if there were no sentiment attached to this striving after objectivity ; only it is extraordinarily difficult to determine what it is. In a national language, even objective matters take on an individual and personal feeling tone ; in the technical languages the shadow of objectivity falls on even the most personal concerns. We would point out once again that we are assuming that national and objective languages never exist in a pure form entirely separated from one another, but that they are always bound together and mixed in many ways. A technical language could have its own vocabulary, possibly even its own grammar, but not its own accent, obviously because it apparently has no sentiments of its own. The so-called languages of commerce, of law, of science, of the arts and crafts are not independent languages, but terminological appendices or additions to some already

en dia hi ha triple nombre de llengües oficials que en la d'ara fa un segle. Ja només queden per reconeixer els patois, i nosaltres no podem admetre que la nostra llengua gloriosa, instrument de cultura, sigui tinguda com un patois indigne." Loc. cit., p. 26.

present national language. Their sign is the *terminus technicus*; and if we are laymen, this always seems to us like a foreign word, even when its roots prove it to belong to the heritage of our own mother tongue. Who has not had the experience of having the naïveté with which he was accustomed to speak of ' property ', or ' theft ', or ' murder ', broken as soon as he came into the company of lawyers or judges? These words suddenly acquired a sharp and treacherous intention and meaning, and became gruesome to us. Even in some poems, if they are too artificial, we feel the frost of the *terminus technicus*, for example when the heroes of Corneille speak of their *feux* and *flammes*, or modish Romantics of their ' beautiful soul '. The most intimate and human things become technical and strange through this commercialized objectivity. Technical terms make our own lives into a ' subject ', and remove it to a distance. To the primitive poetical mind the whole world is known and is of his own kind, and even where it is inimical and threatening it still wears a distorted human mask. But the technical man does away with all this anthropomorphism. The world is strange to him, and therefore interesting. Between I and non-I the *terminus technicus* builds a wall, something that lies in between them. We have called it *interest*. For in so far as the technical man only wants those things that he can use for the purpose in hand, he has to keep at a distance everything that would interfere with his purpose, and must separate out what is useful to him. This purposive filter is interest, and the linguistic equivalent for it is the technical term. According to the purpose it has to serve, it has two aspects : a positive and a negative. The negative interest of the technical man desires to eliminate all anthropomorphic and emotional aspects; it tries to deny, hide, transform, and, where possible, separate and remove them. For man is by nature an autocrat, and would rather be served by machines than by his kind. The positive interest, on the other hand, analyses, prepares, and presents all those

L

things that are of use to man. Their names are then once more made concrete and visual, *e.g.* matrix, screwdriver, shoetree, dumb waiter, manhole, etc. Technical and terminological anthropomorphisms now range themselves beside the elemental and mythical ; and they doubtless contain some elements of sentiment, which we might label ' utilitarian sentiment '.[1]

Let us confine ourselves for the moment to that negative striving after technical perfection, which tries to conquer the world by taking away its soul. It is so rational that it gives the impression of having a positive goal, that of logical knowledge. In reality it never attains this goal because logical knowledge is not its goal at all. If the concepts of logic and scientific knowledge really were the realm and the hunting field of language, at least *one* truth, one pure concept, would have been captured by it in the course of the centuries. And if this *one* thing had become certain, the others would of necessity have followed after, and would have been systematically co-ordinated with it. Then it would have been possible to bring about a unitary logical language through which all men would have been able to communicate, if not their daily needs and their ordinary business, at any rate the categories of their thought. There has been no lack of attempts to raise human speech into the calm, united realm of truth ; but they either failed completely, or, instead of a universal language, resulted in a number of universal sciences : a science of mathematics, of logic, a dialectic, a metaphysic, a science of grammar and their various combinations, mathematical logic, logical grammar, dialectical metaphysics, and so on, but never a logical language. No wonder, for in order to advance human intercourse or commerce, we can lay down rules, create organizations, make treaties and alliances ; but for the philosophical business of knowing the world, we have to

---

[1] I have taken the expression *Zweckgesinnung* from Paul Frankl. For further details *vide* my *Gesammelte Aufsätze zur Sprachphilosophie*, Munich, 1923, p. 254 ff.

be alone. Truth, knowledge, and concepts can to some extent be described by means of language ; but they cannot be expressed and, above all, they cannot be communicated. Indeed, strictly speaking even the presentation of a concept in language is always done indirectly ; for we do not communicate the concept itself, or let it speak for itself ; we communicate the sensations and images, the feelings, interests, desires, fears that accompanied its inception. I can signalize and hand on to others the psychic constellation under which it rose like a sun above my horizon ; but I cannot hand on the concept itself. Humanity gropes about in the fog and cries : " Give us the sun ! " But the great thinkers have never given any other answer from their observatories than a statement of the latitude and longitude in which they were to be found and seen at the moment. And the *language* of science, however strict its logical, terminological, grammatical, mathematical schooling, however unsensual and ascetic, has always given us spectacles, telescopes and magnifying glasses instead of the light itself ; and the majority of men do not know how to handle these instruments. He would be an optimistic teacher who hoped to satisfy the needs of scientific vision with a pair of normal spectacles common to all men. On the contrary, scientific and philosophical interest demand a progressive multiplication, specialization, and infinite ramification not only of technical terms, but even of national languages. The modern natural sciences would never have been born, had not Italian, French, German, English simultaneously come forward to help, and removed the clumsy Latin midwife. In the interest of historic research, every people has to tell us and itself its own past in its own words ; for as long as only Tacitus speaks for the Germans, the science of German philology and history cannot be weaned. Even the critical rejuvenation of philosophy dates from the personal and almost autobiographical turn which it took in the *Discours de la méthode*—not to mention the essays of Montaigne. In essence the language of science is not, as is generally believed, terminological, or technical, or even logical, but dialectical. In the sphere of knowledge and truth every concept must achieve its own dialect. This is not a mere play upon words, but a literal truth. It means that each concept must be so thoroughly enunciated, over and over again, and mirrored in all the languages of humanity, that it finally achieves a form which no longer needs translating. Only then has it exhausted its dialectic, completed its linguistic journey round the world, ended its wandering life from translation to translation ; only then does it become rigid, so that the narrow coffin of a formula can confine the restless one to whom all the languages of the world seemed too narrow.

The formula is closely related to the *terminus technicus* and is interchangeable with it, as the negative interest of the technical man goes over into the positive. Formula and *terminus* are distinguishable, if not according to the objects they have in common within a language, at any rate according to their specific function. The essentially grammatical, *i.e.* predominantly syntactical and morphological functions correspond to the formula ; the lexicographical, *i.e.* onomasiological and semantic functions correspond to the *terminus technicus.*

In his *Philosophie der symbolischen Formen* (Berlin, 1923) Ernst Cassirer has shown with remarkable thoroughness that in all the language groups of the world, formulæ are an expression of a language will that is directed towards eliminating from the world the senses, the gods, the soul, and man.[1] The only fundamental criticism we have to make of his presentation is of the intellectualistic tendency to seek a logical or conceptual goal and interest in grammatical order, whilst in reality it is merely a matter of prose, of chastising the linguistic imagination.[2]

[1] Cf. my review of this book, " Una filosofia della grammatica ", *Cultura*, II, pp. 529–533, Rome, 1923.

[2] To how great an extent prose is directed to syntactical order, and not directly to logical thinking, I have shown in my *Gesammelte Aufsätze zur Sprachphilosophie*, Munich, 1923, pp. 212–232.

We can assume that prosaic thinking is the preliminary school for logical and conceptual thinking only in so far as all language, poetry as well as, or even better than prose, leads man to a philosophical attitude towards the universe. The school of grammar, as experience has shown, more often than not forms small pedants, that of poetry great thinkers. If it is necessary to write good prose to be a sound scientific thinker, then logic proves itself to be the preliminary school for prose ; and this is the exact opposite of what those who aim at training the mind through grammar would have us believe.

The illusory appearance of a progressive grammatical simplification and intellectualization of languages, which is often interpreted as logical clarification, arises above all if, like Cassirer, we limit our investigations to formulæ (or grammatical structures), and neglect the termini (or vocabulary). If the grammatical structure of a language were the whole language, we should have no fault to find. But there are far more actual and complete languages, in other words far more language communities in the world than there are structural grammatical types. Thus a single grammatical structure suffices for nine living Romance languages and their national language communities.

A language community that is based purely on grammatical uniformity is to be found only in the textbooks of comparative grammarians, if at all ; and it should be banished even from these, as a pure figment of the ,imagination, were it not for the historical fact that some languages, whose grammar is similar even to-day, once had their vocabularies and even their phonetic form and accent in common. When a language community is broken up, grammatical structure is the last remaining indication of this community. Many writers therefore like comparing it to the plan or the foundations of a ruin ; but the analogy is an extremely bad one, for in reality the grammatical character maintains itself with such tenacity, not so much because of its fundamental nature, but because of its more external, negative characteristics. I should prefer to liken it to the traces left by the yoke or halter on the neck of a draught animal, which remain long after it has escaped from servitude. Similar grammatical structure is a much overrated proof of a historical language relationship. A common vocabulary is at least as strong a proof, if not a stronger one, in so far as it points to the positive tendency in our speech towards sensual and concrete reality. The onomasiological proof of relationship can be supported by historical considerations of economic, cultural, geographical, in short, factual common interests, whilst the purely grammatical proof remains suspended in the air of abstract, formal thought.

We have seen that the negative tendency to technicality, or grammatical language thinking, can never come to the end of its attempts at banishing the soul from the world ; for the grass of concrete, anthropomorphic thinking grows up again as fast as it is mown. Let us now inquire whether the activities of positive technicality are a similar labour of Sisyphus.

To begin with, as long as it is directed towards purely utilitarian ends, it is clear that no activity, linguistic or any other, can escape from the temporary, the local, and the relative, but remains caught up in a rather aimless activity that eventually becomes an end in itself. For every purpose that is achieved, every interest that is satisfied, loses its value in the act of satisfaction, unless sentiment has implanted eternity in it. As the grass *behind* the scythe grows again, so the grass *under* it fades and withers, and drives the hungry mower from meadow to meadow.

Within the sphere of usefulness of a language we can recognize this state of affairs in the fact that technical terms and words are taken over from each other by different communities, because no language community is sufficiently wide for all purposes. Each must borrow and lend, and there is no end to the exchange of words. It is hoped that by consciously cultivating and accelerating this interchange of words, the children of all languages and nations will arrive at an international language through mutual understanding. Nevertheless this prospect of a practical, technical and terminological unitary language is almost as imaginary as that of a common grammatical or logical language, although the attempts at realizing it have had some success and are less Utopian than the theoretical speculations of men like Descartes, Delgarno, Wilkins, Leibniz and many others. But as long as the *one* permanent interest cannot be found, in which the general understanding of the world can be focussed, the complete realization of a practical common language must remain as before a pious hope. If we postulate humanism itself as this common interest, we are either talking self-evident platitudes, or yielding to a rosy ideology. For men are ' human ' by nature, and therefore all capable of speech ; or we may understand by humanism a spiritually enlarged humanity, and then we are dealing with something special, which must be believed in the religious sense, be defined philosophically, desired morally and realized politically. But, since the dawn of history this has been the cause of the most violent competition among peoples and individuals, bringing in its train all those painful divisions and oppositions of our interests.

We can, it is true, escape from these spiritual battles for a time, by leaping with both feet into the peaceful uniformity of an artificial world language ; but by that means we also discard everything that has a specific vital interest. To begin with, such a language can serve only language cranks and language maniacs who want to speak merely for the sake of speaking, quite regardless of what or with whom they are speaking. Such people, who are concerned with nothing more than speaking, understanding, and answering, do in fact exist. Indeed, in every language or conversation lesson, our interest is neutralized to such an extent in favour of technical facility in speaking, that all other contents of life are made equal and subordinated to the interest in speaking. Such devitalized interest, such ' utilitarian sentiment ', is not capable of forming a living community, though it still has sufficient force to found societies for Esperanto, Volapük, and Ido, or even language academies.

In the present age of technicism, especially, the weakening of primary, spiritual, vital interests, in other words, the relativization of sentiment, is a wide-spread phenomenon. Historically and psychologically it can be explained as the reaction to exaggerated nationalism. During the Renaissance there was a similar reaction against exaggerated sentimental or ' Platonic ' love, resulting in a technical eroticism that manifested itself as gallantry or Don Juanism. In the field of literature, the officious moralizings of the Naturalists during the nineteenth century had as their counterpart the æsthetic technicism of the Parnassians. Wherever sentiment is overdone, it breeds an indifference to itself, which is satisfied with the practices initiated by this sentiment ; and without an ethos it handles the lifeless instruments forged by this ethos.

But no machine can run free for any length of time. Either the instruments rust and the ability to handle them is forgotten, or they create in the man who is always content to use them in a soulless way a feeling of having no spiritual home, and hence the tendency to place his abilities in the service of those who offer most or demand least. . All virtuosity, all technicism, is in essence commercial and prostitutes itself. This, of course, does not mean that the individual virtuoso may not be a perfect gentleman in private life ; but he can never be that in his technical activities. Empty rooms are not immoral, but they can be hired. That is why in recent years international bolshevism, socialism, and communism have quartered themselves on the grammar and vocabulary of Esperanto, and are in process not only of stamping it with their sentiments and their atmosphere, their particular accents on feeling and meaning, but even of making political propaganda for it.

That an academically sophisticated system of forms and words should become a living language seems monstrous; but it cannot surprise a philosophy of language that, like ours, rests on the identity of what is natural in language with what is common usage in language. The whole formal material of Esperanto is natural in so far as it is taken from a number of national languages; but the selective principle by which it is chosen, and the authority that sanctions it, will more and more seem to be no longer the thesis of an individual inventor and his academic supporters, but a customary usage of the esperantist, communistic brotherhood and language community. On the other hand it is just as easy to look upon the whole formal material of grammar and vocabulary as having been borrowed, that is, as having been acquired by use. The natural elements in it will then be the aspect of sentiment, by which this foreign, homeless sand, which is blown about by all the winds, is bound together and made fruitful; and this sentiment in its turn is just as homeless, as European and international, so that the two aspects are closely, even fundamentally related. For by their sense and their meaning, it has always been the tendency and the fate of borrowed forms and foreign words to serve the interests of social classes, callings, guilds, etc., and thereby to forget and deny those of national communities. In this sense, a language formed by international loans and relying on international exchange, must, philologically speaking, seem fundamentally related as well as utterly congenial and adapted to the beliefs and activities, the sentiments and the spread of communism. A history of the spreading of all European borrowed forms, as a history of the development of international thought and activity is not only possible, but eminently desirable.

Esperanto is not without historical precedents. Towards the end of the Middle Ages a criminal language was developed in France, and soon afterwards in Italy, Spain, and England. As far as our information goes at present, it would seem that we must regard the beginning of the French *argot*, to limit ourselves to one example, as a similar conscious, intentional, artificial and academic process as the invention of Esperanto and Volapük. In those times there was even a kind of academy that regulated the modifications in the usage of words. These chosen, secret masters of language in the sixteenth century were called *archi-suppôts*, *archi-boutants*, *arcs-boutants*, *piliers de boutanche*, *souteneurs*, and *poteaux*. The distinguishing characteristic of this language of thieves, vagabonds, beggars, small shopkeepers and hucksters, was the conscious distortion and transposition of the sense of individual words taken from the ordinary French. It was only later that an element of sentiment was added to this utilitarian mask, in that adventurous, fantastic, humoristic and romantic attitude of the Frondeurs, which expressed itself in phonetic variations of certain words by the repression or inversion of individual sounds, or in morphological distortions, by attaching suffixes taken from various dialects and foreign languages. At first it was earnest, objective, sober, and almost pedantic, as indeed the nature of the *terminus technicus* in the criminal world demands. If a sentiment other than the purely negative and destructive could have found a place and could have expressed itself in the technicalities of this *argot*, it would have become a better language than it is to-day. But as it had been conceived, so it had to remain in the school of these naughty, riotous children. To-day it can be only an occasional expedient for criminals or a lyrical ornament in naturalistic or comic literature. The objective interests of criminals and small shopkeepers—for the latter probably were the most active disseminators of this *argot*—and the romanticism of imaginative people have in the long run not been able to combine into a natural, unitary language usage. The disparity between criminal, commercial, and literary utilitarian sentiment has not been bridgeable.

It remains to be seen whether Esperanto will descend to a criminal jargon, or become the language of international commerce, after it has gone through the academic stage of a technical experiment in language and has entered public life. At the moment it is being actively encouraged by the Russian, suppressed by the French, treated somewhat equivocally by the German governments, and politely rejected by the League of Nations. It is a question of power, which in the last resort, however, depends on whether Esperanto-loving communism is capable of creating something positive and original, beyond the mere negation of social order.

If it were given to languages to determine their own fate, there can be no doubt that Esperanto would be spoken on all the markets of the world, in all trains and steamers, governments, embassies and consulates, for it certainly makes that demand. But just as man is autonomous in the intelligible realm of mind and not in the chance events we call reality, so his language is autonomous as a personal style, but not as a means of intercourse or of the creation of communities. In the practical world no language is valid for itself alone, however many claims it may have to grace, beauty, suppleness, comfort, clarity, simplicity, or any other relative and therefore disputable qualities we may think of. The immanent, or, what in this connection means the same, the transcendental proselytizing power of a language does not extend one step further than the sound of its poetry. As a psalter, as Homer, as Dante, Shakespeare or Goethe it can conquer eternity and heaven, but not an inch of earth. It is like the magic forest in the old French Alexander romance, which is peopled by fairies of love, who live there in eternal youth, but die as soon as they forsake its shadows for the light. Such is the realm of languages in poetry :

> Tant com li ombres dure, car ne pueent avant ;
> ja si poi ne passassent, que mortes caïsant.—
> Mais plus aiment les homes que nule rien vivant,
> por çou qu'en cuide avoir cescune son talant.

It ought to be clear that the autonomous power of a language can never suffice for the inception of a human community of interests. For it is interest, that faithless and ever-changing thing, which moves about between words and objects, between poetry and truth, and undermines the whole permanence and the real value of languages ; unless our relative and relativizing interest in nothing and everything be finally bound and made fruitful by a true and permanent sentiment.

Since in language as such no other disposition than the poetic can become immediately active, creative, and binding, there remains to us only the one assumption, that all language communities, whatever interest they may serve, are in the last resort built upon the rock— or, if you will, the sand—of the feeling for poetic style. Church Latin arises out of the sense of style of believers, not out of dogma ; the French of international diplomacy out of a drawing-room sense of style of diplomatists, and not out of French world power ; Esperanto out of the sense of a future world style, that is, out of a love for the desires and interests of men that is as idealistically great as it is cynical, and not out of the technique of communication ; the unitary language of Logic out of the scholastic taste in the supersensual, out of the pedantic delight in playing the schoolmaster to all mundane things, and not out of reality itself. The German of the German Swiss, Alsatians, Czechs, Tirolese, etc., unfortunately is also based merely on a German, that is, a poetic sense of style, and not on any national, political, ethical, or animal ethnographical feeling, or a consciousness of race. The technical languages as well as the national languages are dependent on the poetry inherent in their subject and their interests. Why should not commerce as well as crime, science as well as hunting, the exactitude of definitions as well as the mist of dreams have a specific poetry ? One only needs to feel them and listen to their sound.[1]

[1] Cf. my essay, " La poesia della correttezza ", *Cultura*, II, pp. 312–315, Rome, May 15th, 1923.

The sense of national style is very weak in Germany, and from this point of view the prospects for the continuation of our language community are not very encouraging. But the fate of the German people, its struggle, its fall and its suffering have a poetry that may perhaps be felt more fully and more deeply and be more intensely creative than if Germany had experienced the triumph of victory.

This sense of the poetic is directly experienced neither in grammatical formulæ nor in technical terminologies ; it is felt in the pronunciation, the tone, emphasis and rhythm of the sentence, in short, in all those things the general impression of which is less accurately and popularly called accent. The dialects of the countryside are above all communities of accent, and that is why they sound so tender, heartfelt and poetic to every receptive ear.

If those Catalan students, with whom we started our discussion, decide to accompany the Spanish that has been forced upon them with the tinkle of their homely accent, they have a mocking intention whose import only now becomes clear. The Spanish stranger is to be clothed in the national costume of the Catalans, and the majestic language of the state derided in the loose and comfortable smock of a dialect. For however strongly Catalonian repudiates the imputation that it is a mere dialect, and however true its contention may be, as a spoken idiom it can nevertheless not avoid radiating the colour of its home language, and in this light Spanish becomes an undignified *patois*, or, more accurately, a *jargon* of Catalonia, like the Latin of Folengo, which is a muddle of Mantuan and Italian, or the involuntarily and unintentionally comic Bavarianized German of Josef Filser.

Hanging a bell round the language of the oppressor may be amusing, but is also dangerous, as we can observe in the case of the citizens of Alsace. The Allemannic tongues of these excellent people have played the fool with French with great gusto, partly humorously, and partly from stolid thoughtlessness ; but their sense of German style has thereby also suffered and become impure. Although this question of language is in the last resort a question only of style and taste, it must nevertheless be taken seriously. For the mere fact that a language rests on a common sense of style and a common taste does not make it a work of art. It may therefore not rest content merely with its immortal happiness or beauty any more than the poor artists who labour at the great work, or the wealthy Mæcenians and dealers who pay for it, because they have at any rate some kind of taste and sense of style.

(f) *The community of language as a community of sentiment*

Taste and sentiment are two things; but in the language community they are one and the same. Sentiment binds the ethical man, taste the æsthetic. But since no one likes dividing himself and everyone is intent on preserving his own individuality, the man who makes our taste accord with his own can also without much difficulty win the rest of us, our convictions and eventually even our interests. One cannot in the long run speak the language of a community without suffering for it—and also being rewarded for it. This was experienced, for instance, by Switzerland during the world war, when the majority of its German-speaking citizens took the side of Germany, and all its French-speaking citizens that of France. Whenever a government attempts to nationalize a foreign nation by imposing its own language, it does so in the hope that the bait of taste will catch the whole fish.

Since continued unfortunate experiences have made even the fish cautious, such attempts have in recent times become less and less successful. The opposite procedure is therefore being more and more adopted, by which the sentiments of a nation or a group of individuals are first captured from the side of economic or other interests, and that eventua'ly brings with it a taste for the language.

However, even this calculation is not quite certain ; for since interpreting and translating have been invented there is no necessity for giving up a taste for one language for the benefits to be derived from another. The true sense and the philosophical justification of translation is the maintenance of the autonomy of language taste. Every translation is commissioned, as it were, by the instinct for self-preservation of a language community. Hence translation as a problem of language philosophy is intimately connected with the problem of the language community, and must be considered at this point in our discussions.

If one denies the concept of translation, as the language philosophy of Benedetto Croce does, one must also give up the concept of a language community. There remains only the metaphysical community of the whole of humanity with the whole of the universe as ' the fact of language '. The fact that there is a French, a German, an English language, and therefore the possibility of translating from English into German, etc., is dismissed by this philosophy once and for all by relegating mundane relations to the sphere of ' practical mind '. Here, strictly speaking, there can be only functions, and no real problems ; individual incarnations, and no individual personalities. From this point of view, if our life is not to become a mere senseless treadmill, the only way out is that taken by Croce, who identifies the metaphysical beyond with the present. However, we have to defend not only the identity of convergence and immanence, but the complete unity of both spheres ; and this means that we must also maintain the identity of philosophy and empirical practice, thereby eliminating that tension between them, the over-coming of which constitutes scientific research.

We cannot take this road, since, unlike Croce, we have made spiritual personality, and not individuality, the vehicle of language. For each individual language has the same right to claim universality and dominance over other languages as every other. In fact each is threatened by the others, and without mediation they could not exist next to one another. The open and conscious form of this mediation is called translation.

It sometimes happens that the rulers of two nations employ an interpreter in a purely representative way even when he is not needed to bring about understanding between them, that is, when each is master of the other's national language. Interpretation or translation in this case is a superfluous periphrasis and hindrance ; but it is done because both languages desire to be acknowledged as absolute equals in *one* respect. The translation is a demonstration in favour of constitutional law, that is, a neutral ground is prepared on which both languages can meet as equal representatives of the interests of their respective peoples. In this diplomatic game the translator becomes a mere language being, and really has nothing more to do than be elegant. He can even afford to be inaccurate now and then on matters of fact, since the monarchs understand each other just as well without him ; but he must be ready with his ears and tongue and be the living embodiment of listening and speaking.

In ordinary life there is neither motive, space, nor time for such fictitious and histrionic translation. If a scientific work on the anatomy of the brain is translated from Spanish into German, it is done in order to save German doctors the trouble of learning a foreign language. When a trashy French novel is turned into English, it is in order to facilitate the sale of a strong drink, which our own distilleries cannot turn out in sufficient quantity. In short, the purpose of the overwhelming majority of translations is an economic saving of labour. The translator wants first of all to do others, and only in the second place himself, a service. The practical purpose and economic value of a translation is its mediation. It is a transmission, and the language which it uses functions as communication and is of the same order as any language of intercourse. What it expresses and represents stands in the service of communication ; it postulates both a public and a demand in that public. Even in the case of the representative interpreter there was a demand; but it was not a demand for communication, merely for a living representation of the business of communicating. Communication as such can be represented by the polite, courtly, elegant, subservient, dignified, majestic, or rude manner in which it is done. All sorts of artistic blends can be imagined. Indeed, when it has been represented and has thus become conscious of its own æsthetic value, the desire for communication may even become an artistic motif that itself strives for expression. And now histrionic translation no longer appears as a marketable ware, but, without reference to demand, public, or labour saving, suddenly appears as an end in itself, with its own inspiration, its own aspirations, and its own lyrical feeling. The most extreme and remarkable example of this kind is probably *Der Deutsche Dante* of Rudolf Borchardt.[1] What was once an emotion accompanying the service of translation, now becomes the active agent and creates an artistic race of translators in whom the sense of language produces its final and rarest flowers.

This curious state of mind, to which it is a matter of indifference what is being translated, as long as the translator can express himself through other, distant works and show his own mental adaptability; this histrionic interpreting; this philological poetry, which spread itself in the times of the Alexandrines, again in the period of humanism, and more than ever in our own nineteenth and twentieth centuries, is the polar opposite of folk-poetry. What was merely a formal limitation in the case of the popular poet, has here become a substantial one. Here, too, the format is small, but not as regards literary extent, only as regards the human content, which is not allowed to have a magnitude of its own so that it may the more easily enter into every alien one. Here, too, we have a mnemonic art, but not as regards material

---

[1] Cf. my essay, " Über Borchardts deutschen Dante ", in *Neue Deutsche Beiträge*, ed. by H. von Hofmannsthal, I, vol. 2, Munich, 1923.

things, only as regards experiences, which are not allowed to be original because they have to remain learned reminiscences. Here, too, the shadow of language is over the process, but instead of the shadow of the one mother tongue there are the shadows cast by the many tongues of philology. This muse is to the popular muse as a city hetæra to a peasant girl. We do not wish to make either an artistic or a moral judgment of value by this simile; for there are great and notable masters as well as small, miserable dilettantes in both camps. The simile will not be despised by those who see the hetæra as a part of human society and not as something immoral; for they know that the honourableness of many families lives on the wages of sin. The radiance of national languages would be similarly dimmed if there were no paid translators, and no born and enthusiastic ones.

Speech, even language itself, would become colourless if such artists of translation were not continually renewing its stock from other arts, painting, sculpture, music, etc., and creating a synæsthetic bond in spite of the barriers of language and style. Theophile Gautier was probably the most famous and most gifted form broker of this kind. He never tired of introducing with his magic pen oil paintings, pastels, copper etchings, enamel work, gem engravings, statues, symphonies, etc., into the French language; and in him we can study the soul of this apparently soulless æstheticism. The insatiableness of the striving after form and the will to give expression to things are never satisfied with any form material; they rush from language to language, from image to image, and delight in the ceaseless mutation and recreation of forms.

> Par de lentes métamorphoses
> Les marbres blancs en blanches chairs,
> Les fleurs roses en lèvres roses
> Se refont dans les corps divers.

Art critics may condemn such restlessness as weakness, as a lack of personality and dignity, as the incapacity of

being creative in any one particular art form, as prostitution or dissipated impotence. But it nevertheless has its
valuable and fruitful side in the sphere of language
community. Such poets of translation are the embodied
medium ; and where it is a question of language as a
medium, they do their best service. National languages owe
to these men the enrichment of their style and vocabulary,
and a greater suppleness of their word order. Since they
have no sentiment of their own, they take up those of
their mother tongue ; and since these are not moral but
æsthetic—sentiments of taste, a sense of style—everything
they undertake and achieve is done in the name of that
impersonal and universal force we have called the genius
of a language and have described as a receptive being
incapable of making conquests by itself.

The masters of translation, however, dominated and
filled with zeal by this force, place their will in its service.
They become form robbers, range through neighbouring
languages and the spatially and temporally most distant
literatures and art treasures, and, with the ravenous
hunger of an æsthetic imperialism, seize everything they
desire. But in order to hold it fast, carry it away and
fuse it into the language genius of their own people, they
must break the form and nevertheless take home the
best of it, its innermost soul—a difficult and critical
procedure. This is the Gordian knot of the mind. Who
cuts it, conquers a world of knowledge and experience ;
who unravels it lovingly, gains in addition a wealth of
poetic images.

The delicate and artistic solution would not be possible
if the form could not be broken in such a way that only
its shell falls to pieces, while the inner form is preserved.
Translation as an end in itself and as an art rests on the
relation between outer and inner language form.[1] The
practical and prosaic translator does not concern himself
with these delicate aspects.; he breaks the work and gives

---

[1] This relation has been discussed at length in several sections of
my *Gesammelte Aufsätze zur Sprachphilosophie*, Munich, 1923.

up the whole shell in order to gain only the juice of sentiment. It is a good craft, which even Goethe has praised. " I honour," he says, " both rhythm and rhyme, by which poetry really becomes poetry ; but what is really deep and fundamentally active, truly educative and helpful is that which remains when a poet is translated into prose. Then there remains the pure and perfect content, which, when it is absent, a brilliant exterior may delude us into imagining as present, and, when it is there, may hide." [1] Hence for youth, which has to be educated, and for the masses, which have to be influenced, he recommends the making of prosaic Homer and Shakespeare translations, and reminds them of Luther's Bible : " For the fact that this excellent man has given to us as in one casting and in our mother tongue a work of such diverse styles, with its poetry, history, commands and teachings, has helped the cause of religion more than if he had attempted to copy the individual peculiarities of the original." Nevertheless Goethe recognizes not only one, but two levels above prosaic translation : [2] ' parodistic ', " in which one tries to enter into the state of mind of the foreigner, but only substitutes one's own sense for his." At this level poetry is merely a pleasing decoration, a costume or a rhetorical addition, so that we might call it the rhetorical level. Above it, as the third and highest, is the critical, lyrical level, " at which we should like to make the translation identical with the original, so that the one shall not be valid instead of the other, but shall take its place."—" This type at first met with strong resistance." It still meets with it to-day ; indeed, every system of æsthetics and language philosophy, which identifies what is valid with what exists, and the inner form with the outer, must reject it. For it is as clear as daylight that a German Homer is in no way whatever Greek ; but he may have the same validity, namely, on condition that it is possible to express in the

[1] *Dichtung und Wahrheit*, III, 11.
[2] *Noten und Abhandlungen zum Westöstlichen Diwan.*

German language not only the sentiment of the ancient Greeks, but with it and out of it Homer's own attitude to, and expression of, life.

Whether this is more or less achieved in practice or not, it is at any rate theoretically possible. For to a specific sentiment and meaning there always exactly corresponds an equally definite mental attitude and an inner language form, in respect of which the external forms as an externally conditioned manifold can appear in different guises and have more than one meaning. Every concrete language creation, a word, a sentence, a single suffix or a thick book with many thousands of words, a speech or a poem, in a sense has more than one meaning as soon as one takes it into one's hand, that is, lifts it out of the stream of mental life that flows through and carries it. It is the equivocalness of that which is past and has become fossilized. Who is able to breathe life again into a sloughed skin, and for the second time to recreate that unique thing, which has for ever flown out of it and out of itself ? That life was the inner form, which in the meantime has itself changed and now flows through life in new skins and language forms. The volumes of Shakespeare are such sloughs ; and if we read them with the best understanding and with inner sympathy in their original text, we are, strictly speaking, already translating. Merely listening to and understanding the speech of my countryman and contemporary is a translation of *his* meaning into my own. Wherever and whenever we enter into the speech of someone else, or our own past speech, we are translating.[1] The difference between this unconscious and universal form of translation, and conscious, extraordinary translation lies only in the magnitude of the obstacle and the mental effort of overcoming, bridging, acquiring and reproducing. Each one of us translates and cannot help doing it whenever and wherever he comes into spiritual contact with the metaphysical language community of

[1] Cf. Giovanni Gentile, " Il torto e il diritto delle traduzioni " *Rivista di Cultura*, I, Rome, 15. April 1920, p. 811.

humanity and of the universe. And everyone does it out of the same personal desire to maintain the autonomy of their individual speech, that is, out of the desire to restate in their own language form all those things that assail them with other tongues and threaten to spoil their language taste, bewilder their language faculty, and break the power of their language. Translation is the defensive aspect of our speech. The artistically perfect translations of some national literature must be regarded and valued as strategic fortifications, behind which the language genius of a people defends itself against the foreigner by the ruse of taking over as much from him as possible. About forty translations of the *Divina Commedia* exist in Germany. If no one satisfies us absolutely, and we still expect more, it is a sign of the strength with which Dante's spirit and inner meaning presses upon us, and how uncertain we are that we have as yet penetrated to the final secrets of his sentiment. For this sentiment is identical with the inner language form only, not with the Italian phonetic form, which can be discarded. The two have grown together, but for that very reason are not identical.

If we attempt to analyse this inner language form, we see it as the form of language on the one side, and as sentiment or as inner meaning on the other. But nowhere are we able to find the crucial point at which the one passes over into the other ; for the concept of the inner language form is precisely this identity of speech and meaning. Here translation is at an end. The inner language form is untranslatable, true, and always unique. The being that, in the external language form is called *cavallo* by an Italian and *horse* by an Englishman, in the inner sphere is an actual horse to the Englishman and an actual *cavallo* to the Italian, who here and now enunciates the name and means it to express something that has a meaning. That is to say, the name of the horse-being is by no means identical with the image, the picture, or even with the concept of ' horse ', but, if I may say so, it is the ' horse-horse '. In other words it is not a name or a concept, but a belief, or, as the philosophers used to say, an idea, though this led to all kinds of misapprehensions. Instead of saying ' the idea of the horse ', it would be better to say ' the horse that is felt or believed or willed in language, the mythical horse '. For whenever a belief becomes language, myths arise. In a myth, religious certainty speaks, ceases to rest as certainty within itself, and enters the uncertain path of meaning, where everything psychic becomes relative and therefore attributable, indeed of necessity attributable, to all sorts of things. If we mean something, it cannot be indeterminable. The ' something ' that we mean is our definite goal. Hence the tendency of the mind towards a definite goal is the essential essence of all meaning and therefore also of the inner language form, which is nothing more than meaning expressing itself in language. It is the meaning of language, which is in fact distinguishable from what has actually been said, but can only realize itself in complete unity with it. When we regard language as energy, as being on the offensive, and not merely on the defensive, as continually realizing itself, striving out of the psychic into the external phonetic form and in it giving substance to its infinite meanings, we are directing our attention to the inner language form and our philological activity to this dynamic field. It is here alone that language can be apprehended as energy, here alone that it has sense and life, here alone that its taste, style, and form tendencies are identical with the sentiments and meaning of its speakers ; and it is here alone, therefore, that a language community can also be a community of sentiment.

Externally, and if we do not understand it, a strange language always has a strange sound ; inwardly interpreted, however, it will have strange sentiments only in so far as it has a meaning. Within a national language like the German, all kinds of things can be meant and said, so that it might appear as if the individual languages had no meaning in themselves. Nevertheless their possibilities of psychic expression and meaning are not simply unlimited. Although not restricted and circumscribed, they are nevertheless engaged and orientated in a definite direction. But to determine this direction is a difficult and delicate task. As connoisseurs we can undogmatically indicate such directions, for instance in the manner attributed to the emperor Charles V, who said that one should speak Italian with one's mistress, French with men, German with one's horses and Spanish with God. With a certain amount of general education, it is not difficult to say witty things about the characteristics of different national languages. But how little of that will stand the test of a critical examination !

To begin with, the scientific thinker can only come to the negative conclusion that within a language community everything is original and determined by sentiment, which it immediately realizes in its inner language form and does not have to achieve through translation. And, as we now see, that is at once everything and nothing. Nothing : for even the most characteristic psychic meaning, created with complete originality in the form material of a language, like a poem of Goethe, has to be translated from Goethe's language into his own language by everyone, even a German, who wants to understand it and make it his own ; everything : for no national language, not even that of the obscurest primitive tribe, may be valued so low that we believe it incapable of expressing in its very own way the deepest, highest and most intimate things which can move human souls. The intellectual arrogance of the European and North American prevents him at the moment from acknowledging this fact ; but he is nevertheless beginning to take it into account, for it is this fact that makes it possible to spread the message of Christian love through its missionaries over the length and breadth of the earth. *Nulle secte ni religion n'a toujours été sur la terre, que la religion chrétienne*, as Pascal says. By nature the community of language is as much a fundamental relationship as the community of religious sentiment.   Expressed negatively, this means there is as *little* of the one as there is of the other.

The empirical concepts of a language community live on the dialectic of these opposed views, for a language community is formed by the interplay of linguistic originality and borrowing through translation.   The nets of all the language communities that we know, from the dialect of a tribe to the literary language of a nation and the international languages of commerce, are woven out of poetry and translation, original creation and borrowing, out of own and alien sentiments.   That is why they all vacillate with the same equivocality between the characteristic definiteness of sentiment and the most neutral generalities.   There is in German no word, no language form that has not at the same time got truly German, as well as general and borrowed characteristics, that is not both characteristically national and indifferent.   It is true that historical grammar tries to separate experienced from borrowed forms and achieves much valuable insight into the reciprocal reactions and the loan system between several language communities ; but it is never able to make a watertight division between indigenous and immigrant forms.   A word, whose phonetic form shows it to be indigenous, may be a foreign word because of its meaning, and vice versa.   For example, there is hardly any word that is so characteristic of the German psyche, so truly German because of its use, as the modern foreign word ' *kolossal* '.   In so far as it mirrors a truly national sentiment, it is almost comparable to the famous *Gemütlichkeit* or *Sehnsucht*.   Its inner language form has the most aristocratic, pure-blooded ancestors, like *michel, rîch, küene, degenlich, ungebaere, ungevuoge,* etc., not to mention the gods, giants and monsters of Germanic myths, which had been *kolossal* in our eyes for thousands of years before this word came into our language.   I should almost like to believe that the creativeness of a people with regard to sentiment and feeling is better studied in its so-called loan and foreign words, than in its linguistic heritage. It would have to be proved by investigation, and it would undoubtedly be of value to examine the German mind in the light of its foreign words, and to seek originality in translations. For scientific philology, at any rate, it is more easily visible there than in the truly original, which, by virtue of the comparative method, can only be understood as deduction and translation.

To leave linguistic originality in its specific originality and judge it on its own merits, is above all the task of literary and stylistic, not of grammatical criticism. Nevertheless within their special fields, the history of literature and of language, stylistic and grammatical studies, play into one another's hands to such an extent, that from both sides translation and poetry, the foreign and the indigenous are alternately critically examined. Indeed, the interweaving of grammatical, comparative, deductive, and explanatory methods with the æsthetic, idiographical, stylistic, and interpretive methods must become ever closer if we want to get at the living weft of language communities and characteristics. But, if the mutual contacts are not to become confused, this is only possible under one condition, that each investigator is perfectly clear in each individual case as to which thread it is he is spinning, which of them is the leader, and which the servant from his aspect of knowledge.

If a language, or a coherent group of languages, is examined as a relatively closed community, the student will find that all the other factors that are capable of founding and keeping together a human community, such as the landscape with its mountains, valleys, streams, roads, cities and deserts, politics, commerce, industry, the arts and sciences, the churches and religions, *eo ipso* will contribute to the stream of language. But all these facts, institutions, activities, and interests will be of significance to him not on their own merits, but always as forces and resistances that help to form communities, that is, as

social forces. And the fact of the community, again, he
will have to study from the point of view of sentiments,
which give it life, form it, and in their turn are formed
by it. Nor will he be able to rest content with the
psychology of common sentiments, with the analysis of the
ethos and pathos of his community, but he will have to
lead from them into those things that are artistically
common, the style, taste, and usage of language, specialize
them and make them concrete. Only now will he have
arrived at a point where a scientific grammar can be
dissected out of the community through which he has
ranged, and set up as something valid *in abstracto*, by
which the further movements of a living language can
be measured and observed, explained afresh in their
intimate cohesion with the life of the community, and
understood in their fusion with sentiment and taste.
Most of the errors and onesidednesses of philology arise
because some factor, a historical link, a momentary phase
through which the activity of language passed, is neglected,
overlooked, or disregarded by the investigator. Usually
it is the æsthetic aspect, the final and most important,
which is disregarded.

We shall protect ourselves most effectively against this
danger by the insight, which we want particularly to
emphasize now : that although language furthers and acts
for the social intercourse and the communities of man, it
has not got the power of founding a community by itself,
nor of maintaining one. Language societies arise late,
are impure, and unstable. Men first come together under
the pressure of their natural needs, and only after these
primitive, animal-like communities have been formed
can language arise as an attempt at a spiritual transfusion
and elevation of social existence. Language is neither
root nor trunk, but flower and fruit of social life. It is
therefore in a sense super-social, and this is overlooked
by those who can see in it no more than a practical and
empirical reality within society. The French philologists,
Saussure, Meillet, Bally, Sechehaye and others, and the

German language psychologists and grammarians of the Leipzig school of W. Wundt and K. Brugmann still cling to this narrow concept of language.[1] The æsthetic aspect of lonely self-sufficiency and the religious aspect of super-human influences are always present in language ; but they hope that without being punished, they can overlook these influences or irradiations from other spheres. In fact they are disregarding the central idea of language, banishing themselves from the spiritual home of their subject, and peopling the periphery with the shadowy renunciations of science.

Only where sentiment and taste reciprocally bind each other is language in its element and at home with itself. The inner language form is the temple, in which every external language form is sanctioned. Without this blessing a language community could nowhere and never come about. It is a mysterious process, which fortunately can be made externally visible, namely in rhetoric emphasis.

" When words are used emphatically, they are taken at their word, as it were. Former experiences of the audience are cited literally and appealed to, with visible or invisible inverted commas." [2] By means of emphasis the inner language form is raised to the surface, and the silently slumbering sense of words made to shout, which may be comical, or pathetic and dignified in effect.[3] Emphasis makes the innermost sense of a word to the bold outermost ; it gives point. That is why words that

---

[1] In his posthumous *Cours de linguistique générale*, Lausanne and Paris, 1916, Ferdinand de Saussure with classical exactness and narrow-ness separated the concept of language (*langue*) from the sentiment aspect of language (*langage*), and made the bloodless system of the signs made by speakers the exclusive subject of philology.

[2] Franz Dornseiff in the small but important essay, " Zwei Arten der Ausdrucksverstärkung ", in the *Festschrift für Wackernagel*, 1923, p. 105.

[3] E.g. " Das Schwein führt seinen Namen mit Recht ", or " Der Meinige ? " " Auf ewig und in des Worts verwegenster Bedeutung." *Don Carlos*, I, 9.

are constantly used emphatically by a language community have their meaning narrowed down or specialized.[1]
Out of the plains of general language usage they rear
themselves like mountain tops into the rarer air of a
special community of sentiment. " The members of a
group, who feel that they belong together in religious,
economic, æsthetic, or caste matters, either add some
definite attribute to the words they hear, or have some
specific opposite in their mind. The outsider, and particularly the translator, gets the impression that they
are all talking in ellipses. So to the Greek painters φάρμακον
meant ' paint ', γράφειν ' to paint ', πίναξ ' painting '. . . .
The whole concept of humanity rests on such an emphatic
use of the word human in contrast to *inhumanus-ferus*.
A new accent of value was introduced when early Hellenism
began to be cosmopolitan. γνῶσις got its Helleno-
Christian meaning of ' mystical awareness ', because
generations of mystics added the genitive θεῶ and later
merely added it in thought. The change in the meaning
of the word μάρτυς from ' witness ' to ' martyr ' follows
exactly the same lines." [2] More than that, all persons,
all places receive their own name, their cognomen, by the
emphatic pointing of generic names. The inner meaning
of every proper name is emphatic in origin ; it is meant
sensu eminentiore, κατ' ἐξοχήν, par excellence. Only after it
has penetrated its object with this point of feeling does it
become fossilized and conventional. " In this connection
such wide-spread names like *Aue, Berg, Bruck, Brühl,
Brunn, Burg, Haag, Hof, Kapel, Gmünd, Münster, Ried,
Stein, Weiler, Zell, Altstadt, Neustadt (Villeneuve, Newtown),
Neuburg (Neuchatel, Newcastle), Hochburg, Neukirch,
Mühlberg*, etc., are particularly instructive. Originally
they served only the inhabitants and their nearest neighbours, for whom they were sufficient to distinguish these

---

[1] A number of examples of this process in the history of the French
language is given by Kr. Nyrop, *Grammaire historique de la langue
française*, vol. IV, Copenhagen, 1913, § 215 ff.

[2] Dornseiff, *op. cit.*, p. 106.

places from neighbouring ones." [1] This last statement unfortunately obscures the primary state of affairs, which is the belief in language, the magical projection of a word into an object. This projection takes place because of a sense of community of the speaker with his fellows and with the landscape, which he calls by name and baptizes. " Our Brühl ", the people of the Brühl say ; and the ' our ', even when it is not spoken aloud, breathes that unanimity with which the children of the same earth greet one another. This deep, inner sense of community that is the godparent to every baptismal act of language, is not always so emphatic that it can be directly seen and demonstrated ; it does not always enter consciousness ; but it is always present behind the stage settings of convention, whence it is ready to break forth at any time.

What is commonly called rhetorical emphasis, is merely a pale reflexion or echo of linguistic magic and incantations. We shall best understand what emphasis really is if we imagine typical cases of its strongest, most glaring, and most condensed activity : fearful curses, terrible incantations, superstitious acts of baptism, the calling up of demons and gods, and not merely intellectual quotations from books.

The essential point for us is that the speaking magician, the man who is being emphatic, is completely shut in, and, as it were, fused into the magic ring of the language community involved. In the instant of emphatic expression his relation to language is not that of an individual ; [2] it is not really he who is speaking, it is the word, it is language itself that is speaking. He does not talk, he does not speak, he says nothing that is his own—he is merely lending his voice to the formula. Anyone who knew the formula could do it just as well as he. The

---

[1] Hermann Paul, *Prinzipien der Sprachgeschichte*, 4th. edn., Halle, 1909, § 62.

[2] This is the reason why I had no cause for dealing with emphasis in the essay " Der Einzelne und die Sprache " in *Gesammelte Aufsätze zur Sprachphilosophie*, as Dornseiff expected me to.

active principle, the energy of language, now lies in the word, in the formula, in language itself, not in the speaker. He functions merely as the accidental medium. Through the strength of the formula the magician's apprentice can make a water-carrier out of the broom-stick just as well as his master can. The broom obeys him ; and only because the apprentice has forgotten the *second* formula do we know that he was not the master. That abstract and dead things like words, syllables, parts of speech, formulæ, should become concrete and living ; that linguistic shells should be filled with supernatural powers, is only possible, indeed only thinkable, because a single will, a single sentiment, takes hold of all concerned, because all concerned allow it to take place. But we can only allow that to happen to us of which we approve. An æsthetic element is concerned in every act of suggestion of the will. Whether we call the gate through which an alien will enters into us ear or eye or nose or touch or sensibility or the power of perception, the spirit on guard, who opens and closes the gate and lies awake behind the eyelids, is an æsthetic force—taste. Even the simple savage intuitively feels this when he thinks that his gods and demons, his friends and foes : fire, rain, or lightning, will only obey those requests, commands, invocations, names, and words that are acceptable to them, that is, that are to their taste. If one has guessed the name that is most acceptable to such unreliable beings, if one has found and prepared the linguistic bait they are willing to swallow, they can easily be guided and dominated, for one has entered their language community, which is at the same time a community of taste, of sentiment, and therefore of natural inclination and probable intention.

Once the inner community, that is, the community based on sentiment, has been attained, the æsthetic threshold of the outer language form passed, and the words, names, and magic formulæ found by which agree-ment is achieved, the emphatic enunciation of these words is often no longer necessary to obtain the full effect. For now understanding, the community of sentiment, can save us the trouble. Hence the elliptic character of so many magic words and emphatic phrases. In the example taken from the scene between Don Carlos and the Marquis Posa (footnote 3, p. 188), " *Der Meinige ?* "—" *Auf ewig und in des Wortes verwegenster Bedeutung* ", the emphatic word is not spoken at all. Between such good friends " *Der Deinige* " is obvious without further mention. Even the sentence " *Das Schwein führt seinen Namen mit Recht* ", should really be " *Das Schwein führt seinen Namen 'Schwein' mit Recht* ". It is the peculiar privilege of emphasis that it can either underline or swallow its words. Since outer and inner language form come together in it, sentiment and taste become one in it ; what is meant is already said, what is said already understood before it has been spoken—somewhat as in Dante's paradise words are spoken only in deference to the earthly shell of the wanderer. Magic words do not need to be shouted out ; murmured or whispered their effect is even more certain. If we said before that through emphasis the inner language form is turned outward and the slumbering sense of words made to shout, we could just as well say—and this is the reverse side of the same process—that through emphasis the outer language form is merged once more in the peace of the inner, and the loud words silenced so that they again achieve the inwardness of their essential meaning.

This silent calling and loud silence, this dumb reciting of emphatic expression is possible simply because it binds our minds together in a community of experiences, because it once more calls up, summarizes, and appeals to the common experiences and feelings of those present. The final verses of the comedies of Lope de Vega and his imitators are perhaps the most famous and clearest examples of this side to emphasis. They quote the title of the play, thus making no further announcements, but repeating it as a word that has been fulfilled, whose

deeper meaning has become concrete, meaningful and
valuable through the succession of events portrayed
actively and passively by the actors and experienced
through vision by the spectators, the *Senado* :

> Pues el mar de sus milagros
> Es tan profundo, aquí demos
> Fin a la vida y la muerte
> De nuestro español *San Diego.*
>
> .   .   .   .   .
>
> Corre esa cortina, y dése
> Fin a los Caravajales,
> Cuya sangre resplandece
> Hoy en la peña de Martos,
> Porque fué *Sangre inocente.*

Or, when it is the end of a comedy, it is closed by a jocular
emphasis, an ironically smiling quotation from himself :

> Mi dicha alabo.
>   —Alabalda,
> Y acabando la comedia,
> *¡ Mirad a quién alabais !—*
>
> .   .   .   .   .
>
> Hoy quedamos
> Todos, Señor, con dineros.—
> Para que decir podamos :
> *Dineros son calidad,*
> Pues se alcanza con hallarlos.

If the reader does not believe that the italicized passages
really are emphatic quotations, he need only examine the
endings of some of Calderón's comedies :

> Y aquí,
> Senado, acabe con esto
> " Lances de Amor y Fortuna "
> Del amante más perfecto.

If *Lances de Amor y Fortuna* were not thought of as being
in inverted commas, the poet would have written *acaben.*
Again :

> El " peor está que estaba "
> Nunca ha encajado más bien,
> Que ahora que están casados ;
> Y así : ite comedia est.

N

Naturally only those who have seen or at any rate read the play can fully appreciate the peculiar wit and the full meaning of the emphatic endings. The community to which the sentiment of the play is imparted or suggested is therefore composed almost haphazardly of those members in the audience at a theatre who are willing to pay attention and receive impressions, and of readers. It is essentially an occasional, invisible community of people : Spaniards of the seventeenth century, German, English, American professors, and learned connoisseurs of the nineteenth and twentieth centuries, none of whom needs to know of the existence of the other. In such a variegated and loose way does the inner language form build up the communities in whose inconstant and incalculable psychic spaces the so-called winged words are echoed. One is reminded of the evangelic parable of the sower or the Augustine idea of ' the invisible church ' ; and one realizes that these inner language communities are continually dissolving, reforming, and recreating themselves. They are like the clouds in the sky ; they form dense masses, are torn apart again and evaporate, and recondense into mists that fly over the spatially and temporally fixed empirical language communities. To each of these they can give fructifying rain and from each receive the steaming spirit of the sentiments of taste in language. In this sense they are bound to all languages and dialects on earth, but not chained to any one in particular. So there is a freely mobile, living relation of mutual dependence and interaction between the airy communities of the inner language form and the solid ones of the outer—not unlike the relation between the earth and its atmosphere.

If, like Saussure, we study language merely in its outer forms, grammatical structures, and social systems, separate *langue* from *langage*, and attempt to explain the abstract *langage* out of itself, by " regarding it as a dictionary, all of whose identical reprints have been distributed among the individuals of the community ",[1] we shall fall into the same error as the geographer who thinks he can understand the structure or the relief of a continent or landscape without regard to meteorological and climatic factors.

This dry linguistic study that shuts out the air and the light, forgets that even within closed social and national language communities, even below the uniform grammatical and lexicographical roofs, there are the atmosphere and the atmospheric phenomena of inner language. How many styles and groups of styles float about within the German language at any given epoch ; and how many cf them are not socially, or economically, or politically conditioned, but conditioned by sentiments, tastes, and art forms.

In classical Greek, for example, there are a definite number of ' nominal ' compositions, which are grammatically possible anywhere, but are only used where they are in accord with style, that is, where they correspond to a pathos, an ethos, in short, to a psychic attitude that is immediately determined by æsthetic and literary factors, and not by external social or any other factors.[2] Again, in fifteenth and sixteenth century Spanish we find the imperfect used with a present sense ; and this use has its basis and validity solely in popular romances.[3]

It has been observed that in almost all European languages poets allow themselves a freedom of word order that is denied to prose writers, and that the forms of style born in this way have a greater freedom than the more pedestrian and comical. The neo-French symbolists use prepositions and conjunctions in a way that is despised by all other classes of society.[4] The use of the French *Passé defini* is to-day, after it has become impossible in practical intercourse, in the widest sense only dependent

---

[1] F. de Saussure, *op. cit.*, p. 39.

[2] G. Meyer, *Die stilistische Verwendung der Nominalkomposition im Griechischen*, Leipzig, 1923.

[3] Cf. " Ein Spanischer Brief an Hugo von Hofmannsthal ", in *Festschrift für Hofmannsthal*, Munich, 1924.

[4] L. Spitzer, *Aufsätze zur romanischen Syntax und Stilistik*, Halle, 1918, p. 288 ff.

on style, taste, and the inner language form. To a similar extent the suppression of the *e muet* has become a question of style and taste, so that I would suggest calling this sound the ' ornamental *e* '.

So the plane of the inner language form is crossed by numerous ' isophones ', ' isolexes ', and ' isorhemes ', which are so mobile that they can hardly be confined in an atlas of language taste. Nevertheless, or rather, because of this, it is time that we should track them down systematically and not merely sporadically, as hitherto. We shall not in this way obtain a geography of the atmosphere of languages, just as little as there are atlases of clouds and mists. But if the meteorologists have succeeded in making a typology and casuistry of cloud formations, there is no reason why the philologists should not try in a similarly systematic way to attack the secrets of the inner language form, the levels and gradations of language tastes, the various species of style. They would thereby enter a path along which the historians of literature have long since decided to meet them.

The interplay between the flexible communities founded upon the inner language form and the inflexible ones that rest on the outer, takes on such an inexhaustible variety of forms that it must be regarded and investigated as an historical process, that is, as the history of the French, the German, the English languages. The fundamental rules according to which the game is played, however, should now have become clear. They consist in the continuous weaving of threads between the metaphysical and the empirical community of language, between inner, mobile, emphatic and therefore untranslatable language forms and outer, rigid, metaphorical forms, which, in so far as they are limited, need to be translated, extended, applied, and changed, so that their inertia may not become a dangerous, fossilized obstruction to the thought that has to be expressed in terms of language. Strictly speaking, emphatic forms of speech are as untranslatable as the proper names of a community of language. They are unmetaphorical, whereas the metaphorical side of language is no more than its translatability, its external aspect that we can transcend, as opposed to its inner nature, out of which we neither can nor wish to escape ; for it is as mobile as thought itself, indeed, it *is* thought. To thought the external language forms, the grammatical categories, the geographical language boundaries, do not act as obstacles, but serve as supports, bridges, and transitions. All external language communities, all the systems and structures of language usage, exist and rest on the bosom of linguistic thought, which envelops, carries and fructifies them, like the ocean the earth.

CHAPTER VIII

LANGUAGE AND SCIENCE

LINGUISTIC thinking is different from logical or scientific thinking and yet not different, in so far as there is only one thinking process. As an active, theoretical attitude of the mind, linguistic and logical thought are the same in essence. As often as we try to separate the one from the other, we find that somehow they always come together again. It is therefore not thought as such that we have to analyse ; we can only distinguish the paths it takes, its directions and aims. Linguistic thinking tries to image the world ; logical thinking tries to understand it. Through the power of imagery the world becomes an appearance and, since the mind apprehends and represents it as a pure phenomenon, we remain uncertain whether the world is real or illusory. As long as the mind continues to image or to think linguistically, this will not trouble us. On the contrary, the fact that the world has a face, seems to us eminently satisfactory and pleasing. The mind finds enjoyment in the artistic vision and creation, which we call beauty. Only intuitively, as religious mind, will it have the certainty of belief that there is something substantial about its own images, visions, and dreams. Because of that, uncertainty need not arise ; and as long as the mind sees and creates, uncertainty will not become a dialectical thorn, will not arouse doubt.

At the beginning of scientific thinking stands doubt, and not wonder, as the simple-minded Greeks thought ; for wonder is much more an accompaniment of linguistic or intuitive thinking. Between linguistic and logical thinking there are no comfortable, gentle, unnoticeable transitions, indeed, no progress, no ascending or descending steps ; it is a complete parting of the ways.

What, then, does thought have to do to free itself of the tendencies of language ? It does not cease to image and represent, as though this tendency were a false one ; it keeps it and yet relinquishes it. Thought is not a person or a body and is therefore not bound to space and time. Like a gas, it can act in different conductors at the same time. By turning back on itself, by doubt, reflexion, speculation, it turns away from the appearances of the world, and understands substantial reality within itself. This understanding of reality is called truth.

It is obvious, that in moments of doubting, in.reflexive and speculative aversion from imagery, when thought turns back on itself, it can understand itself, but cannot for that very reason represent, express, and communicate itself. A concept in its logical purity can be represented in no language ; nor is language called upon to represent it, since what is immediately clear—indeed, this clearness itself—does not need the mediation of language.

Only when thought ceases to reflect on itself and the mind looks at the world with new eyes, will it desire in some way to express in language what is substantial about appearances, and the apprehended difference between appearance and reality. This is done in the forms and expressions we call prose as distinct from the forms of poetry, which are poorer in reflexions. Poetry and prose are not two kinds of language, but two species of style.[1] For since truth, concepts, reflexion, and speculation, in short, thought that has turned away from appearances, do not express themselves directly, thought can only communicate itself indirectly, that is, again as appearance and by the circuitous paths of linguistic thinking. This process, by which thinking stops its linguistic activities, turns back on itself, and then continues to speak with a critical consciousness and in a more circumspect style, is known

[1] This thesis has been discussed at length in my *Gesammelte Aufsätze zur Sprachphilosophie*, Munich, 1923, p. 212 ff.

to everyone from his childhood. If he occasionally forgets it, he is reminded by the common warning : first think, then speak.

That it should be at all necessary to give such warnings, which the man of science can hardly repeat often enough to himself, is a sign that there are—not in logic, not in truth and reality, but within language and in the phenomenal world — innumerable seductive, pleasant, easy, hardly noticeable transitions between imagistic and conceptual thinking. With the criteria of inner language the one cannot be distinguished from the other at all, or the transitions determined. Science can mask itself in poetic, poetry in prosaic raiment ; and those who have no logical training and philosophic education must not flatter themselves that they can unmask these masquerades of the spirit.

Since we are concerned with the philosophy of language, it is these transitions and masquerades of the logos in language, the conscious as well as the unconscious, the helpful and the misleading, that are particularly instructive. If we are to judge them correctly, we must not forget that the turning away of thought from speech, the unveiling of the concept, is a logical fact ; the turning of conceptual to linguistic thinking, its appearances, disguises, and representations, is a linguistic fact. If we forget this fundamental law, and confuse the aspect of aversion with that of reversion, we become involved in errors and fall either into sophism or allegory. Sophism is the name of the logical or scientific vice that takes the aspect of the veiling of the logos to be the same as its aversion or unveiling, while allegory sins in the opposite sense, on the side of linguistic thought, by smuggling the logical aspect of unveiled thought, thought that has turned away from contemplation, into the series of modes of expressions and regarding it as identical with the aspect of concrete imagery.[1]

[1] Cf. Croce, " Sulla natura dell'allegoria ", *Nota lette alla R. Accad. di Scienze morali e politiche di Napoli*, 26 aprile, 1922.

Sophisms would not be possible or even thinkable were it not for the fact that language thinking momentarily experiences a kind of arrest or petrification when the logos, the concept, arises out of it. Anything that wants to live in logical thought must die and petrify in linguistic thought. A thought cannot become a concept other than by emerging from the chrysalis of its prelinguistic life, and discarding the dead shell. These dead shells no longer are immediately meaningful language forms ; they are merely a kind of track, footmarks left by the logos as it launched itself. In their resemblance to colourless and rigid formulæ, and in their grammatical schematism, we can still trace and recognize the labours that logical thought had to undertake in order to free itself from linguistic thought.[1] The demand that this freedom makes, in other words, its spiritual necessity, is contained in the ' law of identity ', according to which everything that has been thought must be equal to itself, $a = a$.

This law, however, is not true. In the intuitively apprehended world of appearances, as well as in logically understood metaphysical reality, there are movement, life, activity. Hence our linguistic as well as our logical thinking, to follow the flow of things, must be mobile and changeable, associative and dialectical. There is logically only *one* point at which thought has the possibility, the desire, the will and the compulsion to insist, if it is not to lose itself, on the identity of its objects with itself. We might say that it is along the line of death, where the world of appearances touches the metaphysical beyond, that is, where conceptual, pure, logical thinking has to maintain itself against the phantasies, dreams and imagery of linguistic thinking. Without the law of identity we should be continually confusing appearance and reality. It therefore has its application chiefly where logical and linguistic thought come into conflict, and appearances are mastered by concepts, above all in mathematics and

[1] We have indicated before how successfully Ernst Cassirer has prosecuted these studies.

the natural sciences. Here logical thinking shows its rigidity and exactitude far more than in the historical and philosophical sciences, in which the world of appearances certainly also has to be distinguished from metaphysical reality, but in which the separation is not so absolute that every incursion of the supernatural into the natural is felt as a disturbing factor. The historical and philosophical sciences are more concerned in apprehending the connections and activities by which the metaphysical becomes appearance. This phenomenological tendency of conceptual thinking demands a dependence on, and return to linguistic thinking, which would only be an obstacle to the mathematician and the physicist.

The spiritual educative value of mathematical and scientific studies—apart from their value as knowledge—lies in the liberation from words, in the overcoming of linguistic thinking, dreaming, vague intuition and the shackles of the mythical, magical, and fantastic; in short, in what is usually called ' enlightenment '.

Scientific thinking breaks that emphatic attitude of man which we have described above; that religious belief in language, in prayer, in magic, in meaning and speaking; that close interrelation between sentiments and the words in which they are expressed. The naïveté of the inner language form—by which a ' horse ' became the myth, ' horse-horse '—and all the proper names of things are broken, their baptismal certificates are destroyed, so that there remain only the outer signs, the generic names, the formal order, in short, the translatability and the exchange value of words and languages. In terms of the concepts of mathematics and the natural sciences all languages are external and equal. These concepts can be put in any language, since they merely clothe themselves in the outer linguistic form, but live upon and exhaust the inner. The mathematical concepts of the circle, the triangle, the sphere, of number and so on, or the scientific concepts of force, matter, the atom, attain their full and exact scientific meaning precisely because all imagistic, fantastic, mythical and linguistic thinking that may still linger in them is rigidly excised.

It is due to this negative and abstractive behaviour of the logos, that mathematics and natural science nevertheless grow on the soil of linguistic thought, like light on the wick that it destroys. And since in mental life every destruction is a spur and an incentive to renewed and multiplied creation, the abstractions of scientific concept formation cause an intense hunger after imagination and observant intuition, such as the poet would not have by himself. From the ends of the earth and the depths of the sea, from the whole cosmos of appearances, science gathers material for the senses, arms them with telescopes and microscopes, forces our imagination to look in the same direction as its logical questionings, and, not content with receiving intuitive experiences by the grace of accident or fate, like pious and simple-minded poets, it creates experiences according to the standards of its desire for knowledge, prepares them, investigates, and experiments. So science castigates and enriches, conserves and accelerates, prunes and sharpens, obstructs and drives forward linguistic thought in the service of the logos, which it rapes, deprives of its naïveté, and enriches instead with innumerable children. Through the work of the natural sciences the European languages have had their vocabularies immensely enriched since the end of the Middle Ages. At the same time, although grammatical training and discipline has not been given them directly by the sciences, they have achieved far more than that : they have emphatically demanded and asserted their right to this discipline. The demands made by our civilized languages on the concept forming powers of the natural sciences, will increase in the future rather than diminish. How they will respond to this pressure we can only foresee vaguely and in general terms. There will probably be a further increase in terminology. But the progressive elimination of the differences in national languages, which is frequently feared or hoped for, does not seem to be likely. On the contrary, just because naturalistic thought with its fundamental tendency to abstraction makes more or less the same demands on every language, it forces each one to achieve the highest precision and logical sequence of which, in its own characteristic way, it is capable. The characteristics of individual minds are not destroyed by common tasks and common competition, but are all the more emphasized, and instead of remaining potential are forced into the light of achievement. That is why the differences between Italian and French, or between French and German, have become greater rather than smaller since the rise of the natural sciences. The essential differences in the structure of the sentence in the Romance and the Germanic languages, and between the order and the formation of words in French and German, as well as differences of accent, were less pronounced in the Middle Ages than they are now.

It is possible, however, owing to the continually higher demands made on the civilized languages by abstractive naturalistic thought, and the increasing tension of competitive effort at solving common logical tasks, that one or other language may succumb, that is, be altogether disregarded in scientific literature, to live on only in poetry and everyday intercourse. Here and there we see signs of some languages dropping out of scientific world competition, ever since it began in earnest. The scientific research worker can already grasp almost all that is of importance in his work by reading French, German, and English. Important work in other languages is made accessible through translations, because it is felt to be isolated and would otherwise be in danger of being ignored.

The higher naturalistic thinking ascends into abstract technicalities, the more exclusive it becomes. It has no immediate need for the co-operation or the understanding of the masses, and cannot use the untrained help of amateurs and laymen at all.

At this height, however, where the estrangement and separation of logical from linguistic thinking is greatest, is the speculative or reflexive turning point at which the abstract concept becomes dialectical, and logical thinking discovers its true nature and at the same time its unity with linguistic thinking. This return and approach of the logos to language can be represented in many different ways : as the transition from mathematical to historical or from naturalistic to metaphysical thinking ; or from the concepts of reason to those of intelligence ; or from the abstraction to the idea ; or from the rigid, postulated identity of thinking and being, to the moving reality of identity, and so on. From our point of view we can best regard the transition in question as one from the negative to the positive aspect of the inner language form.

Since we cannot think without speaking, or speak without thinking, each activity presupposes the other. They are so closely dependent on one another, that we can just as well regard and value thought as speech, or speech as thought. The more naïve and natural view is that which supposes and recognizes thought only where there is also speech, so that the latter is seen as the premiss of the former. From this standpoint, then, nothing is recognized that is not language, that cannot be apprehended and seen as expression, communication, and representation. It is the æsthetic point of view, which is incapable of seeing the naked logos or any silent and formless thought, and which is willing to honour only the representational faculty even in the greatest thinkers and scientists. If one is serious about this no doubt possible and justifiable attitude, and carries it through in the strictly scientific sense, one will come across language forms that are present in an external sense and yet have no linguistic meaning ; empty words, hollow gossip, thoughtless phrases, unimaginative, unrealizable forms, which have no linguistic content or meaning, in short, which have no inner language form. We shall then understand that it is the inner language form which is the essential part of language, and that the outer form is purely fortuitous and illusory. Nevertheless, we cannot disregard the outer as long as we take up the æsthetic attitude ; for how can we recognize the inner form if we have not got the body ? If we refuse to recognize the outer form, it inevitably follows that we must also give up the inner ; and then æsthetic contemplation would destroy its object and itself. If the inner language form were no more than language seen from the inside, that is, from the side of the speaker, that would be the end of the wisdom of philosophers. If the inner language form is denied, speech and all thought are denied as well. But thought does not destroy itself ; it stops and retreats at this abyss, turns back upon itself, and becomes reflexive.

Thought carries out this retreat by contemplating its own imagery and speech. Everyone knows that he cannot and may not express everything he thinks ; and he knows this because he observes his own imagery and speech, because he thinks about his thought. In this way we attain to the second and truly logical standpoint, that of self-consciousness. The negation of the inner language form has therefore in reality not taken place at all ; it has only been considered and consciously avoided. We can therefore not speak of stepping back from negating to positing the inner language form, nor of a logical transition from the mathematical and scientific to the metaphysical and historical method of concept formation. There has been no transition at all, but a return of thought into itself. The linguistic direction of thought, which at first was external and free from doubt and which did not distinguish between outer and inner, regarding expression and imagery, appearance and reality, sound and meaning as identical and of no account, is startled out of its dream and critically illuminated by the logical concept. The latter does not, therefore, destroy and negate the former, but stops it in its sleep-walking, in order to point out the correct way. This desire to orientate is earlier than the " halt ! ", which thought calls out to itself. At the instant of calling a halt, thought already knows whither it wants to go. In order to enlighten the world, we must already have understood it ; to abstract from its appearances, we must know its nature ; to cut out linguistic thinking without destroying it, we must already have transposed it into its non-external form and know what it can and what it cannot do. What it can do is to apprehend the whole world of appearances as being and becoming, as motionless and moving appearance. In this sense we may say that the first stage of language is the onomatopoetic, or, to suggest a more comprehensive term, the ' phenomeno-poetic '. For every kind of sense impression, not only that of hearing, can immediately express itself through language. This immediacy is no more binding for hearing than it is for sight or smell ; it is not binding at all, but because of its fundamental originality is the immediacy of freedom, an *origo poetica* of the spirit. We can find no final reason why Hölderlin should express the eternal yearning in the heart of man by singing of sunlight and the ether, whilst Leopardi chooses the night and moonlight. In the same way we cannot give a proof why the German child should say *mä* to a sheep and the Italian *bä*. This irrationality of language, this dreamlike fluctuation of the poetic spirit, which demands to be bound and strengthened even at the stage of primordial creation, cannot be removed from the world by literary or etymological criticism. It is simply there, and its very indestructibility becomes a problem for conceptual thought. Why does language fluctuate, why does it not conform to the law of identity ? Why does it not use the same word for the same thing at all times, or a different word every time ? Why is language not even consistent in its fluctuation, in its changes ? The only possible answer is, that it does not regard the concept as something rigid, external, and opposed to itself, but as something plastic within itself.

This plasticity of the concept is in fact the same as that which presents itself to our æsthetic judgment as the inner language form. It is the deeply felt and truly active spiritual principle of language, even though it does not always attain its fullest expression. To our logical judgment this same spirituality of language no longer presents itself as a mere language form, but as a form of thought, a concept.

All scientific concepts, the mathematical and naturalistic as well as the speculative and historical, are forms of language and of thought at the same time. They are a form of language if we take their æsthetic, a form of thought if we take their logical validity into consideration. That one and the same thing can be concept and language at once seems to be a contradiction ; but it has a logical basis. We must remind ourselves again that in philosophy ' the one ' and ' the other ' *together* form that living unity which bears difference within itself, and that the things of the mind can be distinguished only if we do not separate them, but think them as a unity.[1] I have shown elsewhere that the conceptual systems of the great philosophers are at the same time the inner language form of their thought, that, for instance, the *cogito ergo sum* of Descartes is his thought and the language form of his thought, and that a syntactical change in the one would also be a violation or falsification of the other.[2]

Let us examine some further examples of the peculiar way in which the language forms are separated from concepts and at the same time united with them.

An intuitive fool once said he could quite well understand that the astronomers were capable of discovering the distances, sizes, movements, and velocities of the stars ; what baffled him, however, was how they knew what the stars were *called*. Well, the astronomers do not know the names of the stars, and do not want to know them. In fact it matters so little to them, that any and every name

---

[1] Cf. H. Rickert, in *Logos*, II, p. 26 ff., and R. Kroner, *Logos*, XIII, p. 90 ff.

[2] *Gesammelte Aufsätze zur Sprachphilosophie*, p. 212 ff., and particularly p. 227 f.

suits them, provided it refers to the particular star they are discussing, and to no other. They give to celestial objects the names of ancient gods, or letters, or numbers ; only the convention must be rigid, so that there may be no confusion. Astronomical names are external and have no immediate inner language form ; they are not really *nomina*, but *pro-nomina*. The whole language of the scientists and mathematicians is in this sense pronominal ; it points and refers to things, is demonstrative and relative. Their minds are not busy with words, they do not say anything, they operate. As regards their linguistic nature, numbers are pronouns ; as regards their mathematical nature they are operations or functions. In so far as these operations are carried out by arithmetical thinking, they do not need names. Hence, instead of numeral adjectives, the mathematicians can substitute letters or even the things themselves, wooden balls or stones, or mechanical, physical, and chemical quantities of matter or force whose relations they are investigating. It makes no conceptual difference whether the operations in question are carried out arithmetically and the numbers recited or written down, or whether they consist in working a calculating machine, or whether they are carried out as experiments in a laboratory ; for as far as the concept, the scientific substance, is concerned, experimental operations are the same as the method of calculating by reciting numbers. And that is why the origin and essence of the inner language form of numbers is an operation. This fact has frequently enough been noticed in the languages of primitive peoples. " The Ewe, for example, count on their outstretched fingers, beginning with the smallest finger of the left hand and bending up the finger they have counted with the index finger of the right. After the left they proceed in the same way with the right. . . . In Nuba the gestures that accompany counting are as follows : Beginning with *one*, the fingers of the left hand are pressed into the palm by the right hand in order, starting with the little finger. The same

o

is then done to the right hand. For twenty, both fists are pressed horizontally together. Von der Steinen reports that the Bakairi failed to accomplish the simplest operation of counting, if the objects to be counted, *e.g.* a handful of maize, were not immediately accessible to touch. . . . In Sotho the word for five really means " complete the hand ", that for six " jump ", that is, jump to the other hand. This active character of the so-called numeral adjectives is particularly clear in those languages that form their expressions for numbers by having a special description for the way in which the objects to be counted are grouped, set down, or stood up. Thus the Klamath language has a great number of such terms, which are formed from the verbs for placing, laying down, and setting up. A particular group of objects that are to be counted has to be spread out on the ground, another has to be arranged in superimposed layers, some have to be divided into heaps, others arranged in rows ; and to each such ' placing ' of the objects there corresponds a different verbal numeral adjective, a different *numeral classifier*, according to their characteristics. The movements needed in setting up these objects are accompanied by definite bodily movements, which are thought of as being done in a particular order. The latter do not need to be confined to hands and feet, the fingers or toes, but may be extended to any part of the body. In British New Guinea counting starts with the fingers of the left hand, and then continues to the wrist, the elbow, the shoulder, the neck, the left breast, the chest, the right breast, the right side of the neck and so on ; in other parts the shoulder blade, the clavicle, the navel, the throat, or nose and eye and ear are used." [1]

We see that the clumsiest counting efforts of the savage show the same fundamental relation of concept and linguistic form as the most difficult and abstract calculations of a master of applied mathematics. For the negro as well as for Einstein the theorem holds true that

[1] E. Cassirer, *Philosophie der symbolischen Formen*, I, Berlin, 1923, p. 183 ff.

the inner language form of number is an activity of thought, a grasping and manipulation and transportation of objects from standpoint to standpoint, and that external language, the expression, communication, and representation of this active adjustment of points of view, is a phenomenon accompanying it and co-ordinated with it. Because of this relation of co-ordination, external language forms, mathematical signs, numeral adjectives, gestures, etc., can accompany the inner activity of calculation like the shadow the dog. They can just as well remain absent or vanish, or they can be employed as assistants or vicarious substitutes, or they can even become the inner activity themselves. That depends on the task we have set ourselves and the practised abilities we apply to it. If the mathematical task lies in regions we have often traversed, the arithmetical operation becomes an almost automatic function, which we hardly need to carry out. We merely need to set it going and to represent it by external mathematical language forms, like logarithms. On such occasions mathematical thought appears condensed and externalized, as its own shadow and substitute and identical with its language forms. But if new regions are to be discovered, it must actively seek and build the road, free itself from the shadow of language, relinquish familiar formulæ and signs, in order to create new language forms, new orientations and functions through its own initiative, and clothe them in new formulæ, signs and external characteristics. On such occasions mathematical thought appears independent of its language form, and becomes the light that dissipates the shadow, to throw it in other directions.

The co-ordination of thinking and speaking in the mathematical sciences is at once free and bound ; on the one hand, therefore, mathematics may have validity as a language, that is, as a system expressing conceptual operations, on the other as a logical activity, that is, as a systematic attempt to attain freedom from language. We might call it a language, which allows only pronouns

in place of nouns, imperatives in place of verbs, copula-
tive equations instead of adjectives and adverbs, and
whose fundamental attitude towards the whole colourful
movement of life is summed up in the one sentence :
" Put this and that equal to that and this ! " This is
not in the true sense of the word a language ; it is the
bare expression of the purely logical will that operates
on the world of appearances, the world of linguistic
thinking. The purpose of the mathematical co-ordination
of language and concept is the liberation of the concept
from the senses. It is a kind of pledge, in which both sides
purify each other, become more spiritual, and free themselves from the senses by serving each other as substitutes.

In the speculative and historical sciences the purpose is
the same : the liberation of thought from the senses. The
relation of logos and language, or inner and outer language
form, also remains the same in so far as it is a free and
bound relation determined by the purpose for which
knowledge is sought. But in practice the relation becomes
different. It becomes more intensified, becoming more
free on the one side and more closely bound on the other.
Seen from the outside, the language of historians and
usually of philosophers also remains that of common
humanity ; it is not laced into the Spanish boots of a
technical convention. Only occasionally do philosophers
demand such asceticism of it ; but that is an exception
and a misuse. Since it can move about freely, and revel
to its heart's content in its nominal and verbal wealth,
it cannot pledge itself to the logos as it does in mathematics, and cannot become a substitute for it as often as it
likes. Nevertheless it is in the service of the logos, and shall
and will and must serve it—but only as Faust served his
' master ', " auf besondere Weise ", in his own way ; it strives
hard and often errs but remains conscious of the right way—
in its " dunkeln Drange sich des rechten Weges wohl bewusst ".
It is a relation of love, not that of a contract, though this
sounds somewhat fantastic ; for how can language love
the logos, or images a concept ? And yet the expression

is justified in so far as the logical and scientific thinker can only contemplate, express, communicate and represent his knowledge if he loves it. Understanding unites with contemplative and creative thought in the Platonic *eros*, provided we regard it philosophically, and not historically or, worse still, mythically ; and in this embrace the logos, which otherwise would be something general, something that stands alone in the world, becomes *ours*.

Allen gehört was du denkst ; dein eigen ist nur, was du fühlst.
Soll er dein Eigentum sein, fühle den Gott, den du denkst.

Without eros not only the cosmos but our thought first of all would fall to pieces. There would be so much reason and abstraction, that thought would be unable to find the way back to itself. This danger does in fact continually threaten mathematical and naturalistic thinking, for it has no eros, or rather, it has not got it as unharnessed passion but as a desire for knowledge that trains our purposes and is trained by them—and this is both more and less.

In all sciences, that is along the whole front of linguistically expressed science or scientific literature, the relation of linguistic to logical thought is fundamentally determined and regulated by the tone of the spiritual logos. Where it is active, as in the natural sciences, its mood becomes more sober, whilst in the more contemplative sciences it can become intensified to the point of intoxication. Its fluctuations can, as it were, be read on the thermometer of psychology ; but we must not believe that this glass instrument makes the weather. The natural temperatures of thought are no more than the tensions between its subjects and its objects, or its vehicles and objects. Therefore the study of these tensions, what we may call the psychology of scientific *Weltanschauungen*, is no longer a matter for philosophy but one for philology and the literary sciences.[1] An examination of the systems of

[1] In this connection we must certainly not think of Jaspers' *Psychologie der Weltanschauungen* (Berlin, 1919 and 1922). For he takes every kind of psychic attitude to be life, every experiencing of the

philosophy, the methods of mathematics and the natural sciences, the *Weltanschauungen* of history, in order to discover by what they are naturally determined, or, what comes to the same, to discover their spiritual eros, cannot lead us to hope for more than an understanding of their *langage*. That is a great deal ; for the whole meaning of a thinker appears in his *langage*, his specific way of expressing things and his inner and outer language forms. On the other hand it is very little ; for the meaning of his expressions contains, in an undistinguishable mixture, all that he believes because of his religious convictions ; the intuitive knowledge and the errors of his uncertainty ; his phantasies ; what he knows and apprehends through his reason and intelligence ; what he desires on the strength of his convictions ; or what he pretends to himself and others because of his vanity. All these can be beautifully represented in his language form and may mislead us. True, the eroticism of the scientific spirit should not allow prostitution and adultery ; but the linguistic part of that spirit is at once spirit and flesh, and where the one is willing, the other is weak.

The chastisement to which the historical and speculative sciences are subjected by the scientific formation of concepts only takes place partially and in the modified form of a positive and, as it were, inner asceticism. The logos calls language back to its inner life, and makes it once more conscious of its better self. Language is persuaded to stop following merely its own euphonies, turn away from the seductions of its rhymes and rhythms, and seek its beauty in truth, in the love of logic, whose vehicle it has to become. The effect of this definite,

experiences of life to be *Weltanschauung*, and so describes and casuistically classifies them. For him the human spirit is no more than an abstract patient, and the doctor of souls diagnosticizes with uncalled-for curiosity. He may have the honest desire to help, but has no means of bringing about a cure. This amusing game is played with astounding thoroughness and German seriousness. Such things are treated by the French in a much lighter and more matter-of-fact way, more like a conversation.

positive, and liberal education is easily seen if we examine a language with a feebly developed logos, one, for example, which has no philosophic and historical literature or schooling. Such a language is a *patois*, or at most a dialect. Poetry alone, however deep its springs and however great, is not sufficient to lift a language from the level of dialect to that of literature ; and daily intercourse, the language that goes from mouth to ear, is also not sufficient as long as it is restricted to serving immediately practical ends and needs. Only when speaker and listener take thought of their language and give a backbone of logic to the intuitive spontaneity of their expression, can they free themselves from the spatially and temporally conditioned externality of their speech, which we call dialect, and create a written language, a literature. A literature that is merely poetic, that has no scientific writings, is no more than written dialect. It is as yet unfledged. In this sense we have to look upon the whole of the literature of the Middle Ages that was written in the vulgar tongue as bound to dialect and as spiritually unfree. For in those times speculative and historical, indeed all scientific thinking, belonged to Latin and existed in the mother tongues only vicariously and because they borrowed from Latin. The Middle Ages certainly possessed original poetry, but no prose of its own ; its scientific thought was dependent and not free. In these times of a coarser romanticism, when the mediæval spirit is again being extolled, it is well to be reminded of the views of Hegel, which still hold good. " This is the great principle, that in the absolute relationship to God all externality vanishes ; with the disappearance of externality, which is the estrangement of the self from itself, the state of subjection, too, is dissolved. And with it praying in an alien tongue, and the prosecution of science in it, are at an end. In language, man is productive ; it is his first external expression, the simplest form of existence that he reaches in consciousness. What a man thinks, he also thinks inwardly in terms of language

If he has to express or feel through a strange tongue the things that touch his highest interests, this first form is broken and strange. But now this break with the first emergence into consciousness is healed ; it is essential to freedom to be able to be in one's own sphere, to speak and think in one's own language. This is infinitely important, and without this form of coming into one's own, subjective freedom would not have existed. Luther would not have been able to complete his Reformation without translating the Bible into German." [1]

The education of a deeper inwardness through philosophic thought can, of course, be overdone. Through such exaggerations the spoken expression of the individual will become dim, un-external, uncommunicable through too much concrete matter-of-factness—as we can observe in certain prosaic German philosophers—or the whole language as it is in general use becomes stiff and unsuited to the individuation of personal thinking through a too highly developed system of concepts. The scientific conventions of French prose are an example and a warning of this.

But we can leave these pathological cases of linguistic eroticism for the logos ; poetry will see to it that they do not cause any harm in the long run.

[1] *Vorlesungen über die Geschichte der Philosophie*, III, 230–231.

CHAPTER IX

IN poetry the relation of inner and outer language form finally becomes clear and throws off that restless, apparent existence with which we have hitherto been concerned. We have continually found that there is a certain ambiguousness and impurity in the fact of language, be it speech, conversation, or language usage, as long as we regarded it as the vehicle, mirror, imitation or echo of psychic meanings, or as the medium of mental activities, or as the sign and symbol of objects and facts that have been thought ; in short, as long as we brought language as an existent into relation with any other existent that was not itself language. We found that religious conviction, by being expressed, did not lose its subjective validity, but did in fact lose its individual characteristics and remained as mere meaning or intention ; that scientific knowledge, concepts and eternal truths became externalized into catch-words, formulæ, and terminologies which every fool could rattle off ; that the immediate experience of joy and pain was at once petrified and grammaticized through use ; that the will assimilated itself to desire, action to talk, and purity to its impure expression in language, so that they could easily be confused ; things could no longer be distinguished from their shadows, nor life from its stage. We therefore had to appeal each time from the outer form of language to its inwardness ; and in this way we arrived at a conception of the inner language form, which has gradually grown so comprehensive that we should do well to test its carrying power.

Each time something new entered this concept. When it was a matter of the language of religion, the inner form was a conviction or a belief ; in scientific expression it was understanding or the process of arithmetic ; in the expression of feelings the capacity for being moved ; in objective or in technical expression it was interest ; in the expression of the personality with the help of style and feeling it was a psychic intention, and so on. According to the direction in which the meaning of the speaker pressed, as distinct from the actual words used, the inner language form took it up and became its believing, loving, thinking, feeling, meaning, and willing vehicle.

In addition we have defined the inner language form now as something spiritual, and again as something mental, and it was never clear whether it was a philosophic, psychological, or even sociological concept. This multiplicity does not arise from any confusion of thought— or at least we hope it does not—but is owing to the fact that we did not regard language only as a spiritual and creative activity, but, by way of deduction, also as a natural function of the mind and as a medium for thought and the exchange of ideas. Naturally the concept of the inner language form had to follow this development and assume those aspects through which our whole conception of language passed. As many conceptions as there are of language, so many will there be of the inner language form. If the mind takes to words, that is, spreads itself into the personal, psychic, bodily and finally corporeal, for the reason that language is an activity, this effective work is the inner form principle. Philosophically or speculatively we can only understand and apprehend it as a whole, that is, as a principle ; but empirically, in its individual manifestations, only through the externality of language forms, as a kind of embryonic form, as the psychic language forms that underlie those of style and grammar. So to the speculative eye the inner language form is the creative principle of the speaking mind, whilst to the eye of the empirical scientist it appears as the psycho-physical relation, by which he has to reconstruct each time from what has been spoken to the mind of the speaker. Because of all this, the inner language form is the meeting place of the philosopher and the linguist ; for here the mind appears in no other form than that of language, and language is nothing more than the mind incarnate. Here it is a question only of language as creation, and no longer of language as religion, nature, life, community, logos, or anything else. It is true that in the connections we have studied hitherto it was also creation—the religious, natural, living, communal, logical creation of language ; but what was created in and through it was always something different to itself. Hence its inner language form remained largely symbolic there, and received its validity, its meaning, from some other belief and striving than the purely linguistic. But if the nature of language is exhausted in symbolizing what is not language, how then can it have a being of its own, and for that its own symbol, in other words, a pure inner form ? The concept of inner language form after all, expresses the fact that the speaking mind speaks its speech, forms its forms, creates its creations, or in simpler words, that every language has its rule, which in itself is nothing religious, or logical, or natural, or arbitrary, but again something linguistic. The specifically linguistic character of language is its linguistic rules, which we call grammar ; and what is specifically characteristic about speech is its self-creativeness, which we call poetry. Without its poetic character all speaking would be a mere external activity and would have neither its own inner, nor an outer and other sense. How should our speaking be able to give form to a religious or scientific thought, or even to some everyday wish or need, if it were not able to create itself but instead remained caught up and confused in a chaotic babble of tongues ? " Man speaks at each moment like the poet, because, like the poet, he gives expression to his impressions and feelings. It does not matter that this is done in the tone of ordinary conversation or familiarity, for there is not the slightest distinction between this and the other forms that are called prose,

prose poetry, narrative, epic, dialogue, drama, lyric, or song. And if the ordinary man will not mind being regarded as a poet, which he is because of his humanity, the poet may not take it amiss that he is coupled with common humanity; for this relation alone explains the power of poetry on all human minds in the narrow and in the highest sense. If poetry were a special language, a 'language of the gods', human beings would not be able to understand it; if it rises up, it does not rise over, but raises; true aristocracy and true democracy come together at this point also." [1]

Nevertheless the objection is raised again and again that it is impossible for all our speaking to be poetical and artistic. Not every expression of meaning through musical sounds is music or through colour, painting. Am I a musician when I whistle to someone, or an artist when I smear a cross on the wall? Yes and no. If we say of someone that he is no artist, we can mean two things : either that he does not paint, but does something else, like cobbling or carpentry; or that he tries to paint but succeeds only in doing it badly, that he is a painter but not a notable one. The first is a question of definition or orientation, the second a criticism or a judgment of value. In the second sense we can say that the ordinary human being is not a poet, and his talk not art. But this is at the same time an unspoken demand that he should nevertheless make an effort to raise his conversation to the height of art and to express himself poetically even when writing a business letter or giving orders to his cook. There are people who attempt to comply with this demand, and who clothe the most banal occasions in flowery purisms; but they merely become the laughing-stock of their fellow-men; for

> Quand on se fait entendre on parle toujours bien,
> Et tous vos biaux dictons ne servent pas de rien.
> (Les Femmes savantes, II, 6.)

---

[1] B. Croce, *Foundations of Æsthetics*.

This seems to show that prose, the language of intercourse and of science, can have nothing to do with poetry and art even in the first sense of orientation and definition ; that there is in fact an important difference between the linguistic forms of expression of the poet or artist and the non-artist ; and that in ordinary speech and in scientific language one is not only a negligible or a bad artist, but no artist at all and has, indeed, no call to be one. How can we reconcile this with the view of Croce quoted above, that man speaks as a poet at every instant ?

If all these possible aspects that we have considered and affirmed are true, then a linguistic expression like " Rose, bring me my slippers and give me my night cap ! ", should first be poetry, secondly negligible as poetry, and thirdly not poetry at all. However absurd this may sound, it is in fact true. For in so far as this sentence is expressed in language, it contains these three aspects, and we are therefore constrained, first, to distinguish it from poetry as non-poetry or prose, secondly, to identify it with poetry as the expression through language of a wish, and thirdly, to interpret it with regard to the sphere of life which it touches as a sentence whose orientation is largely practical and whose artistic value is insignificant. What is fundamentally poetry, does not always need to be so in fact ; for the occasions on which it manifests itself are different in innumerable ways and do not always need to have a poetic significance. There is an element of poetry in every linguistic form we can think of ; but we must distinguish elemental poetry from that which is expressed or is in the process of being worked out, just as we distinguish the latent or immanent spirit from the manifest, or potential from active force.

It might be that the above sentence about the ' slippers ' and the ' night cap ' had appeared in a poetic work, for instance a comedy. In the *Bourgeois Gentilhomme* we find something like it : " *Nicole, apportez-moi mes pantoufles et me donnez mon bonnet de nuit !* " Nevertheless the sentence as such would not be poetry, but would only *belong* to it. It would no more contain elemental poetry, that is, the essence of language, than if it had been said by any good citizen of France instead of on Molière's stage. Its poetry is not due to the fact that it has been said by Molière or that it has been said in French, but to the fact that it is language and that, for instance, the person Nicole or Rose was addressed by *vous* or *you*, as though she were more than one person. In this polite language form, which regards one person as many, debases the ' I ' and exalts the ' thou ' to ' you ' or ' vous ' or ' Sie ', and gives a kind of majority to the other person, even when she is a servant girl, we see not only modesty, politeness, and good breeding, but above all the magnifying power of the imagination with its multitudinous accompaniments of fear, jealousy, trust, hate, and love, which make everything, even our fellow-men, into something vast and chimerical. Though her master may see nothing mysterious in Nicoline or Rose, something of mystery nevertheless still clings to her name ; and if she should have a lover who sighs to her as " Rose " or " my little Rosebud ", primeval poetry begins to stir its linguistic powers of expression into words like :

> Du bist wie eine Blume,
> So schön, so hold und rein,
> Ich seh' dich an und Wehmut
> Schleicht mir ins Herz hinein.

Furthermore, the imperatives " bring me ", " give me ", " *apportez-moi* ", and " *donnez* " are created and sustained by the poetic imagination ; for in sober and prosaic language there are no immediate expressions of the will, no true imperative forms. Our will expresses itself directly in actions and not in words. Man uses language only when his actions are in some way obstructed. Only the passive, lazy, weak will, the apparent will, the will of imagination, can become a subject for linguistic expression. Imperatives are poetic impulses of the will. They are images, parables and metaphors, the shadow and reflexion of our will translated into poetry; not an objective willing, but a subjective and imagined willing, a yielding, confiding and commanding through speech, and not an active realization of our will. We hardly need to prove what complete inventions and fables the words ' bedroom slippers ' and ' night cap ' are ; for the bedroom and the night do not need shoes and caps, but, through poetic licence, man attributes his own needs, purposes, and clothes to the house and the night, to all things that come within the purview of his language.

The good burgess does not think of all these things when he orders his bedroom slippers and night cap in Molière or anywhere else on earth ; nor is he conscious of any poetic services or debts. In his stead language creates on Parnassus, and he himself is a Parnassian only in so far as something linguistic is happening *in* him while he speaks his ordinary language. The muses only assist him as the king the carrier ; for if kings did not build, the carriers would have nothing to do.

So language may be compared to a communal building scheme, in which poets and common men act together as kings and carriers in such a way that neither can do without the other. To understand it fully, therefore, we must be familiar with both. But the perfected, self-sufficient magnificence of poetry is reserved for those special festive occasions on which the imagination shows itself not only as an element of and the medium for language, but at the same time as form ; occasions on which it turns its inner language form outwards. If, therefore, the essential element of language is brought forth into the light and represented as the purest expression of itself in that work of art, a perfect poem, we may well say that in æsthetic criticism philology has its beginning and end, its Alpha and Omega. And this is true of any particular branch of that science.

With respect to historical grammar we have already shown that its categories are so handled by the poet that a comparative, a subjunctive, a conditional sentence only find their fullest and most moving fulfilment in the language of poetry. Through poetry, every grammatical form becomes a form of experienced speech.[1] And if we enter the sphere of phonetics, we find that even the most external aspect of language forms, their actual sounds, is spiritualized to such an extent by the poet that it ceases to be something external. The less poetic spoken prose is, the greater the emphasis on clarity becomes, since we attempt to make ourselves understood through it. At the level of prose both speaker and listener wrestle with the relative opacity of the phonetic material, as with a veil that has to be penetrated by thought. At the level of poetry this difficulty is regarded as having been overcome. The clarity of expression is a supposition that has been more or less fulfilled and no longer is the goal or the problem. This is the reason why poets, actors, elocutionists and singers—particularly when they lack practical training—regard it as beneath their dignity to be clear and intelligible. It is in fact beneath their dignity, for they want to be and must be *expressive*, which, according to the way one looks at it, is either more or less than

[1] E. Lorck, in *Die Erlebte Rede*, Heidelberg, 1921, restricts this term to the figure of true indirect speech, and E. Winkler, in *Germ. Monatschrift*, XII, 1924, defines the Romance imperfect as the form of ' *Einfühlung* ' into the past. These attempts to arrive at the foundations of a grammatical category show us that it is of a poetical nature. But all grammatical categories whatsoever are experienced and apprehended intuitively (*eingefühlt*), that is, they are poetical as regards their spiritual value and psychic origin. In some cases we may have to dig deeper than in others to reach these common roots. If, for instance, the Romance future tense did not express an experienced, felt, intuited, longed-for consciousness of time in the same way as the perfect or the present, how would it be able to describe the possibility, the necessity, the uncertainty, the certainty, the intention of an event, and to bring together views that are logically exclusive ? Or how could the prepositions as a means of orientation in space and time describe all kinds of inner relations if their topological and chronological functions did not have the attributes of dreams or phantasies or poetry, if they were merely logically thought and not psychically experienced ? The poetical principle of motion has been very well demonstrated in the case of the French neuter pronoun by Leo Spitzer in *Idealistische Neuphilologie*, Festschrift, Heidelberg, 1922, p. 120 ff.

intellectual clarity. In itself, lyrical, exalted, or sung
language need not be less clear than the spoken word.
As far as we know, there is no phonetic or acoustic
natural law to prevent the singer from making his text
clear ; [1] but there is in him an artistic and poetical will
that forces him again and again to rush past the preliminary conditions of clarity, so as to be more certain
of achieving his own special object, eloquent expressive-
ness. Measured by the clarity of prose, this can equally
well be the more primary, spontaneous and natural, or
the later, higher, and more artistic, just as poetry is
something primary in language as well as something that
has been developed consciously. It does not seem to me
that modern phoneticians are well advised when they
expressly avoid poetic examples in their presentations of
the science of phonetics.[2] It is of course true that all
hopes of determining, and representing *in abstracto*, the
psychic expressive value of individual sounds or groups
of sounds through poetic texts or other onomatopœias
must be buried. Such speculations about the isolated
object will have to be left to the play instinct of symbolic
poets or children. Arthur Rimbaud was both when he
wrote the well-known sonnet about the vowels :

A noir, *E* blanc, *U* vert, *O* bleu, voyelles,
Je dirai quelque jour vos naissances latentes. . . .

In this field it is the abstract that is inexact and unscientific ; for the primary, spontaneous, human, and
natural aspects of psychic expression do not run about
naked in language like dogs in the street, but are clothed
in historically determined language customs, in individual
occasions and relations. If we try to dissect those aspects
out of their relations, we find that they have no permanent
core but are a transient breath or perfume, which belongs
as inevitably to the poetical language forms as the foam to

---

[1] Cf. the sensible views of Otto Jespersen, in *Phonetische Grundfragen*,
Leipzig, 1904, p. 104.
[2] There are, however, some notable exceptions, *e.g.* the excellent
handbook of Spanish pronunciation by T. Navarro Tomás, Leipzig, 1923.

P

the wave. If we try to collect that foam, we destroy it, and find nothing in our hand but water. In so far as all those means of expression with which poetry charms our ears—rhyme, rhythm, metre, assonance, the melody of the sentence—have a psychic meaning, they are an efflorescence, through which the innermost elements of language come to the surface, so that in any one particular situation they appear to be external. But in so far as their sense and meaning are concerned, they still remain the innermost essence of language.

Phonetics and phonology would not be a science and could never take up a historical point of view, or rise to historical concepts, if there were no poetic urge in language to bring our deepest feelings, meanings, and thoughts to the surface in the form of sounds. The less poetic a language is, the less material there is for phoneticians, and vice versa. Its phonetic body is equivalent to its poetic capacity. Voiceless and shadowy languages, like the system of mathematical symbols or the codes of telegraphy, or languages that exist only in writing or in schools, like Middle Latin or Esperanto, are poor soil for the philologist or the philological historian. Half-baked literati of translation, it is true, are at present making much to do about the poetry of Middle Latin, with its pious hymns and sequences and the light-hearted songs of strolling scholars ; and for that reason philological science will at some time have to inquire into the pronunciation and the phonetic history of Middle Latin. But as a language it lives more on its antique echoes and on paper than in the voices of men. Its poetry therefore is also not much more than a reflexion ; it is arbitrary, dallying and disconnected and, though we do not wish to minimize its charm, we miss its living emotional basis. Only when song and music electrify the exhausted Middle Latin body, are some church songs occasionally able to give us the impression of artistic cogency so as to satisfy even the critical listener. On the whole, however, the poetry of the Middle Ages is to folk-poetry like a drama that is read to one that has been tested out on the stage.

To phonology language is the actress of the spirit, without whose voice poetry, and with it all human emotions, thought, desire and knowledge that strive to express themselves, would have to remain dumb. Its relation to poetry is therefore a peculiarly privileged one, in so far as the voice of language is clear, transparent, truthful, free from pretence, and reliable only in poetry. Where this clarity is absent and the purity dimmed, the muse retreats, and language becomes that double tongued, unreliable buffoonery we have described at such length.

Poetry is the true element and essence of language. Here, where it can be symbol and medium, where it acts its own self, that is, ceases to be and to have effect as symbol, medium, and actress, the misleading alternation of inner and outer form comes to rest. Inner and outer language form become completely equivalent, without the compulsion of a magical belief or will, and without the reservations of the mystics.

The black poodle in Goethe's *Faust* is not merely *called* poodle, it *is* a poodle ; not, it is true, a zoological specimen, but a dream image of this species. Nor is it any arbitrary specimen, but this particular one that is æsthetically valid only in *Faust*, whose ' core ' turns out to be a wandering scholar, who in his turn is Mephistopheles, and Mephistopheles again is " *ein Teil von jener Kraft die stets das Böse will und stets das Gute schafft* ".[1] This force, too, is imaginary, and exists only in Goethe's imagination and feeling ; it is not evil in any objective and logical sense, but in the sense in which Goethe and his readers feel and imagine it as that evil which is a force and plays many parts, which is supposed always to achieve the opposite of what it sets out to do. So it is also something mythical and imaginary. As long as we keep to the words of the poet, we cannot escape from the

[1] A part of that force, which always desires the evil, and always achieves the good.

labyrinth of dreams and phantasies. For here words and things, that is, outer and inner language forms, are as one.

If we misunderstand this position in the slightest, we are led to raise impossible questions, for instance, as to who the Beatrice of the *Divina Commedia* is. Is she the historical Beatrice Portinari of Florence, or a concept, or a symbol, or an allegory of theology and the church, or the grace of God and his revelation ? There is only one answer : that the Beatrice of Dante's poem is herself a poetic creation, that she is the Beatrice of the poet's inner vision. She is as little Portinari as Gretchen in *Faust* is Friederike, or as the Nymphenburg palace in Munich was built and inhabited by nymphs. Only the man who gave it that name wished and dreamed that it might be so, that this beautiful palace with its gardens, woods, lakes and fountains might be thought to be the work or the habitation of nymphs. The etymology of the name Nymphenburg is nothing more than the critical insight into this poetic dream of the Bavarian prince who built the pleasure palace.[1]

In the final instances of their science, all good etymologists are fortune hunters and interpreters of dreams. Through hundredfold experience they know that they cannot do much with their knowledge of the shifting of consonants or of meanings, if fortune does not smile on them and whisper the dream that gave life to the word they are tracking. Moreover those etymologies that are considered by the expert as well established, and as presenting no further problems, are usually the most problematical from the point of view of the philosophy of language. Thus Alois Walde says : " At the instant of its conception every word is perfectly clear etymologically. Through the further development of language this etymological transparency has in many cases been

---

[1] In the interests of historical accuracy we might point out that the name has an Italian origin : *Borgo delle ninfe* and goes back to a suggestion made by the Savoyan mother-in-law of the Archduke Ferdinand Maria, who thus merely fulfilled the dreamword of his *suocera*.

dimmed or even completely destroyed, through phonetic changes or through changes in meaning, or through the loss of the root word, so that it is only scientific investigation which is able to trace the lost relationships. This may happen within a single language ; thus the original connection of *luna*, the moon, was with *luceo*, to shine, so that it meant ' a shining heavenly body ' ".[1] Granted that there is this connection between *luceo* and *luna* ; there still remains the question whether the moon got its name from shining, or whether shining did not get its name from the moon. We only know that in Latin there was a comparison of ' moon ' and ' shining ' ; what we do not know is whether the reason was a ' shining moon ' or a ' moonlike shine ', whether the moon entered into the shining or the shining into the moon, or whether they met half way. A logical solution cannot be found ; for first, not all shining belongs to the moon, secondly, the nature of the moon is not exhausted in shining, and thirdly, linguistic comparisons of this kind are not logical acts of thought at all. They are the dream of a poet, in which things come together, not because they are being differentiated or because they are being identified, but because they are thought and felt together in an emotional unity. When etymology teaches us that the Indo-Germanic words for *father* and *mother* go back to the mumbling of a child, it is admitting that though it may be able to follow and explain the transformations of the names for father and mother in different languages, it cannot solve the riddle of the child that first formed them. But we do not find these riddles only at the beginning of the chain of etymological transformations, as the term ' primary creation ' would lead us to hope. Like a treacherous, destructive force they run through the whole chain of rationalistically welded links and over and again lead us to question the linguistic correlations of etymology. No student of the Romance languages ever doubted that

[1] Alois Walde, *Lateinisches etymologisches Wörterbuch*, Heidelberg, 1910, p. XI.

the French verb *aimer*, to love, is the direct etymological descendant of the Latin *amare*, until Gilliéron suddenly showed the possibility, in fact the probability, of its having at some point been derived from the Latin *aestimare* through *esmer* and *êmer*.[1] In a short communication about the Italian *farfalla*, " butterfly ", Leo Spitzer gives us a memorable example of the way in which, in the history of language formation and transformation, primary creation and development, poetry and imitation are fused together.[2] He is trying to find the relation between the Latin *papilio* and the Italian *farfalla*. Possibly, he thinks, *phalena*, ' night butterfly ', might have had something to do with it, though it is doubtful. It seems more likely that the Arabic *farfàr*, light-heartedness or talkativeness, had an influence, as in the Sicilian *farfareddu*, restless child, Neapolitan *farfariello*, little devil, French *farfardet*, sprite, and many other examples of a common popular belief in the dæmonic, psychic, and spiritualistic attributes and meanings of the butterfly. That would more or less explain the *f* of *farfalla*, and possibly the *r* as well. But in addition we must obviously suppose that the words *palpebra*, " eyelid ", and *palpitare*, to palpitate, had an influence, which is suggested by the Sicilian *parpagghiare*, to wink, Southern French *parpaiouna*, to flutter, and similar words. So that *farfalla* is more in the nature of a rhythmical than an etymological descendant of *papilio*. The permanent element in the transformation of forms is the double beat representing the fluttering of the eyelid and the butterfly ; and as the true etymological root of *farfalla* and even of *papilio* nothing remains but the expression through language of the movement of winking and fluttering, which the eye and the butterfly have in common. Every time the mill of etymological

---

[1] W. von Wartburg, *Französisches Etymologisches Wörterbuch*, denies this relation to *aestimare*. However that may be, the point is the inherent uncertainty of any given etymological derivation in the present state of our knowledge.

[2] *Archiv für das Studium der neueren Sprachen*, vol. 141, p. 146 ff.

development sweeps away the onomatopoetic dust from the word for butterfly, language creates it anew. I can strengthen this theory by a quotation from Mörike's *Peregrinalieder*; for here, where the etymologist turns poet, the poet can teach the etymologist :

> Spielenderweise mein Aug' auf ihres drückend,
> Fühlt' ich ein Weilchen die langen Wimpern,
> Bis der Schlaf sie stellte,
> Wie Schmetterlingsgefieder auf- und niedergehn.

By quoting such thoughts and examples we have no intention of raising the suspicion that etymology is a dreamlike and windy discipline. On the contrary we intend them to show that it will have to cling much more carefully to the facts of experience, the clearer the consciousness becomes that its objects and methods deal essentially with poetry and the dreams of poets, and that, as the history of words, it is the sister or even the double of the history of literature. If etymology reconstructs vanished language forms to the measure of present ones, that may be less audacious than the reconstruction of a vanished form of poetry by the historians of literature, because it is dealing with less complicated structures. But both remain patchwork, and to pride oneself on the pseudomathematical exactness of such scaffolding argues mere carelessness of thought. It remains a fundamental truth that words can no more be calculated or deduced from each other than poems from other poems, for in both an irrational force is active, whose products cannot be apprehended without intuition. Routine, and familiarity with the mechanisms and functions of language usage, are useful and necessary to the linguist ; but they only too often form in him the habit of an unquestioning certainty, which has repeatedly to be broken by the realization that he is dealing with an essentially fantastic, æsthetic, and therefore capricious object.

While on the one hand the student of language is constantly in danger of forgetting that the nature of language is poetic, the historian of literature is equally in danger of forgetting the other philosophical aspect, that the nature of poetry is linguistic. Now that the mischief of the moralizing pursuit of literary history has been somewhat alleviated, the naturalistic direction is again gathering strength in the guise of ethnography, geography, or nationalism, or under the banner of psychology, psycho-analysis, biology, sociology, or phenomenology in general. It is hopeless to attempt to close all these false approaches, for new ones are continually being invented and advocated by doctrinaire, intellectualistic, unphilosophic and unintuitional minds. The most illuminating thoughts and warnings will never bring such aberrations to reason. In a certain sense even these aberrations have their value, in so far as they have to be diligently followed so that the knowledge that they do *not* lead to the goal may become unshakable. For instance, one must have read—if not written—a book in which it is shown that the poetry of the French is not merely poetry in the simple human sense of the word, but the expression of French national feeling, thought, and will ; or that Corneille is not simply a poet, but a mouthpiece for the aspirations of statesmen ; that Montesquieu is more than a great prose writer, namely a prophet and singer ; that the importance of Balzac does not lie in his mastery of the epic, but that he has to be understood as a spiritual magician and phe-nomenon ; that the poetry of Germany has to be under-stood as the fruit and the mirror of its tribal characteristics and its landscapes ; that the highest product of Heinrich von Kleist's art is not *Der Prinz von Homburg* or any other of his dramas, but his suicide, the fact that he overcame the bondage of life. At some time everyone has to wade through such attempts at apprehending the importance of poets apart from their poetry—and in present-day histories of literature he can find innumerable examples of this kind of thing—in order that he may become tired of missing the point and repentantly return to anchor himself in the realization that for the science of literature there can be no higher or deeper object than poetry itself. Poetry is so wide and so universal, that the whole of mind and spirit, nature with its landscapes, nations, tribes, and their political, social, religious and other aspirations can find room in it ; it is so powerful that all these things do not remain as mere raw material, but are transfused and transformed by it into its own being, that is, into language. It is the function of poets to remove the things of this world out of their practical, empirical, and natural reality, in order to make them live again in the realm of art, and make them real and active in language.

How, then, could the science of literature deal with anything else than the linguistic activity and reality of mundane and of eternal things ? And how else shall we know and judge them than by the power and the capacity of language and the concept of language ?

We have tried to integrate this concept through the various activities of the mind and the most important fields of culture. At first we saw it in its uttermost questionableness and abstraction as the concept of a medium of media ; then it began to breathe and be filled with life, only to reject it again, in order to rise from the medium to the symbol of things, to suffer further differentiation and articulation into the concepts of outer and inner language form. So it became flexible and at the same time firm, that is, capable of making us understand the creative, transcendent, and dynamic as well as the conventional and static behaviour of language, and providing an adequate foundation for the empirical science of language. We have extended the concept to include the inflexible sounds of language ; the signs of writing and of gestures ; the most volatile tenuousness of thought ; the free creation of a moment, and the forms whose nature has remained determinate for thousands of years ; the stylistic peculiarities of individuals ; and metaphysics, which reaches beyond all human communities. By such extension the concept of language might well be shattered, were it not closed, strengthened, and unified by the identification of outer and inner language form as realized in poetry. Language that appears as poetry is individual and universal, national and common to every man, formal and objective, experienced and created, temporal and eternal, rooted to its environment and endowed with the wings of the spirit, understandable and beyond understanding, open to the infinite and romantic manifoldness and disjointedness of life and yet closed within the autonomy of its intuitive, classical, creative will. It is at rest within itself in contemplation and in freedom from tendentiousness; and, like a sun, it radiates its light in all directions.

Now that we have transformed the concept of language, and regarded it from many points of view and in many forms, we by no means believe that we have exhausted the subject and caught or circumscribed the nature of language. Many readers, who are used to the philosophizing of the schools, may miss the final exactitude of definition and feel that instead of analysing the concept of language we have been presenting it in a succession of more or less logical or speculative visions. Perhaps more of the intuitive nature of that which we believe to be language is contained here than is meet for a scientific work. We beg that though there is too much of language and too little of logic, the reader may forgive us; for " out of the fullness of the heart the mouth speaketh ".

APPENDIX

NOTES AND TRANSLATIONS

Page 3. " Names are sound and smoke,
An all-enmisting heavenly force . . .
Feeling is all in all . . .
And when thou'rt wholly blessed in thy fee ings,
Then name things as thou wilt."

p. 22. Reverence (*pietas*) is great for parents and relations, but greatest of all for our country.

p. 23. " Here I take my stand.   I cannot do otherwise."

p. 25. " The Salian hymns are hardly understood enough by their own priests."

p. 33. " To say God's Name in time seems possible to thee ?
—It is not uttered in Eternity."   Angelus Silesius [1]

p. 33. (note) " 'Tis nature's work that man should utter words,
But whether thus or thus, 'tis left to you
To do as seems most pleasing."

p. 34. " Where is the Fairest, him I love ?
Where is the Bridegroom of my Soul ?
Where is my Shepherd, where my Lamb
For whom I suffer so much dole ?

Where is my Spring, ye cooling springs ?
Oh say, ye streams, where is my Stream ?
My Fountainhead, whereto I run,
My Source, whereon I ever dream ?

Where is my Bower of Bliss, ye woods ?
Ye levels, say, where is my Plain ?
Where is my verdant Mead, ye meadows ?
Ah, point the way to him again !

Where is my Dove, ye feathered creatures ?
Where is my own true Pelican,
He who will make me true and living ?
Ah, would my weary search were done !

[1] Angelus Silesius : *Sämtliche poetische Werke, herausgegeben und eingeleitet von Hans Ludwig Held*, Munich 1924; J. E. C. Flitch : *Angelus Silesius, Selections from the Cherubinic Wanderer*, 1932.

Ye mountains, where is he, my Summit ?
Ye valleys, speak, where is my Vale ?
Ah say, I wander hither and thither,
And still I seek him, still I fail.

.   .   .   .   .

Ah God, where shall I farther seek him !
He is within no earthly form."

p. 34. "Thou art the Time to come, great sun of morning
Across the levels of eternity.
Thou art the cock-crow in the night of time,
The dew, the early matins and the maid,
The stranger thou, the mother thou, and Death.

.   .   .   .   .

Of things thou art the full epitome
That keeps the final secret of itself—
To every thing another thing thou art :
To ships a coast, and to the land a ship."

p. 38. " The great king Karl sat at the helm
And never a word he spoke,
He steered the ship with a right firm hand
Until the storm had broke."

p. 50. " All that in terrestrial kind and fashion
Is uttered in song,
Aspires to the skies ;
Below, the many fall to naught together ;
Others with the spirit's flight and power
Rise like the Prophet's winged steed
Rise aloft and pipe indeed
Without the gates of Paradise."
(*Der Westöstliche Diwan,* xii.)

p. 55. " The plaint of Syrinx sounds from yonder reed,
And Philomel's deep woe from out this grove,
That thicket has received the pearly tears
Shed by Demeter for Persephone,
And from this hill the Cytherean cried
' Alas,' so vainly to her beauteous love."

p. 92. " . . . . and in the way
He speaks within, I go declaring it."
(Dante, *Purgatorio,* xxiv, 54)

p. 92. " He lends the gift of speech to those who yet deny Him."

p. 99. " . . . . Meanwhile the kingdoms fall,
Peoples and tongues pass by : she sees it not."
(Leopardi, *La Ginestra, o il fiore del deserto.*)

p. 99. " We instinctively tend to crystallize our impressions in order to express them in words. And thus we confuse the true feeling, which is a continual becoming, with its unchanging external object, and still more, with the word that indicates that object . . .

Thus each one of us has his own way of loving and hating, and these loves and hates reflect the entire personality. Yet language indicates these states of mind by the same words for everyone ; it has only been able to determine the objective and impersonal aspects of love, of hate, and the thousands of other feelings that affect the spirit. We estimate the talent of a novelist by the power wherewith he uses a multiplicity of juxtaposed details to extract the primitive and vital individuality of the feelings and ideas he attempts to record from the common level to which the use of language has brought them. But in the same way as it is possible to go on interpolating indefinitely between two points of a variable, without ever covering all the ground, so also do we fail to betray in its completeness all that our spirit holds by the mere facts of speaking and of having associations of ideas which are juxtaposed without interpenetration. Thought and language remain incommensurable."

p. 100. " Excited folk have chanted to me about speech being so poor—Oh, so very poor. By God, no. Speech is rich, it seems to me, overpoweringly rich in comparison with the poverty and circumscriptions of life. Pain has its limits : the body faints, the mind becomes stupefied. It is the same with happiness. But the human need for communication has invented sounds that delude us into thinking that these limits do not exist. Is it only idiosyncrasy ? Am I the only one with whom certain words seem to run down the very marrow of the bones, to awake premonitions of experiences which do not exist ? "

p. 108.   " Nature is a temple, where living piers in lines
             Utter at times uncertain words and sighs ;
          Man passes by between the wood of signs
             Which gaze upon him with familiar eyes."

p. 129. " I have essayed many things, drawing, engraving in copper,
          Painted in oils, and in notes, much too have I recorded,
          All was inconstant, no less, nothing learnt now avails me.
          One gift only I wrought to give me the hand of a master :
          A talent for writing in German—and so, luckless poet, I ruin
          Life and Art together, set out in the poorest of dresses."

p. 130. " If flame of fire were issuing plainly from the windows
of a house, and if someone inquired if there was a
fire in there, and another replied yes, I can hardly say
which of the pair to deride most. And it would be
the same sort of question and answer if someone should
ask me (after the reasons given before) whether love
of my own mother-tongue is in me, and I should just
answer yes."

p. 147. " For peace and quiet and getting on
Believe me, you mustn't put people wrong :
That's a timely word to a friend of ours—
Lefranc Esquire of Pompignan.

For an impudent discourse, loud and long,
Fit only to please a vulgar throng,
Paris presents this crown of song
To Lefranc Esquire of Pompignan."

p. 147. The Rispetto was a popular love song in ottava or
sesta rima, sung in Tuscany. The Sicilian Strambotto
was similar, but more often satirical.

p. 148. " O face so lovely in its flowery whiteness,
What power hath given you such a wealth of beauty ?
The stars caress you with their twinkling brightness ;
Where'er you pass, the air bows down in duty,
Where'er you pass, the wind no longer blows,
You are the garden's only perfect rose.
Where'er you pass, the air awaits your leisure,
You are the garden's only beauteous star :
Where'er you pass the air forgets all pleasure,
You among flowers the sum of sweetness are.

When you go by before my habitation
Methinks the sun's bright orb is your attendant,
Your way is marked by clear illumination,
Where'er you go you leave the way resplendent.
And yet the light you scatter in your strolling
It burns not like my flame, beyond controlling :
The light you scatter faints and comes to languish,
My burning love not death himself can vanquish.

Tell me, O fairest, how 't were best to cure it !
What shall I do that I may find salvation ?
I go to church but cannot long endure it,
I stumble in an Ave's recitation.
I go to church and nothing can I say,
I keep your name in mind the livelong day
I go to church and not a word can find,
Your lovely name is ever in my mind."

[*Translator's note* :—This is very freely rendered, and in a more
sophisticated vocabulary than the original, *e.g.* " bianco quanto

la farina "="as white as flour" will not do in English verse.
The parallel to these forms is found in the early Elizabethans
of the Petrarchan tradition ; so that a change of vocabulary
is almost inevitable for the form of the original to be kept.]

p. 148. " O Love, O Love, what have you made me do ?
          You send my mind in fantasy astray !
          I can't repeat a Paternoster through,
          Nor half an Ave can I rightly say ;
          I can't begin the Creed, and all through you
          I start for Mass and find I've lost the way ;
          And I must go and be baptized anew
          Since loving thee has made me Turk or Jew."

p. 152. " I long to weep so much that I must break
          Like Mary Magdalene with my woe,
          And a great river of my tears I'll make,
          Which shall be ever in torrential flow,
          Which shall be ever full of rocks and stones :
          If thou should'st leave me, thus shall be my moans,
          And by that river flowers shall ever be ;
          Thus, if thou leav'st me, will I weep for thee."

p. 152. It is dangerous to rouse the lion, the tiger's fang is
          fatal ; and yet the most terrible of terrors is still a
          man in fury.

p. 154. " Six little words there are that take up all my day,
          I should, I must, I can, I shall, I will, I may.

          Only with thy constant teaching can I know each day
          What I should, I must, I can, I shall, I will, I may."

p. 155.   " At the back of father's house
                      There's a pond so cool,
                  I shall make myself an eel,
                      An eel in father's pool.

                  If you make yourself an eel,
                      An eel in father's water,
                  I shall be a fisherman,
                      Fishing for his daughter.

                  If you become a fisherman,
                      Fishing for me there,
                  I shall be a little lark
                      Flying in the air.

                  If you become a little lark,
                      Flying in the air,
                  I shall be a hunting-man
                      To get you in a snare.

If you become a hunting-man
To get we with a gun,
To the convent I shall go
A little convent nun.

If you should make yourself a nun,
A nun for convent-teaching,
I shall be a preacher too,
And win you by my preaching.

If you would be a preacher too,
To win me by your preaching, O,
I shall give myself to you
Because you love me so."

p. 156. " I think of thee if o'er the waves his glimmer
The bright sun flings ;
I think of thee when the moon's face a-shimmer
She paints in springs.

I see thee there if on the distant highway
The dust cloud wakes ;
In silent night, if on some narrow by-way
The wanderer quakes.

I hear thy voice whene'er with muffled thunder
The great wave heaves,
And oft when all is still I hearken under
The silent leaves.

I am with thee : thou art not distant from me—
Ah now thou'rt near !
The sun goes down, the stars' light falls upon me,
—Would thou wert here ! "

p. 158.   " Were I but a little bird
And had two little wings,
To thee I'd fly, my dear ;
But as it cannot be
I linger here.

Were I even far from thee,
Yet in sleep were near,
Talking to thee, dear ;
Yet it breaks when I awake
All alone, my dear.

No hour of the night is told
When my heart is not awake
To think of thine,
Since thou hast given a thousandfold
Thy heart to mine."

p. 171. " They may not farther than the shadows' bourne,
If by a span they pass, then dead they fall ;
Yet men they love and long for more than all,
To have her joy of one each waits forlorn."

p. 178. " By slow metamorphoses
Marbles white and marble flesh,
Rose-red flowers and rosy lips,
Shape themselves in forms afresh."

pp. 188 & " Thou'rt mine ? "
192. " For ever, and in the boldest meaning of the word."

p. 193. (i) " Since the sea of his miracles is so deep, let us
here end the life and death of our Spaniard
St James."

(ii) " Ring down the curtain and make an end of the
Caravajales, whose blood shines forth to-day in
the mountains of Martos because it was *Innocent
Blood*."

(iii) " I praise my fortune "
" Praise it,
And, ending the comedy,—
' *Beware of Whom You Praise* '."

(iv) " We remain to-day, all of us, sir, with money.
So we should be able to say [1] ' *The Rank's the
Guinea's Stamp*,' for quality is attained with
money."

(v) " And here, Ladies and Gentlemen, we end *The Casts
of Love and Fortune* of the most perfect lover."

(vi) " The saying, ' *It is worse than it was*,' has never
been truer, for now they are all married ; and so
Ite, comedia est." [2]

p. 213. " Every man has thy Thought : only things felt are
thine own,
If thou wouldst make him thine, feel thou the God thou
hast known."

p. 220. " You speak at your best when you're best understood,
And all your bright nothings are simply no good."

---

[1] Literally, " *Money is Quality*." The title is a quotation from
Gongora. (Pointed out by E. M. Wilson, the translator of Gongora.)
[2] Cf. *As You Like It*. Rosalind's Epilogue : "I charge you . . .
to *like* as much of the play *as please you*."

Q

p. 222.   " So lovely, sweet, and pure
                    That like a flower thou art,
                 I gaze on thee, and sadness
                    Wells up within my heart."

(Heine)

p. 225. " You vowels, A the black, white E, green U, blue O,
          Some day will I reveal your hid nativities."

p. 231. " Pressing my eyes on hers in a playful manner
            I felt for a moment the long eye-lashes
              —Till sleep should fold them—
            Like butterfly-pinions they rose and fell."

A. P. R.

INDEX